CALIFORNIA
SOUL

CALIFORNIA SOUL

An American Epic of Cooking and Survival

KEITH CORBIN

with
KEVIN ALEXANDER

RANDOM HOUSE
NEW YORK

Published in the United States by Random House, an imprint and division of Penguin Random House LLC, New York.

RANDOM HOUSE and the HOUSE colophon are registered trademarks of Penguin Random House LLC.

Photos from the author's collection.

Library of Congress Cataloging-in-Publication Data
Names: Corbin, Keith, 1980– author. | Alexander, Kevin (Food writer), author.
Title: California soul : an American epic of cooking and survival / by Keith Corbin with Kevin Alexander.
Description: First edition. | New York : Random House, 2022
Identifiers: LCCN 2022002253 (print) | LCCN 2022002254 (ebook) | ISBN 9780593243824 (hardcover) | ISBN 9780593243831 (ebook)
Subjects: LCSH: Corbin, Keith, 1980– | Cooks—California—Biography. | African American cooks—California—Los Angeles—Biography. | African Americans—California—Los Angeles—Biography. | Street life—California—Los Angeles—Anecdotes
Classification: LCC TX649.C665 A3 2022 (print) | LCC TX649.C665 (ebook) | DDC 641.5092 [B]—dc23/eng/20220124
LC record available at https://lccn.loc.gov/2022002253

Printed in the United States of America on acid-free paper

randomhousebooks.com

1st Printing

First Edition

Book design by Susan Turner

*To my Granny Louella; my dad, Samuel; Truett; Branden;
and all those who lost their life in our struggle before
they got a chance to see themselves in these pages*

Granny Louella Henderson, cooking at her stove,
1989.

They say every man is defined by his reaction to any given situation.
Well, who would you want to define you?

—NIPSEY HUSSLE, "I Do This"

CONTENTS

PART FOUR

CALIFORNIA
SOUL

Prologue

Watts, California. August 2018. Morning.

THE FIRST THING I REMEMBER WAS THE WHITE CAMARO.

I'd been back in Watts for three days. A year earlier, I'd moved to Oakland to work as director of operations for the LocoL Restaurant Group, but I came back frequently to see my family and check on the original LocoL, in Watts. On this visit, I was making my rounds with my younger brother Marlon and his four-year-old son, to say goodbye to family before catching my flight back to the Bay. Around nine A.M., we left my mother's house in her new Toyota Venza and drove through the Jordan Downs projects where I grew up, to see friends and soak up some of what I had been missing in Oakland. I made one last stop, at my aunt's, and then headed to LocoL to work until my flight to Oakland. As we drove away from her house, we passed the white Camaro.

As soon as we went by, two dudes jumped out. Looking

quickly, I saw they had guns—and not just any guns. These motherfuckers had AK-47s. Instinctually, I knew they were Bounty Hunter Bloods from our rival project, Nickerson Gardens. There was a war going on, and they were here to kill.

As they started shooting, I screamed at my brother, "Go! Go! Go!" Bullets hit the windows and doors. The headrests exploded. I turned to the backseat and tried to get my nephew to keep his head down. The Venza bucked over the bumps in the road as my brother hit the gas and made a right turn onto Grape Street. We flew through the Stop sign on 102nd. Less than a minute later, we were at LocoL.

Somehow, miraculously, no one in the car was hit. My nephew was in shock, too little to understand what had happened. But the car itself looked like a murder scene. Both headrests had bullets lodged in their poles. The dashboard was shot up. The back hatch was riddled with holes.

What happened next was the result of instincts sharpened from my years in the game. There was no thinking, no back-and-forth, no debate. There was no screaming and hollering, just a lot of energy and quick movements. I knew I had to leave a body in Nickerson Gardens before they even got back to their hood. My homie Montana came out of LocoL's kitchen. I told him what had happened, and he got in my mother's car. I hopped back in, and we drove to her house to grab a couple of .45s and a 9-millimeter.

I came back to LocoL just as my cousin was pulling up. When I let him know what had gone down, he didn't hesitate. "I'm going, too. We can use my car."

Less than five minutes later, my cousin, my brother, Montana, and I were parked on Compton Avenue, out in front of a liquor store across from the Nickersons. We were looking for any Blood, anyone affiliated. And soon enough, a dude in his twenties wearing a red hat came out of the store. He would do.

With my 9 mm in one hand, I cracked open the door and turned to look over my shoulder. And in that moment, seeing the faces of my brother and Montana, I paused. This shit didn't feel right. I got back in the car, shut the door, and put my gun down.

"Fuck this," I told my cousin. "Let's go."

As we drove away, I watched the young dude in the red hat get in his car, oblivious to the fact that his life had been so, so close to being over.

I was done. This was the end. I had to get out now for real.

OVER THE COURSE OF MY forty years, I've played lots of roles.

I've been a bogeyman, one of the demonized teenage drug-dealing gangbangers America was so scared of, who grew up in the '90s in the worst projects in Watts during the height of the country's infatuation with gang culture and gangsta rap.

I've been a prisoner in some of the most dangerous maximum-security prisons in America, surrounded by inmates serving life sentences for murder, making moonshine in my cell and stabbing people in the yard for survival.

I've been an ex-felon who tried to go straight and worked his ass off to get promoted in a civilian job, only to be fired because of his past and left wondering if gangs and crime really were the only paths available.

I've been a press-friendly selling point, the "feel-good"

hire at an ambitious restaurant that was supposed to revitalize my community.

I've been the chef and face of a fine-dining restaurant that headlined national "best" lists and hosted private dinners for Jay-Z, the cast of *Black-ish*, and John Legend.

And after the George Floyd murder, as Black Lives Matter took off across America, I was bandied about by white folks as part of some sort of "woke" narrative to help assuage their guilt. I've had white women in Beverly Hills pull up alongside me and apologize for the way police pulled me over. I've had random white people in my Instagram DMs telling me they love me.

The book you're about to read isn't a gangland morality tale or a prisoner-makes-good drama or a chef memoir that paints my life as a "uniquely American" success story. Most of those stories end when the protagonist is deemed transformed enough to step through a magic door and enter mainstream white society. I know that song all too well. My magic door was supposed to be cooking. But when you're a Black man coming from where I come from, that door may open, but you never make it all the way through.

This book is my opportunity to ditch the tropes and tell my whole story—the story of what it's like to grow up Black in America under some of the worst circumstances; to see unspeakable tragedy; to commit acts of violence and crime; to get locked up and then locked up again; to attempt to go straight and find the system unforgiving; to find a passion and go for it; to succeed and fail and be forced to fight for your place at the table. This book is called *California Soul* not just because that's the type of food I cook or because I'm uniquely tethered to the place where I was raised, but also because I've poured my soul into this story and I want you to know that, when you read it, you're staring at a piece of me and my truth.

Anyway. Let's start at the beginning.

PART ONE

Corbin and his cousin Branden,
"BL," at a birthday party in Watts
when the author was seven.

1

Family Business

WHEN SOME PEOPLE SAY THEY GREW UP IN THE DRUG GAME, THEY mean it metaphorically.

That's not what I mean.

My mom spent part of her pregnancy with me in jail on a drug charge. When I was a baby, my uncle used to carry me around and sell drugs out of my diaper. When I was a little kid, I lived in a drug house with my mother in the Jordan Downs projects, in Watts, until it was raided by the police.

So, when I say I grew up in the drug game, this shit ain't an allegory. I mean it literally.

I grew up *in* the drug game.

My mother, Lydia Garner, was one of eight kids and rebellious from a young age. Though she spent a lot of years living with her deeply religious grandmother, by the time she was fifteen, she had been kicked out of her house for buying a pair of Levi's 501 jeans—church rules said girls couldn't wear pants—and ended up moving in with her aunt.

With weekend-long poker games and people always coming through drinking and partying, my aunt's house had a completely different vibe, and my mom began to assimilate to that lifestyle. Her cousin Bertie Jo was a drug legend, famous in Watts for two things: (1) having the only private swimming pool in Watts; and (2) creating and controlling the PCP trade in South Central in the 1970s and '80s.

Just to be clear, that pool wasn't used for swimming. It takes lots of liquids to make PCP.

As a teenager, my mother started selling PCP for her cousin and witnessed up close the power, influence, and money at the top of the drug food chain. She saw bribes get delivered to judges, policemen, and anyone else whose wheels needed greasing. She saw fancy cars, clothes, and jewelry. But she also saw the dark side of the game. After a disagreement with her cousin over money, she was almost killed when a man beat her up and tried to give her a "hot shot" of heroin in the neck, to make it look like she'd overdosed.

Thankfully, she's always been a fighter. She fought off that man and had no problem fighting anyone else, man or woman, who might cross her. People didn't expect that from a slim, pretty girl with a big smile. My mom was, and still is, an alpha—more so than most men. She had a presence, and whenever she came into a room, it was like a spotlight came out the ceiling and shined down on her. Even if you weren't looking at my mom, you knew where she was.

In 1979, my mother had my older sister Kadeisha, but before she was even born, Kadeisha's father was shot and killed by the police. A year later, my momma met my dad, Samuel Corbin. About fifteen years older and married with a whole other family in another part of Watts, my dad had a good job at the Department of Water and Power, but he knew the other side as well. He was part of an old-school safecracking crew, and his older sons controlled the drug game in Watts's Front Street neighborhood. On the undeniable force of her personality alone, I'm sure my mother charmed him from the beginning, because soon after they met, on November 21, 1980, they had me.

Because my dad had another family, there are no pictures of all three of us together in the hospital, no blue balloons tied to the mailbox when they brought me home. As soon as she could, my mother took me back to the dope house where she was living and got back to it. Life resumed.

Growing up in that house, I had no set rules—no scheduled nap times or square meals, no one to wipe my ass or tell me to brush my teeth. Life was a random accumulation of events. Even now, I see it more in imagery and scenes than stories. I see myself dropping firecrackers through mail slots with my uncle. I see another of my uncles jumping out of a car and running from the police as we played trash can basketball in the project streets. And I see the police raid that sent my mom to jail.

These were the days of L.A. police chief Daryl Gates and "Operation Hammer," when hundreds of SWAT team cops would brutally raid suspected drug houses in South Central.

During one raid, on Dalton Avenue in 1988, the cops fucked up the houses so bad, spray-painting "LAPD Rules" on walls and smashing furniture with sledgehammers and axes, that the Red Cross was called in. On another, after everyone was handcuffed, Gates brought Nancy Reagan through for a tour. Posing for the photo op, the First Lady commented, "These people in here are beyond the point of teaching and rehabilitating."

When our house was raided, we weren't lucky enough to get a celebrity appearance. Maybe it was too early in the day. I remember getting ready to go to school when the SWAT police came charging in with sledgehammers and guns, looking more like RoboCops than beat cops. I remember the sound of everything breaking: the door, the table, the walls. Smash. Smash. Smash. It was scary as hell.

Because of the raid, my momma went to jail, so she left me, Kadeisha, and my two younger brothers, Kevin and Bam, with my Granny Louella. Even after she got out, my mother knew the demons of her drug addiction were too much and that the best care we could get was with Granny. Still, she tried to help in her own way, leaving money she made from selling drugs with Miss Margaret at the candy store for my Pa Pa to pick up and turning her county check over to my grandparents.

This is where my actual memories begin.

GRANNY'S HOUSE AT 10617 JUNIPER Street in Watts was always buzzing. Part of that may have had to do with the fact that she didn't own a key, so the door was always open. You never knew who was going to be on the couch in the morning, recovering from last night or kicking things off today.

But it was mainly about the food. In our neighborhood, my Granny was a legendary cook. Everything about the way she kept her house was designed to feed the masses, whether she knew you or not. In her backyard, she had live chickens and an occasional pig, which she and my Pa Pa would butcher themselves and roast in a pit in the front yard. She had citrus trees and a vegetable garden and grapevines. Granny had come out to California from Alabama as a child in the 1940s, during the Second Great Migration, and a piece of that southern country upbringing had stayed with her. In her younger days, she fed everyone from her yard. Only the staples were store-bought. You wanted ice cream? Go churn it yourself.

She kept two deep freezers and two refrigerators in her garage, plus another refrigerator in the house, and she would pack all of them. When she cooked, she didn't do it just for the family; she cooked with the intention of feeding the whole block. She'd get up at five A.M. on the weekdays to make bacon and eggs and grits for all of us kids. People used to say they knew we were coming from Louella's because they'd see us happily eating bacon sandwiches on our walk to school, our faces shiny with grease. On the weekends, she'd cook the big meals, getting up early to put on one of her floral muumuus and get started. I remember watching her stand over a big old sink of water with her greens, meticulously cleaning each leaf like you might clean clothes on a washboard. In all the times I ate them, never once did I taste grit. She did the same thing with her chitlins, cleaning the intestines one at a time, incorporating love and care from the beginning, never skipping steps.

She would make giant pots of gumbo, huge vats of bubbling chili and rice; pull every last bit of meat off the neckbones for beef and potato burritos. She was like the food Pied Piper. Folks from all over would smell my Granny's cooking and conveniently wander by right when it was ready, so every night was like a party. My Pa Pa and his friends would sit out on the porch drinking Thunderbird and Night Train, listening to music and laughing and joking and telling stories from the sixties as they shoveled down my Granny's meals. We'd have neighborhood kids and cousins and our brothers and sisters running through, grabbing a quick bite of a burrito, before sprinting into the backyard to play tag. And my Granny, tired from hours of cooking, would go sit in her favorite chair in the corner of the living room. On the table in front of her would always be five things: a cup of coffee; a Pall Mall Red cigarette; a lottery ticket; a cake; and a twelve-inch turn-the-dial television with a clothes hanger as an antenna, so she could watch her *Murder, She Wrote* or her Westerns. She loved John Wayne.

Every day, there would be a different big-ass cake on that table: German chocolate, vanilla, pineapple upside-down, Sock It to Me. Anytime someone new came to the house, the first thing my Granny would ask them was "When is your birthday?" and then "What's your favorite type of cake?" It didn't matter if that kid never showed up again in his life, on his birthday, my Granny would have his favorite type of cake waiting on that table, ready for him, or anyone else, to take a slice.

Granny was soft-spoken and the sweetest woman I knew. But if you crossed her or pissed her off, you'd become very familiar with her favorite word: *motherfucker*. "Sit your motherfuckin' ass down now," she'd say to us often. "You motherfuckers are driving me crazy." It was hard to blame her. My Granny had already raised eight kids, and now, because of drugs or jail, she was raising *their* kids, too. Most grandparents just needed to occasionally take their grandkids to the park, or buy them a Nerf football for their birthday, and they'd come out looking like the greatest grandparents in the world. But this was a woman who would get up at the crack of dawn every day to feed a bunch of kids who were not even hers.

Granny was the "big momma" for our neighborhood. Around my way, big mommas were the cornerstones of the community as well as of their own families. As in my case, they would fill a parental role for their grandkids, but they were also like the parents for the entire hood. You might be fourteen and think you're the hardest kid, beating everyone's ass in your grade, but if you came home and pissed off a big momma, she'd tell you to go pick a switch to get your own ass beat. And you'd do it. And she might do the same for your friends.

Before she retired, Granny had worked for years cleaning white people's homes all over L.A. For a while, she was a live-in maid in a beachfront house in Malibu owned by the actress who'd played Jane in one of the original Tarzan movies. My mother used to tell me about visiting Granny there during the summers in the 1960s and getting to ride horses along the beach with all the rich white kids. After that employer left the area, Granny got a job cleaning rooms at the Holiday Inn. It was a long way from Malibu.

Even after Granny retired, she never got to take it easy. There were no vacations, no excursions to the beach or the movies. On the first of the month, she'd go to the grocery store. On the fifteenth, she'd go back to the grocery store. Other than that, she was in the house morning, noon, and night. But that didn't mean my Granny didn't hustle. She had way too many mouths to feed.

She would hold poker games in her house, make bets on the ponies, and occasionally sell a little weed—all from her chair at the corner of her table. She cooked chili and rice and peach cobbler for my mom to sell. She sold her beef, bean, and cheese burritos out of my auntie's liquor store on 103rd, keeping an eye on me as I played on a jerry-rigged *Ms. Pac-Man* machine in the back.

As the oldest grandson in the house, I was the one she had to give the most attention to—making sure I was home when I said I'd be, keeping up with my bullshit. She'd get angry, but she also developed a soft spot for me, allowing me to do things the other kids couldn't. She had no problem with my curly-haired, ashy-elbowed, chubby-cheeked eight-year-old ass staying up late playing bartender at her poker games, fetching beers for her friends from behind a toddler door in the kitchen (and sneaking under tables to take change out of the money buckets), riding my bike over to the projects to deliver her pony race picks, or going to the store across the street with a note for the man at the register so I could get her a new pack of Pall Malls.

It didn't seem like much, but in those moments, I could feel her love.

Her husband, my Pa Pa, was known as Turkey Red, mostly because he was, as my Granny might have put it, "a Louisiana-red motherfucker." He was six foot two with red hair, freckles, and a big, booming laugh, which you'd hear while he hung out with his friends on the front porch drinking, playing music, smoking, and grilling barbecue. Pa Pa wasn't trying to be a chef, but he had moves. He used to doctor up his store-bought BBQ sauce with cut lemons or sugar. He'd make chili from scratch, adding steak meat where most people used ground beef. Pa Pa also knew how to put a bike together from spare parts, repaint it, and make it seem new. He was the bike man for the entire neighborhood.

But there was a rule with Pa Pa: Don't. Fuck. With. His. Shit. When his son kept sneaking sips from his Night Train and Thunderbird, Pa Pa poured a little bleach into one of the bottles in the fridge before going to bed. When his son came in and snuck a sip, he nearly choked to death. That was Pa Pa's lesson: *Don't fuck with my shit.*

And that wasn't even the craziest example. Once, another of his sons was making my younger brother cry. My grandfather came out of his room. "Stop bothering my goddamn grandson." But my uncle kept at it. My grandfather looked at him. "I told your motherfuckin' ass to leave my grandson alone. I best not see your ass when I come out this room." My granddad returned to his room and . . . next thing I saw, he'd come back out with a twelve-gauge shotgun. My uncle took off running and had almost made it up the street when my granddad leaned the shotgun on the gate and shot him right in his head with buckshot, flipping him over. The buckshot just scarred him, but that was how strongly my grandfather felt about protecting us. *He would shoot your ass.*

Of course, even Pa Pa couldn't escape the wrath of Granny. They never really fought in front of us, but we all knew when tensions were high. My Granny would beckon one of us to come to her corner of the table. After taking a drag off her Pall Mall, she'd look at us and say, "Go tell that motherfucker I married to come here."

I may have loved my Pa Pa, but right then, he was on his own.

———

GRANNY WAS ALIVE TO WITNESS World War II, the Korean War, segregation, the civil rights movement, the Watts Riots, assassinations, and the crack epidemic, but she didn't talk about any of that shit. She was part of the Silent Generation, and she took that to heart. Granny wasn't sitting you down and giving you life lessons. She wanted her grandkids to look at her with admiration, love, and respect and did not paint a picture of pain and strife. She may've been silent, but there was a pride in that silence.

She'd seen both sides of the world—the side where her kids rode horses on the beach in Malibu and the side where those same kids scrounged in the streets for enough loose change to buy a three-dollar crack rock. She knew it was going to be hard for us as Black kids growing up poor, coming from where we came from, and she didn't give us false hope. She didn't tell us "America is great. There's equality. All you've got to do is hit your books, and you can be anything you want." But she didn't weigh us down with the negative, either; didn't burden us with her plight. There was truth in her silence, too.

And yet, you knew she wanted us to do the right thing. She wanted more from us, though she'd resigned herself to the fact that she didn't have the ability to take us to that higher level. But she was hopeful. She believed in the universe. She cared. When I got kicked out of school in the third grade for fighting, it broke her heart. Her love radiated off her, and everyone around her could feel it.

She taught us to look out for one another. If I wanted to go somewhere and didn't want to bring my younger brother along, she'd look at me and say, "All you motherfuckers are going together, and you're going to dress alike, too." But most important, I was raised to consider my cousins as close as my siblings.

Which brings me to Branden, aka BL.

Between them, my Granny and her sister Dolly had fourteen kids. And for most of their lives, before Dolly moved into the projects, they lived either next door to or around the corner from each other, in houses all over Watts.

Branden was Dolly's grandkid—so, technically, my second cousin, but we didn't make those kinds of distinctions. We were all just cousins. His mother, like mine, was on drugs, and he grew up in his auntie Darlene's house in Jordan Downs. He may've been a year younger than me, but from the time we were little, we were like phantom twins. Even as a kid, Branden had something in him that commanded respect. He carried himself differently.

Athletically built, with almond-shaped eyes and a bullet-shaped head, Branden suffered from alopecia as a child. This made his hair fall out in patches—we used to tease him that his head looked like a map—likely, a result of the stress he felt from dealing with his mother being in the streets. But he was a natural-born leader and one of the best athletes in our projects. When he played football, the whole neighborhood came out to watch.

He was also incredibly smart, in the gifted program at our school, with a quick, cutting wit. He loved practical jokes. You never wanted to be the first to fall asleep at a sleepover with Branden, or you'd end up with flour all over your face. He liked to slap-box and was so naturally strong that by the time we were in middle school, he could pick you up and slam you on a table just messing around.

Branden wasn't a people pleaser; he was quiet and observant. When he did talk, he got straight to the point, never afraid to tell you to your face exactly what he thought. Dude was fearless. Of course, it helped that he was essentially a thoroughbred fighter. His father, Bruce Bullard, had been famous for knocking motherfuckers out. And, like my mom, Branden's mother, Kathy Miller, was well known for being one of the toughest women in the streets.

When we were still in elementary school, older fellas in our neighborhood used to set up fights in abandoned houses—the same places where they'd hold dogfights—with Branden taking on kids from other neighborhoods. Grown-ass men would stand around betting money on the kid fights, eyeing us like we were pit bulls. But Branden was a safe bet. He never lost.

If you were his friend, he was incredibly protective. Once, an older dude from the neighborhood snatched our friend Greg's chain off his neck. When Branden heard, he immediately found the dude, snatched the chain off his neck, and put it back on Greg. Branden wouldn't let you disrespect or bully him, and it was the same for anyone under his care. When he found out one of our aunties was getting beaten by her husband, and none of her four sons would do anything about it, Branden, as a young teen, went over and shot the dude. The beatings stopped.

From a young age, I always felt like I was observing, taking things in, acting like a sponge for information. I never had imaginary friends, but I was creating characters out of myself. I was trying to figure out my own identity, so I would try on pieces of Branden's to see if any fit. Nearly everything Branden and I did growing up was determined by or in reaction to each other.

We came up together, but there were differences between us. Branden loved having a lot of people around him and under his care. He didn't mind others taking some of the shine off the things that made him glow. We were both alphas, but different kinds. Branden was a lion. He liked being among his pride. I was more like a tiger, preferring the space and solitude to handle things solo.

The dynamics between us reminded me of Chris and Gordie in *Stand by Me*. I watched that movie all the time. I loved that it seemed like the kids were raising one another. They were all growing up on their own together and developing identities along the way. They experienced things. They'd get in fights with each other, run from dogs in a junkyard, swim across a swamp and get leeches on their nuts, stand up to older bullies, find dead bodies. They didn't start out tough and courageous, but in each situation, someone found a way to step up. They found their bravery, or their intelligence, or their vulnerability, and made it work for them. They didn't know what was going to happen; they just embarked on the journey. I loved that shit.

Plus, there were no fucking parents around.

Of course, our *Stand by Me* moments were a little different. We would find the breaker box for a whole row of houses in the projects, cut the power, and run away. When the projects had swings and sandboxes, we'd play on those. When they took away the swings, we played in the sand. And when they took away the sand, we shot marbles in the dirt where the sandbox used to be. It didn't matter. We made everything in the projects our playground.

The kids with strict parents would go home when the streetlights came on. But for Branden and me, night just meant a different kind of trouble to get into. Everything in the projects intensified at night. The smells of drug smoke and urine and trash were stronger. People acted crazier. Danger became more palpable. Branden and I would see things no kids should ever see: dead bodies lying in cars shot up after an ambush, kidnapped folks being moved into new safe houses. We became desensitized quick, and those experiences helped us build our street résumés. By the time we got to middle school, we'd seen things other kids hadn't. We knew how to react. We had an advantage.

But just because we saw grown-up things, it didn't mean we had to be adults. Occasionally, in the summer, a group of us would lie in the project's gym field at night and have a sleepover. Keeping my eyes on the sky, I'd count the stars, listen to the crickets chirping and the owls hooting, and convince myself I was on a real campout deep in the woods, just like the kids in *Stand by Me*.

In the morning, when we woke up and started moving around, bats that had been sleeping among us would fly off, freaking most of the kids out. But I wasn't scared. I'd watch the bats fly across the sky and wonder how far they could go.

2

What's Going On

THE SENSATION OF BEING IN THE PROJECTS IS LIKE A SONG. WHEN you first hear it, you might pay attention to the lyrics, or the chorus, or the bass line. But with so much happening, it's hard to isolate all the individual parts. Eventually, it's just music. And that's the busyness of the projects, the flow and energy of the people: kids shouting and laughing; dudes making bets and gambling; tires screeching; the smell of weed, of piss, of sulfur from the crack; the bold color of the art and graffiti on the buildings; cars blocking traffic; teenagers jumping out to talk to their friends; and other cars honking; big mommas coming out their houses telling those young boys to move their fucking cars out the street. There's hugging and laughing and dancing and kids practicing cheerleading and throwing footballs and playing trash can basketball. There's drug selling, fights, and gunshots.

Just hanging out in the projects is like a drug rush. Everything is heightened. And if you spend enough time there, it definitely rewires your brain. Your synapses are always firing. You come to expect that sensation, to crave the chaos. You need it. The projects, in a strange way, are addicting.

And because they're a world unto themselves, that high can last as long as you want. You never have to leave. When I was coming up, Jordan Downs was its own underground shopping mall, with everything you could possibly need.

Hungry? You snagged a burger or tacos from Miss Irma; or a burrito from Miss Irma's mother, Miss Dot; or, if it was a Friday, some fried fish and French fries from the Muslim lady Miss Wajeha's tent.

Wanted something sweet? You went to Miss Margaret's Candy House.

Sick or in pain? Mister Fred had a whole pharmacy stocked with red devils, Valium, and any other kind of pill you needed.

Wanted a car fixed or a paint job? You'd go find Papa.

Need new clothes or a pretty decent fake Rolex? You'd see Dead Eyed Paul or Cynthia Curtis.

A bike? Big Al or my Pa Pa Turkey Red would hook you up.

A mixtape full of slow jams? Tunc would make you something special.

A driver's license or a ticket fixed? You went to D-Mac, and his girl at the DMV would handle it.

Wanted someone to spray-paint a picture of Black Santa and his reindeer on your window for Christmas? Joe had you.

And if you needed someone to cook your drugs? You came to me.

As kids, being in the bubble of Jordan Downs was like living with the largest extended family you could imagine. As you got older, you started seeing the downsides to that environment and wondering how it got that way. But to understand this you need to understand Watts. And to understand Watts, you need to understand how all these Black folks came to live in South Central L.A. in the first place.

When both sides of my family moved to Southern California from the South in the forties, everything was booming: movies, defense, aerospace. Demand for workers was at an all-time high, and the federal government used an executive order to ban hiring discrimination by government contractors, so a huge number of southern Black families (more than 340,000 during 1942–45 alone) headed west as part of the Second Great Migration.

Getting jobs was easy. Getting housing was hard. The Veterans Administration and the Federal Housing Administration wouldn't finance homes for Blacks, which meant that of the 125,000 new homes built in L.A. County between 1950 and 1954, only 3,000 were "open to non-Caucasian occupancy." Plus, white people didn't want Black folks living in their neighborhoods. With *Shelley v. Kraemer* in 1948, the Supreme Court ruled this shit illegal, but nothing was enforced, and if a professional Black person still somehow managed to find a way into a white suburban L.A. neighborhood, the harassment that followed made the actual living part impossible. In 1959, a Black psychologist moved his family into a white area and, in the first few months after their move, reported one hundred incidents to the police, including gunshots through the windows, two undertakers sent with reports of a "dead homeowner," and the words "Black Cancer Here. Don't Let It Spread!" painted on the front of their home.

With neither the patience nor the money to endure this shit, most Black folks ended up overcrowding into the only part of Los Angeles that didn't fight to keep them out: South Central. Forced to live in deteriorating pre–World War I housing or illegally built rental properties, they tried to make the best of it, but they were boxed in. To the east, Alameda Street became known as "the cotton curtain" separating Black L.A. from the white working-class "sundown towns," so named because Blacks were not safe there after sundown, thanks to the racist L.A. County Sheriff's Department and the local "Spook Hunter" gangs.

If Black folks did manage to get somewhere, that caused different problems. Though Compton had resisted Blacks for decades, by 1969 there had been enough of a demographic shift in the city for voters to elect their first Black mayor, Douglas Dollarhide. Compton was supposed to be an example of a successful inner L.A. suburb for Black professionals. But white flight and construction of the Century Freeway—which cut up the area while somehow avoiding all the white neighborhoods—meant that almost all the retail businesses along Compton Boulevard closed down.

The rest was predictable. Banks, seeing Compton in decline, stopped giving home and small business loans, meaning the

shitty housing couldn't be fixed and new businesses couldn't
open to replace old ones. Dollarhide tried, but the all-white
L.A. County Local Area Formation Commission rejected plans
to annex unincorporated industrial land in order to fund schools
and other services. With no other options, the city was forced to
raise property taxes, pushing most professional Blacks out. Who
wants to pay ridiculously high taxes to live in a city with rapidly
worsening schools and business districts? Author Mike Davis,
who has written extensively about the L.A. government's
fucked-up history toward minorities, called Compton's treatment under Dollarhide a "white embargo," saying, "Compton
might as well have been Haiti or Cuba."

For Black folks around L.A., Compton became the lesson.
First, they'll do everything they can to keep you out. And if
they can't keep you out, they'll do everything they can to keep
you poor.

BY THE TIME I WAS growing up in Watts, no one needed remind-
ing. We'd *been* poor since the 1940s, when the government built
giant projects to provide housing for factory workers during the
war. As Watts grew Blacker, city officials started ignoring it,
and the area festered with shitty public services, inadequate
schools, and laughable hospital care.

The police, however, paid Watts special attention. Their
"stop-and-frisk" policy basically ensured that many young
Black men in Watts had a criminal record by the end of their
teens. And that often meant they couldn't get a real job. Even
when the L.A. economy was revving, the unemployment rate in

Watts for men was close to 30 percent. The combination of civil negligence, police harassment, and economic abandonment could stay dormant for only so long.

On August 11, 1965, this powder keg exploded with what would become known as the Watts Riots. Two Black men from Watts were pulled over a block from their home for drunk driving, and when one refused to be handcuffed, the local police precinct—whose motto at the time was "Let's Shoot a Motherfucker Tonight," aka LSMFT—responded to a call for backup with twenty-six vehicles. The spectacle of all those lights caused a crowd to gather, and as they watched the men—and then a few of the women who came to the men's defense—get beaten, it became just too damn much.

Throughout the week of rioting, my family was right there in the mix. My mother remembers being on her porch listening to her fifteen-year-old cousin play his bongos as the National Guard drove by in an armored jeep shouting at everyone to go back inside their homes. When her cousin was slow to stop playing, they shot him in the legs.

After a week of looting, burning, and National Guardsmen with shoot-to-kill orders emptying .50-caliber machine guns into apartment buildings, thirty-four people were killed, over a thousand were injured, and almost four thousand were arrested.

Before the riots, the commercial district by my Granny's house on 103rd was vibrant. There was a movie theater showing first-run films for a quarter, a tailor shop, restaurants, a mortuary, a Schwinn bike shop, Pappy's Burgers for fifteen cents, an accountant, doctors—everything. But it all burned. When the riots were over, that area became known as Charcoal Alley.

After the riots, Martin Luther King, Jr., visited Watts.

While he was there, a young man came up to him saying, "We won!" When MLK asked what he meant—as thirty-four people had died, and everything had been destroyed—the man said, "We made them pay attention to us."

Now, to be from Watts meant something. We were the Black people who finally couldn't take it any longer. After the riots, the major gangs in South Central came to an organic truce among themselves, from the Slausons and the Gladiators to the Parking Lot gang out of Jordan Downs. Gangs at that time were about the low-level shit—petty crime, selling weed, settling scores with fists, knives, and bats. Of course, there were still neighborhood rivalries and small squabbles during this truce, but a few of the gangs actively became more politically aware and community oriented.

For example, the Parking Lot gang, which included several of my uncles, renamed themselves Sons of Watts, and devoted their time to helping parolees and running security for local events, even taking the step to incorporate as a nonprofit. Sons of Watts worked with Community Alert Patrol (CAP), a group of neighborhood cars that followed police around at night, acting as a check on their power. Huey Newton's much more well-known Oakland-based Black Panther Party, which formed several months later, even based its policing of the police on CAP's tactics.

In this changed environment, Watts was freed up to experience a brief cultural renaissance. Artists made junk art out of the leftover rubble and showed it at Markham Middle School (where, decades later, I would go) and then around the country. Along 103rd Street, right by Granny's home, the Watts Happening Coffee House, an arts center, and studios opened up in 1965 where so many of the old businesses had burned down.

Budd Schulberg, the white Academy Award–winning screen-writer, founded the Watts Writers Workshop, which for a time was, as Davis put it, "one of Hollywood's favorite feel-good philanthropies," even receiving a grant from the National Endowment for the Arts. The Watts Summer Festival—partly a commemoration of those who'd died in the riots, partly a joy-ous celebration of the creativity bubbling up in the city—launched in August 1966.

But as the images of the riots faded, so did white liberal interest in Watts. Philanthropy projects were abandoned. MLK was killed. Malcolm X was killed. Bobby Kennedy, too. No one was going to help us. We had to help ourselves. But we're resourceful motherfuckers. And if the aboveground, legit econ-omy wasn't going to deal us in, the projects would go ahead and make our own game underground. So, our economy shifted. If a bank wouldn't give Miss Margaret the money to open a candy store, she'd do it out of her house. If Pa Pa couldn't get a line of credit to purchase bikes wholesale, he'd take broken parts from a scrapyard and build a bike his own damn self. And if no straight business would employ young Black men from the projects, those young men would gravitate to the one trade where money could always be made: drugs.

With the gang truce of the late 1960s fading away, the best way to sell those drugs now was through gangs that had started to loosely align themselves under the banners of Raymond Washington and Stanley "Tookie" Williams's Crip set or Sylves-ter Scott's Pirus and their Blood alliances. At first it was weed, sherm sticks (cigarettes soaked in PCP), and other low-level, stepped-on shit. But in the early eighties, as the CIA-backed cocaine trade exploded, the drugs got more serious—as did the money and the crime. There was no going back.

After all, voids needed to be filled.

IN APRIL 1992, WATTS WAS on fire again.

Thanks to the acquittal of the four police officers caught on videotape beating Black motorist Rodney King, the entire city was going up in flames. In South Central, the rioting was so bad that businesses would actually open their doors for us to take shit and then pay us to burn them down when we were done, so they could collect the insurance money. But something even crazier was happening on the streets of Watts.

In my city, gangs were everywhere (and still are). Just in the 2.2 square miles that make up Watts, you had the Front Street Watts Crips, the Bacc Street Watts Crips, the Circle City Pirus, the Watts Franklin Square Crips, the Fudge Town Mafia Crips, Nut Hood, the Ten Line Gangster Watts Crips, the Compton Avenue Crips, the Hat Gang, the Bebop Watts Bishop Bloods, the PJ Watts Crips in the Imperial Courts projects, and the Hacienda Village Bloods in Hacienda Village. And that wasn't even counting the Latin gangs. But by far the two biggest were the Grape Street Watts Crips, out of my own Jordan Downs projects, and our bitterest rivals, Nickerson Gardens' Bounty Hunter Bloods. The war between our two sides had gone on for years.

But during the five days of riots following the 1992 acquittal of those four cops who beat Rodney King, the Grape Street Watts Crips and Bounty Hunter Bloods (plus two of the other biggest gangs in Watts, the PJ Crips and the Hacienda Bloods) were in each other's projects—not to shoot, but to celebrate a truce. Although the timing made it seem like the truce had something to do with the riots, it wasn't about that. Negotiations had been going on for years (often at former NFL star Jim Brown's house through his Amer-I-Can program), and the first parts of a treaty among these gangs had been signed the day before everything blew up with King. By the week of May 4, the riots had ended and Crips and Bloods were walking shoulder-to-shoulder in front of news cameras celebrating the peace treaty.

The early nineties were a pivotal time for Watts and the rest of South Central. Dre and Snoop were topping the *Billboard* charts. Movies like *Boyz n the Hood* and *Menace II Society* (filmed in Jordan Downs) were packing white movie theaters. News coverage of the riots, the gang truce, and the drug trade exposed the true-life versions of the Black stories that had recently taken over popular culture. There could've been a renaissance similar to the brief one that followed the riots in 1965; white culture had seen the danger and the bombast, and they wanted a taste. This time, though, there were no real economic benefits trickling down to the people of Watts. But following the gangs' truce, there was definitely a new kind of tranquility on the streets.

Except on the Markham Middle School playground.

During my time there, middle school in Watts was essentially an experiment in what not to do for schooling. For elementary and high school, each of the projects and main rival gang territories remained more or less separated, with the members of each gang attending a different school. But during the years when everyone was hitting puberty, feeling insecure, and overcompensating by trying to act tough, the kids from all the various projects were schooled under one roof.

We started at Markham with no reason to have a beef with any of the other projects—except an inherited beef. As a kid, you didn't question why certain gangs and projects were your allies or your enemies. Just knowing that certain kids were from another project was enough for you to hate them. And with no organized sports, there was no chance for a *Remember the Titans*-style camaraderie to develop among the different projects.

In the spring of 1994, the OGs from all the different projects marched along Compton Avenue past Markham to commemorate the second anniversary of the march after the Rodney King riots. Normally, each kid would sit outside in the corner of the playground closest to where his project was. The Nickersons would sit on the southwest side, Imperial Courts on the southeast, Haciendas in the northwest, and those of us from Jordan Downs in the northeast. Essentially it was Bloods on the west side, Crips on the east.

One day, I was chilling with Branden and our homies Rah Rah, Greg, Bruce, Smokey, and Truck, eating the snacks we'd bought from the student store. (Cool kids didn't eat no regular lunch.) We had started off in our respective corners of the playground, but when the OGs marched by, everyone ran to the fence, which was technically on the Nickersons' side of the playground. Normally, we might get in squabbles over the basketball court, or someone might get jumped if they happened to be alone outside their territory, but we were never all together in such close quarters.

If it had been a film, seeing Bloods and Crips walking shoulder-to-shoulder like that would've inspired us to also squash our petty beefs. Seeing Nickerson dudes like Klepto, Snotbox, E.T., Cruz, Little Rick, Cane, and all the PJ Watts dudes like Lil Tony, Fred-O, Karon, and Poo-Butt surrounding me and my homies, we should've realized that we were all from the same city, all facing the same problems, and all looking for some sort of common ground to stand on like the OGs. But we're talking about a bunch of thirteen-year-old project babies.

I don't know how it first kicked off, but inevitably, someone in the crowd got bumped, and that dude shoved back. And then the shouting started.

"Fuck Booty Hos [our derogatory name for Bounty Hunters]!"

"Fuck Fake Street [their derogatory name for Grape Street]!"

"Fuck Peanut Butter and Jelly [everybody's derogatory name for the PJ Watts Crips]!"

We were like a pile of bone-dry kindling stacked on top of one another. All it took was one match to set it off. Maybe Klepto from the Nickersons first threw a carton of milk. Or maybe I threw a water bottle. At this point, recalling the exact flashpoint is impossible. And, truthfully, it doesn't matter. All that matters is that, within seconds, as the OGs marched by chanting "Peace," a huge brawl broke out right by the fence among a bunch of middle-schoolers.

I was throwing punches left and right and tossing people off my back, trying to stand my ground in the midst of the chaos when, after a few minutes, Officer Nebbles and his security crew came through to break it up, grabbing a few of the most flagrant offenders and throwing them in the back of their golf cart. It just so happened that Markham Middle School had a police substation right on campus, where they'd lock you up until a real patrol car came to haul your ass to jail.

Though this brawl has always stuck out in my mind, in a way, it was just a bigger version of the skirmishes that went on throughout middle school and of the problems they created. We may not have come into school with an actual beef with the other kids, but by the time we graduated, we remembered the ones who jumped us in hallways or on the playground, and we wanted to hurt them. The truce may've been in place, but eventually it would end. After all, Watts is small. You knew you'd see them again.

GROWING UP, I GENUINELY ENJOYED math and history, and I thought of myself as smart, but I was deeply insecure at school. When the teacher had each student in the classroom read a paragraph from a story, I remember counting how many people came before me and figuring out which paragraph I'd have to read, and then I'd spend the whole time reading it over and over again to myself. By the time the teacher got to me, I was able to read it fluently and fast—and appear to be a better reader than everyone else. I thought I could have it both ways—be tough out of school and a nerd inside. That's how I got my nickname, Fresh. In the beginning, Branden used to call me "Freshman," as a sort of tongue-in-cheek way of saying that, in school, I was a nerd.

"What up, Freshman," he'd say with a smile when I rolled up on him with my books.

The nickname stuck, but I didn't really like it, so I short-ened it to "Fresh" when I was tagging things. Eventually, every-one else started calling me Fresh. There's a certain irony in the fact that I got my nickname on the street because of my love for the classroom. I'm an information junkie. I like knowing things, period. But when I say I loved the classroom, I genuinely mean the *classroom*. Growing up in the midst of chaos, I loved the predictability of class, knowing that for an hour I could let my guard down, if only a little bit.

It was hard to focus on education with everything else going on. Danger was everywhere and real, almost a tactile part of life. As we grew, we became more attuned to escaping it and navigating the city to avoid the other gangs and the older kids. Our instincts sharpened real quick. While walking to school in the morning, when the gangs would be shooting at one another, we learned to travel quickly through open spaces and to hit the ground and hide under cars when we needed to. We knew it was safer to move in packs—any solo kid could be picked off by roving groups from other projects and neighborhoods. But as we grew older and hit middle school, gangs could just assume our affiliation and shoot on sight. So, traveling in those same packs that had once pro-vided comfort suddenly became dangerous.

In our neighborhood, there was always talk of "genera-tions," almost like your graduating class from the streets. The people in your generation were usually the kids who came up within three or four years of you. More than the gangs or even, in some cases, families, your generation was where your allies and loyalties forever lay.

Hierarchies within generations were established early on, in elementary school. Elementary school served as a kind of boot camp. You'd get into little scuffles within your own group or, occasionally, with kids from different hoods—at a fast-food joint or the Will Rogers pool that sat in the middle of Watts. At this point in our lives, for the most part, we were figuring things out with kids from our own neighborhood for when it really started to matter—in middle school, when we were crowded into a building for six hours every day with the same kids we were trying to avoid out on the streets.

It wasn't like the school administration didn't understand this. In fact, the principal and the staff did things to try to temper the violence. For example, we were made to keep to different areas of the playground, and most kids from a specific project would have their last class of the day scheduled near the door where they were let out of school, the exit closest to their project. But things didn't always work this way. In eighth grade, I ended up with my last class over by where the Nickerson kids got let out. If I didn't time it right, they could catch me on my own and jump me, so I started bringing a .357 pellet gun to school, keeping it in my locker and retrieving it every damn day before last period. That way, I could at least flash it, and buy enough time to get back to my side of the neighborhood.

You know how some animals can see more gradations of color than humans? Well, middle school made us start seeing everything in shades we couldn't see before, through a lens of potential threat. We couldn't just *go* to school. We needed to consider where we entered it, which door we used to leave it, what time of day we went to a certain part of the school, who was surrounding us when we went to the bathroom or the play-ground. Everything was calculated for risk and reward, includ-ing what we wore.

In South Central, clothes were another way to fence us in. But this time, we did it to ourselves. To this day, there is no such thing as just wearing gear to support a team you like. Everything means something else. Purple Vikings or Lakers gear means Grape Street. Red Nebraska hats mean you rep the Nickersons. Burgundy Phillies gear, the Pirus. Houston Astros hats, the Hoover gang. Chicago Cubs, Compton Crips. Denver Broncos, Denver Lane Bloods. Seattle Mari-ners hats, Rollin' 60s Crips. White Sox caps, any enemies of the Rollin' 60s (because S-O-X stands for "6-0 killer"). That's a lot to think about for kids barely into their teens. With all this extra shit weighing us down, it's no surprise that, by the time we hit middle school, we thought we were already grown.

At Markham, I continued getting into fights and finding other ways to fuck up, mouthing off to teachers and generally being a pain in the ass. Even my Granny grew tired of my bullshit, and in seventh grade, at the age of twelve, I moved in with my mother in an apartment complex at 103rd and Juniper, right across the street from Jordan Downs.

After our house was raided when I was little, my mom had learned that there was a threat on her life from a dude in our neighborhood who was known as a killer, and she went to live with relatives in Kansas City for a few years. While in KC, my mom had my baby brother Marlon, and when the dude who threatened her went to prison, she came back to Watts. As soon as she was back, she dropped my brother at my Granny's house and went straight into recovery, staying in a sober-living home for several years, studying for her nursing degree, and getting a job at the post office.

I was proud of my mom for cleaning up and making it back home, but ours wasn't exactly a smooth reunion. I wasn't used to having a mother, and she wasn't used to being a mom. We didn't know how to communicate, and we didn't get any guidance or counseling about what we had both been through prior to getting back together. We bumped heads on everything—from going to church, to doing homework, to going out with my friends. After having total and complete freedom for almost all of my childhood, I found it ludicrous that I should suddenly have to follow the rules of a woman who hadn't been a part of my life up until then.

Despite all my rebellious bluster, glimmers of my school-loving nerd side tried to break through. I remember, in eighth grade, there was a teacher-student swap day, when the teacher would pick one student to lead all her classes. A few days earlier, my favorite teacher, Mrs. Banks, was explaining solids, liquids, and gases and I'd asked her a question.

"So, what about sand and dirt?" I asked. "They seem like they're solid, but they operate like liquids."

It was a serious question, but Mrs. Banks thought I was being a wiseass. To show me what it felt like to deal with kids like me all day long, she chose me to be the teacher on swap day. A few days later, I stood up in the front of the room and taught her classes—all six periods.

During first period, I was nervous standing up there in front of my classmates. I had the lesson plan in front of me, but I didn't know what to do with it. I compensated by making jokes and entertaining the class, and though they loved it, I could feel that I wasn't actually in control. And I damn sure wasn't teaching them anything.

By the next class, I had learned my lesson—and the lesson plan. And I realized something important: the teacher sets the tone for the class. If I was taking this seriously, then the class would take it seriously. If I knew the material, the class could learn the material. It didn't mean I couldn't still joke around, but I would do it on my terms. And I loved that. Controlling the energy of the room made me feel powerful, and heard.

After school, Mrs. Banks told me how happy she was with how I'd done. I was happy with myself. I could even imagine teaching one day. The nerd side of my gangster-nerd persona could've won.

3

Kitchen

WHEN I WAS BORN, MY FATHER LIVED IN WATTS'S FRONT STREET neighborhood, outside the projects, and already had his original family, so I didn't know much about him. I knew they called him Big Sam. I knew he was born in Arkansas, had twelve siblings, and had moved to California as a child. I knew he'd been involved with the Black Panthers as a teen. I knew he got drafted and sent to Vietnam and came back with three Purple Hearts, a necklace of shriveled ears and teeth from kills, and a different personality. People who knew him before and after

Vietnam say that the experience, and his exposure to Agent Orange, fundamentally changed him.

I've come to understand there was a duality to my father. On the one hand, he was a war hero with a steady job at the Department of Water and Power, a man well known for his ability to bake and hand out incredible sweet potato pies on holidays. But on the other hand, he was addicted to drugs, ran the streets with my mother, and robbed businesses all over L.A. with his safecracking crew. Just look at what he brought back from Vietnam—was the real Big Sam more the man with the Purple Hearts or the one with the necklace of human trophies? I don't think I ever knew.

During the summers, my younger brother Kevin and I lived with my father and his family. I don't know how his wife, Nettie, originally came to find out about us. Obviously, the fact that we were born to another woman while she and my father were married must've caused problems, but we never saw it. For all his flaws, my father never shut out one of his own children. I wouldn't have blamed Nettie for not wanting us around; we were reminders of my father's mistakes. But she opened her home to me and Kevin, clothed and fed us, and treated us just like her own sons, Bo, Manuel, and Truett.

Bo and Manuel were a lot older, so they were in and out, and mostly on the streets. But Truett was only three years older than me, and during summers, I stayed in his room.

Truett was a big motherfucker. My father is six foot six and lanky, and Truett had every bit of his height. From a young age, he was massive, like a bear standing on its hind legs. Like Branden, Truett was one of the best fighters—not just of his generation. I mean anywhere. By the time he was thirteen, he was knocking out grown men on a regular basis, but he had nothing but love for his younger brothers. During those summers staying in his room, I became close with him. For most of my childhood, Truett was my protector.

I remember, one summer, Kevin and I were bothering my dad about wanting to swim, and so, to make us happy, Truett went out in the backyard, dug a big-ass hole with a shovel, and filled it up with water. "There," he said. "Now you got your pool."

Being kids, we were happy as hell, but when my daddy got home and saw us splashing in that nasty, muddy-ass water in a hole in the middle of his backyard, he was not amused. He sent us to the tub to get cleaned up and then came in with his belt to give us a beating, but Truett stood in front of him. He didn't say anything, but his intention was clear: *You're not going to hit my little brothers.*

Like my other older brothers, Truett repped the Front Street Watts Crips. In late September 1994, some Front Street fellas had gotten into it with Crips from "Bacc Street" (another crew a neighborhood over, on Back Street, though no Crip sets use the letters *c* and *k* together, because that stands for "Crip killer"). The next day, those dudes pulled up, saying they wanted to talk it out. The two gangs had been cool, but when Truett went over, they shot him and drove away. A few days later, he died in the hospital. He was sixteen.

I didn't find out until after Truett was gone. I'd just gotten home from school when my mother told me everything: about the shooting, about Truett going to the hospital, and about my father pulling the plug earlier that day, when it was clear Truett wasn't going to make it.

Immediately, I punched a wall in my mother's apartment, ran out the door and down the stairs, and cried my eyes out. I was a hurricane of emotions. I was angry at my father and my older brothers and sister for not reaching out to me sooner and letting me know Truett was in the hospital, so I could've at least said goodbye, and devastated by the fact that I would no longer be making any new memories with him. I would never again see him driving his scooter down 103rd to come pick me up; never again run into him at the Will Rogers pool and feel proud as he stood up for me in front of my homies; never spend another summer sleeping in the same room, hearing his stories. Those were all in the past now, and the thought of that was so overwhelming, I could barely move.

I was thirteen. He was my idol, and the one person outside of my Granny who seemed to love me unconditionally and wanted to protect me. It hadn't been my parents who'd forced us into a brotherly connection. Truett had taken it upon himself to make sure we had that. Maybe, if I'm being generous, that was why neither my mom nor my dad told me about Truett sooner. Maybe they didn't understand the bond he and I had. Maybe they thought we were just estranged half brothers. Not being told was like losing him twice.

With his death, my balancing act of keeping one foot in school and the other on the streets fell apart. I had nothing but anger inside me. This fury and frustration didn't have a specific target: anybody opposing me needed to feel my pain. I had no proper way to express myself. I was trapped in my thirteen-year-old emotions for years and years, traumatized by Truett's death.

The world had fucked me, so, from there on out, I thought, *Fuck the world*. The nerd was gone. I was going to be a gangster.

We put Truett to rest the same day my mother married my younger brother Marlon's dad, Mitchell. For a few days, I was actually trying to decide if I should go to the funeral or the wedding, but in the end, I wanted to go to both. So, my brother Kevin and I put on the white tuxedos we'd have to wear at our mom's wedding later and headed to my father's house to join the procession to the church. Outside, Truett's homies, all wearing shirts with his picture on them, were buzzing. Apparently, dudes from Bacc Street had been talking, and word was they were going to come by and shoot up the funeral. Everyone outside the house waiting for the limos was on high alert, with cars parked strategically to block off the house and protect the family inside. Sure enough, just before the limos came to pick us up, Bacc Street came through in a car and shot at the house and at everyone in the front yard.

After the commotion and the screaming had died down, and we realized that no one had been hit, the limos came and . . . we just went along to the church. After the funeral, Kevin and I didn't even get a chance to go to the grave. We got dropped by the limo at Century and Avalon and waited at the bus stop in front of the McDonald's until someone picked us up and drove us to Carson Street. We had a wedding to get to.

WHILE HE WAS ALIVE, TRUETT had always made sure our older brothers gave me money. And considering he was a scary motherfucker, they listened. When Manuel was convicted of murder and sent away to prison for "juvenile life" (meaning he wouldn't be released until he was twenty-five), Truett started going to Bo.

Bo was thirteen years older than me and shorter than my other brothers, with a dark complexion. He had issues with kidney failure, so his eyes were always red from dealing with dialysis. Bo was quiet, but when he spoke, he spoke with purpose, even if he wasn't direct. Say you owed him money. Instead of just saying, "Fool, give me my money." He might say, "Man, have you ever seen this movie? Well, there was a scene I loved where this one guy does a favor for another guy, and when it came time to pay him back, that other guy doesn't follow through on his promise, and next thing you know, that man ends up missing. Yeah, I love that scene." And then he might chuckle to himself. "Anyway, what's up with my money?"

Bo was old-school, and he'd seen a lot. I think he got in a habit of never wanting to incriminate himself, and what started as a coded way to talk about illegal activity became just his way of communicating, period. And while I appreciated his careful nature, that shit could be infuriating.

Bo: "You going to the store? Man, it'd be cool if you grabbed a soda."

You go get him a soda and ask for two dollars back.

Bo: "What you talking about? I never asked you to buy me a soda."

After Truett died, I kept coming to Bo with my hand out, and eventually he got tired of hearing me in his ear and decided to teach me something to keep me out of his pockets. Behind his quiet demeanor, Bo was a master hustler. He always saw a bunch of angles on how to flip a dollar. And one of those was drugs.

This wasn't a *Karate Kid*-style Daniel-san tutelage moment. Bo wasn't like, "Come back tomorrow, and we will start your education." He just happened to have a new package of drugs one day, when I went over to his house at 107th and McKinley with my hand out, and he decided to show me something. He knew better than to tell me to "go get a fucking job," because that wasn't the way to earn in our family. His way of saying he wanted to give me a set of skills so I could make some money was to show me how to cook cocaine and turn it into crack. I was going to learn how to "cook work."

Bo was a good teacher. He was patient and laid back, didn't move fast at all. Most people in the streets, it's all about speed, but that wasn't him. He took his time. Execution was important to Bo. And so was quality. He was never someone to try to take one kilo and stretch it into two, or push the limits. He just taught me how to cook pure, grade-A-quality crack cocaine.

With me sitting at the kitchen table of the house Bo shared with his wife and kids, he showed me everything—how to use a scale to weigh out the drugs; how to taste-test and cook down the product to check its purity; how to work a stove; how to do temperature checks; when to add the water. He'd ask me, "What are you looking for? What are you tasting for?" You had to have kitchen intuition, listen to the sounds. You know how if you lay pieces of chicken in a hot pan, you can tell the grease is too hot by the way it's sizzling? Well, if you pour water on cocaine, you can tell if the water is too hot by the way the coke sizzles, too.

Cooking activated all my senses. Sight, smell, touch, sound, taste—everything was heightened. And it focused me—because there were real stakes at play. You were cooking with money, basically—your money, other people's money—so, you really couldn't fuck around.

But even after Bo taught me to cook, I had no use for the skills for a while—so, he kept fronting me quarter pieces, which were seven grams. Bo told me I could sell it however I wanted, but he needed a hundred dollars back; I could keep everything else I made on top of that. If I was smart at the time, I could've made two hundred dollars and doubled my money, but as a fourteen-year-old kid, I had no idea what I was doing, so I would sell off little five-dollar baggies to the smokers in the neighborhood and make just enough to pay back Bo and buy some zoom zooms and wham whams.

Thanks to Branden, all this changed during our freshman year in high school.

JORDAN HIGH SCHOOL WASN'T MARKHAM Middle School, and that was a fucking relief. Made up mainly of kids from Jordan Downs and the surrounding Grape Street neighborhood, Jordan High had none of the same tension with the Nickersons or the other projects, but it created another unavoidable dynamic: a blurring of lines in the neighborhood.

The teachers and administrators may've come from out of town, but the security guards and janitors and lunch ladies and everyone else were usually from Watts. (If they were going to work at Jordan, you'd better believe they were going to be from the neighborhood, lest they put their lives in danger every day.) If your family had influence in the neighborhood, you had influence in the school—and my family had lots of influence. While I was at Jordan, my uncle was head of security, so we had certain privileges, like using his office to hook up with girls. At the time, drugs were moving through the school regularly, distributed by janitors and other staff members to certain students to sell. It got so bad, in fact, that we had a real-life *21 Jump Street* situation in 1996, when I was a freshman. Several L.A. cops posing as students uncovered a massive weed operation at the school. One of the girl cops, a cute Latina, who was probably twenty-three but managed to pass for seventeen, had gone with some dudes to a weed house, cased the spot, and brought the whole thing down. Cops arrested one of the older security guards from the neighborhood and took duffel bags of money and weed out of that house. But the undercover sting didn't have the intended effect. Once the cops were gone and the offenders were arrested, the coast was clear for new drug operations to start up. After all, voids needed to be filled.

If you were interested, Jordan High provided excellent drug networking opportunities, and Branden took advantage, establishing a connect through a Mexican student who fronted him an ounce of cocaine. Ever since Bo showed me what to do, I'd been dying to test my cooking skills solo, but Branden was hesitant, saying he didn't want to take the chance. Once he got the ounce, he planned on bringing it to another cook the next day. Looking back, I can't blame him. I'd never cooked on my own in my life. But that night, after Branden hid the coke in a cabinet and went to sleep, I quietly got up and brought it to the kitchen. I needed to know if I could cook.

While Branden slept, I went through everything Bo had taught me. I worked the stove. I checked the purity. I did temperature checks. I listened for just the right time to add the water. I was locked in because I knew the stakes were serious. I couldn't fuck around. When Branden woke up in the morning, he went to check on the cocaine, and when he discovered it wasn't there, he lost his mind. I stayed quiet at first, but after a while, I showed him what I'd done. He was mad, surprised, and grateful all at once.

But now was the moment of truth. We needed to find a smoker to test it. Given that we were in the projects, this wasn't difficult. A few minutes later, we were watching this dude smoke the drugs and waiting to see what he thought.

"Seven out of ten," he said, a smile on his face.

Personally, I think he might've undersold me, but from that moment, we never looked back.

BEING A PART OF A gang can be bad for you as a person, but it doesn't make you a bad person. Where I grew up, gangs weren't the scourge of our community; they *were* the community. Gangs organized backpack giveaways, BBQs, and parties for the whole neighborhood. They paid for outings to roller rinks. OGs handed out lunch money. Hell, Grape Street once even rented out Magic Mountain so the people from our projects could have it all to themselves.

But the same people passing out lunch money and back-packs to kids were also the ones getting those kids' parents addicted to drugs, which was why they couldn't afford those things in the first place. The people throwing the neighborhood parties were also the ones driving by other neighborhood par-ties and shooting into them.

Growing up in the projects, most of us didn't come from "traditional" families, so we built a family together to figure out how to survive. We were all trying to become comfortable in an uncomfortable circumstance. Gangs were just the water we swam in. And like all families, gangs have good and bad apples. But just because they hung out didn't mean every kid I came up with in elementary and middle school gangbanged. There were drug dealers and robbers and killers, but we also had teachers, electricians, plumbers, and nurses. Actors and artists. And everything in between.

Some gangs have strict, rigid hierarchies, with a kingpin at the top, but I don't know shit about that, because that's not how we, or any of the other gangs I know of, operated. Even in the early days, when Tookie and Raymond combined their crews to form the original Crips, it was never about some sort of central leadership. It was always a loose network of affiliated crews. Still, when I tell people I was a member of the Grape Street Watts Crips, they expect stories of gang initiation, and they always seem slightly disappointed there was no blood oath, no pricking your finger, no made-men Mafia shit, no riding around with your lights off and killing the first person who flashes their lights at you and other urban myths.

When you tell people you sold drugs, they expect the same sort of story—like we had to go to a drug dealer clearinghouse and file for permits with the correct Crip ward boss so he could clear us to sell in the neighborhood. Maybe give us a sticker to put on our car or something. But that wasn't how shit worked.

If you were Grape Street and you lived in the projects and people knew you, that was your stamp of approval. It didn't hurt if your family's legacy in the area involved drug dealing. After all, as any politician can tell you: name recognition is name recognition. Beyond that, it turned into capitalism and everything that that entailed. And during my high school years, with the truce in place and the daily threat of war out of the way, that capitalism jumped off.

I can't overemphasize how much the gang truce in Watts impacted those years. I was partying in the Nickersons on a regular basis and would eventually even buy drugs over there to cook for our crew. We would play football together, go out to the clubs, date ladies from one another's projects—everything. Together, we were like apples and grapes, a fruit basket. But most important, the truce allowed a lot of people in our community to reach a certain age. From 1992 to 2002, we had probably the lowest murder rate our city had seen up to then. Fewer of us were getting buried before our time.

Once Branden had his steady connect and it became clear I could cook, we decided to get serious about the drug game. In May 1996, there had been a huge FBI bust of a major drug enterprise that spanned four states. Eleven dudes from Watts, many of them Grape Street OGs, were locked up, meaning there were a lot fewer experienced cooks left on the street. This gave us an opening. Our first order of business was to establish a base of operations. After a few months trying to sell drugs outside, we realized that having a house was crucial. First off, customers feel much more comfortable coming inside to conduct business. Sure, the crackheads would buy wherever, but working people wanted to do it in private, and they were the ones who had the real money. And so, using our Grape Street network, we took over a house in Jordan Downs where my boy Rah Rah's cousin lived. It wasn't that complicated. Rent at the time was twenty-one dollars a month, so we paid off basically a year's worth of his cousin's rent, found her another place to live, and took over the house. From there, we put together a crew, eleven of us in total, all teenagers, all living together on our own.

By this time, my mother was clean and had bought her first house, a few doors down from the apartment we'd been living in, but she wasn't doing anything but praying I'd change my ways. She couldn't tell me shit. After all, I'd been in the streets unsupervised since I was eight. So had Branden. And Rah Rah. And most of our other friends. Watts had a way of making you grow up quickly.

But my mother and I maintained one form of connection: if I was planning something dangerous, where I might not come back, I made sure to tell her. As someone who'd rededicated her life to God, she didn't approve, but she appreciated the honesty. I'd known too many kids who kept everything they did in the streets from their parents, and when those kids got killed, I'd seen those parents destroyed by never knowing the truth behind what had happened. Those of us who knew didn't say anything to the parents, so as not to risk them going to the police. (We just retaliated.) Those mothers and fathers never found any solace. I didn't want that for my mom.

Fifteen felt like just the right age to go get mine. There was no real structure to our business or how we lived. We knew that people would have money on the first and the fifteenth, and that we'd better have product available then. But other than that, there were no rules, no schedule, no curfew—nothing. If drugs came in, I cooked them. If we were hungry, we ate. Tired, we found a place to lie down and sleep. The closets were piled up with new clothes from Mensland in the Carson Mall and Hip Hop Zone in the Marketplace. Iceberg, Rocawear, Enyce, Guess—everything. We'd put on a new outfit, wear it for a week, changing only our underclothes when we showered, and then throw the old clothes away. You can believe no one was doing any fucking laundry.

Days and nights bled into one another. It was all about the hustle. We started getting money right away. This wasn't like New York, where you were taking over blocks. It wasn't a territory game. You grew your business by the quality of your drugs and your creativity in marketing them.

We had a few different schemes. One was to dye our product a certain color to separate it from the others' product. Another was to keep a few of the local crackheads happy and hooked up with freebies when they brought in anyone who would spend real money. Naturally, we worried about undercover cops, but being in the projects actually protected you from the undercovers, because everyone knew everyone else, and no undercover was going to risk their life walking into a project dope house. If they were going to do anything, they would pay a crackhead twenty dollars to get them to buy from us using marked bills. But if a smoker had been buying from me for a year and never had twenty dollars in his life, I would know something was off. I learned to trust my instincts.

Oftentimes at night, we kept a youngster outside in the parking lot with a walkie-talkie, so they could report back on what they were seeing, who was coming around, everything. If our back porch light was off, we were in business. Lights on meant the shop was closed. If police happened to be watching and filming, you wanted it as dark as possible. If someone came and knocked on the door and we recognized the voice, we'd let them in. Otherwise, we'd just tell them they had the wrong house. It wasn't like we were innovating on our own. These were SOPs (standard operating procedures) sorted out through trial and error by the OGs who'd already navigated the streets before us and then handed them down.

Once a customer was inside, we'd ask what they wanted, and when they gave us money, we'd pull out the built-in cutting board (a project kitchen specialty) and show them rows of dope: one row of tens, another of twenties, and one of fifty-dollar pieces. I'd point out the section you could pick from and let you choose your own rock. This way, any bitching about its being short was on you. On a rare occasion, a female smoker we knew and trusted would come through with a white guy who was a whale. Once we'd reasoned he wasn't an undercover, we'd let her use one of the rooms upstairs, smoke him up, and run him through two or three thousand, a hundred at a time. Every day was different, but we were making steady money. Then, almost by accident, our drug operation went national.

EARLY ON, WE RAN INTO a little problem when one of our crew, Greg, stole a kilo of coke from one of my big cousins, G AL. In the interest of keeping himself alive, Greg linked up with a dude he knew from Long Beach who already had a drug operation in Texas, got on a bus, and left. About a year later, he came back. The Texas enterprise had been busted by the cops, and Greg had gone to jail for a minute, but as soon as he could get out on bail, he had come home with a plan for us to act as the supplier for projects in other cities. Again, in Watts this wasn't new. We'd seen the older homies who'd gotten busted supply drugs all across America, from Minnesota to fucking Jackson, Mississippi, so we knew it could be done. And we'd seen the money coming in from out of town when their girls would go to Western Union to pick it up. But now that Greg was all worldly and shit, he helped us come up with a plan.

We'd talk to the homie with the car wash, who had all the dope, and get him to front us a kilo of cocaine with the promise that we'd bring him back $20K. Our pitch was that this was extra money for him, since it normally sold for $16K. Then, four of us would get on a Greyhound bus headed to whatever city we had our eye on, each with nine ounces of coke hidden in our Timberland boots. When we got there, we'd spend the day at a mall, kicking game to girls and, hopefully, finding one who had her own place and a car. If she was feeling us and we felt like she was someone who might know a man who knew a man, we'd get her phone number, to hook up with her later and have her show us around town, specifically places in the hood like the barber shop or sandwich spot or wherever hood niggas hung out. The only requirement was it had to be close to the projects.

Once we got in the shop, inevitably someone was going to talk to us, ask where we were from. After all, we dressed different, we talked different, our vibe was totally different. We knew we'd stick out, but that was good. Through those conversations, we'd end up meeting hustlers. Or, if they weren't hustlers, they were someone who could put us in contact with the hustlers or whoever was making moves in the projects. But it had to be in the projects—because, though the way they dressed and talked may've seemed foreign as hell to us, the project mentality all over America is the same. It may sound different coming out of our mouths, but all project dudes speak a common language. So, we could tell if dudes were scammers, or trying to jack us, or for real. That shit looks the same no matter what hood you're from.

Once we found someone we might vibe with, we'd sit on it for a while. We wanted them to come to us, to need us. We didn't need to advertise what we were there to do. Watts and L.A.—those names already rang out. And for the dudes we were looking for, they were like a drug dog whistle.

Once we'd established our outpost and made the right local contacts, we'd begin shipping drugs on the regular. We did it in a variety of ways, from lining a car with drugs and using a car delivery service, to boxing the drugs and using UPS or FedEx to ship them to a safe address close to our spot and having someone sit in front of the house to intercept the package. Using these methods and some others I'm not even going to get into, we started moving product and expanding the Grape Street network to Memphis. Then Atlanta. Even Des Moines, Iowa. All over the damn place.

Unlike the Grape Street OGs, who'd been shipping drugs to other cities for a while, we weren't trying to just move keys. We were creating Grape Street embassies, outposts, starting our own Grape Street chapters in these places. Our power didn't lie in the amount of weight we could move, because, honestly, it wasn't that much. Our power was in our name: "Grape Street Watts." And soon enough, it would be everywhere.

I HAD MANY ROLES. I was in operations. I was in sales. I was an enforcer. But, of course, I was also the cook. I took pride in my cooking skills. That talent became a part of my identity. First of all, no one else in my generation could cook, and that made me feel like I was smarter than other people, separating myself out. I may've never passed a chemistry class, but I became a young hotshot chemist, the dude you needed to see if you wanted to stretch your dope and make a nice profit. And because the feds had cracked down on older cooks, demand for my services skyrocketed.

As I got more reps, my cooking improved. I could basically cook crack on anything with a heat source—a gas stove, a hotplate, even a microwave. All I needed was a saucepan, a heat-treated beaker or measuring cup, and something to stir with. If you're fancy, you might use an electric cake mixer or a whisk, but most of the time, you were unbending a coat hanger and using the little hook at the end to whip the drugs.

Bo had given me the foundation to be able to cook quality crack, but once I started seeing how the chemical reactions worked, I couldn't help but experiment. Everybody used baking soda or vitamin B12 to a certain degree, to stretch the coke. But that's as deep as their thinking went. The problem with this was once that shitty, stepped-on crack hardened, it wasn't going anywhere. It clogged pipes and created a low-quality experience. (I didn't test it myself, but there were plenty of fiends willing to be in my focus group in exchange for free drugs.)

This was where I was able to separate myself. The majority of drug cooks thought about it like amateurs at home looking at a recipe book. I thought about it like a professional. Every chef has a secret ingredient, and when cooking drugs, mine was water. I used more than most. Water kept the pipe clean and the entire experience unique. But water's real secret weapon was its weight. It's a heavy substance, and if you know how to use it, you can technically make the same volume of drugs heavier. And since drugs are sold by weight and not volume, you end up with more product to sell. But you have to have the touch.

I'd do a dry cook, melting a little bit at a time while folding in some water. You needed the cocaine base to get to a pancake batter texture, which takes some patience and know-how, almost like cooking a roux. You needed the bottom layer of baking soda, the middle layer of water, and the cocaine oil at the top to blend together, like with an aioli. I'd whisk and whisk and whisk and, as the air cooled it down, the paste would thicken. With reps, I learned when to stop and just how thick it should feel as the outer shell hardened against the cold air without breaking. This was all trial and error. It wasn't like breaking an aioli in a restaurant kitchen, seeing that shit separate in your food processor, and having a chef come over and tell you to add more egg yolk and spin it again. Bo wasn't watching over my shoulder, and none of my friends knew how to cook, so that forced me to make serious decisions on my own.

When it was the proper thickness, I'd methodically pour cold water on the outside of the beaker while dipping my hand in a cup of ice water and letting it drip onto the inside. When it's hot, the crack is a darker color, but as it cools, it gets lighter. Once the top of the mixture was solid, I'd pour ice water in a little at a time, until the drug was completely submerged, and swirl it around the crack. In the same way you can tell fried chicken is done once it floats to the top of the oil, I knew the crack was ready when it fully cooled, released from the beaker, and started to float at the surface, solid and hard and ready.

Once I knew my limits, and knew what I could stretch, I pushed the product as far as I could. It worked like this: If you brought me a kilo of coke (about thirty-six ounces, worth $16K at the time, wholesale), and it was relatively pure, I could cook it straight, and you could make $36K, or about $1K an ounce. But if you wanted me to stretch it, using baking soda and varied quantities and temperatures of water, I could potentially give you back between an extra quarter and an extra half a bird (between nine and eighteen ounces), which meant you'd make up to another $18K. Depending on who you were, my fee for the initial cook would be around $3K plus $200 an ounce for everything I gave you over that initial thirty-six ounces. So, if I produced an extra eighteen ounces, you paid me $3,600 on top of the initial $3K.

It may sound expensive, but I was worth it. Once I got to the actual cooking, I was like Tom Brady on game day—totally locked in. But that didn't mean I couldn't have fun, too. Some people just stand over the pot watching it the whole time. Not me. Sure, when I first started cooking, I had that freaked-out, new-parent look, because I didn't know what to expect. But I was so confident now that I'd go over to whatever rock house I was supposed to be cooking in, put on some music, dance, and chop it up, because I knew the timing so well.

I didn't bother keeping my process a secret. I was like a chef performing for the guests in an open kitchen. Tom Colicchio could make a dish right in front of you and tell you what he was doing, but that wouldn't mean you could go re-create it. If you watched me cook work and could do it yourself, then— good, do it.

But let's be real: you weren't gonna do it like me.

4

Dear Mama

ON DECEMBER 31, 1996, MY GRANNY PASSED AWAY FROM BREAST cancer.

We'd known she was sick for a while, so Christmas that year felt especially meaningful. Granny always had a silver tree, but this year, she insisted on a white one. She fixed up the whole house with white and red bows. She bought more gifts than I'd seen her purchase in her whole life. Granny even gave my mom money to buy her new jewelry

For Christmas dinner, she cooked a feast that was epic even for her—from rabbit to pig's feet to gumbo. And you'd best believe there were cakes. Normally, my Granny was so concerned with getting everyone else fed that she'd wait until the very end of the night and then fix herself a plate and eat off a tray in her bedroom. But this night, she started having chest pains, so my auntie took her to Martin Luther King Jr. Community Hospital in Compton. The next day, when my mother went back to the house to pack up a bag, she saw the plate by Granny's bed. Her Christmas dinner was completely untouched.

Granny was still in the hospital on New Year's Eve. At the end of our visit that day, she asked everyone else to leave except for my mother. My Granny was born on New Year's Day, and I remember telling her I would see her the next day, on her birthday. When it was just the two of them, my Granny took her new rings off and handed them to my mother.

"Give these to your sisters," she said, staring my mother straight in the eye. "I want you to take care of your brothers, and take care of your grandkids, and take care of your daddy. Can you do that for me?"

My mother, who at this point was clean, with a good job and a house, was ready to take all that on. "Yeah, Momma, I can do that for you," she told her, holding back tears. Later, my mom would tell me that she knew this would be the last time she saw her mother alive. Knowing that my mom could take care of the family now, Granny, our big momma, would finally be able to let go.

My mother walked out and drove us home. But as we pulled up to her house, we got a call from my auntie telling us to go back. We rushed back over, but a doctor told us we were too late. Granny had died a few minutes earlier. Louella Henderson was only sixty-four years old.

There were more than five hundred people at my Granny's funeral and service. It took nearly four hours for everyone to get a chance to view the body. They even had to start turning cars away at the cemetery, because the parking lot was all filled up. Granny put so much love into the world and never expected anything in return, and when you do that purely and honestly, the world takes notice. Her passing was a great loss to Los Angeles.

GRANNY AND TRUETT DYING WITHIN a few years of each other shook me up. Both had been my protectors, and both had loved me unconditionally. With them and Branden, I wasn't posturing; I could be myself. But without two of the people who had been the rocks in my life, I had less of a sense of who I was or why I did the things I did.

As I started selling and cooking drugs, school fell by the wayside. I had completed ninth grade at Jordan High, but I got kicked out in tenth—allegedly, for a fight, but more because Branden and I had too much influence, and the administration wanted to break us up. Given that Branden was Jordan's star football player at the time, I was sent away to Gardena High. Two months later, I was kicked out of Gardena for fighting and sent to Locke High, back in Watts. Two months after that, same thing: I got into a fight in the cafeteria. But this time while I was waiting in the office, a principal, a counselor, and a security guard all came in.

"Keith Corbin," the principal asked. "Are you related to Truett Corbin?"

"He was my older brother."

They looked at one another like they'd seen a ghost. Truett was at Locke when he was killed, and his death caused a war between Front Street and Bacc Street, whose territory was across from the school. The principal looked at the counselor and the other administrators.

"How is this boy allowed to go to this school?" he asked. No one answered. "I'm sorry, but there's been a mistake," he said to me. "We're going to fix this, but you can't stay here. It's too dangerous."

By the spring of 1997, I was back at Jordan High to finish tenth grade. But considering I'd been kicked out of three in one semester (including this one), I'd lost my taste for school and dropped out. And to be fair, most school administrators had lost their taste for me. For the rest of tenth grade and all of eleventh, I didn't think my decision mattered much. But as everyone else's lives went on, I found myself bored as hell. I'd get up early and stand outside the school to watch the girls walk in. Then I'd go back to the projects and play video games and sell drugs. I could feel my mind dulling, and I was always missing out on whatever my homies were talking about when they got back to the house. Mostly, this revolved around how the girls at school were looking.

Growing up, we didn't have any sort of proper respect for women. Not having our mothers around, we didn't show deference to them, and the behavior we saw modeled by the older fellas was stereotypical player shit—the more women you sleep with, the more powerful you are. I was no different. I'd lost my virginity early, as a sixth-grader, and I'd been sexually active ever since. My whole crew was the same way. Plus, Rah Rah and Greg were light-skinned, so you can believe the girls liked them. We'd holler at girls from high schools all over South Central and beyond, places like Gardena and Westchester, looking for the pretty girls with big houses. Riding out to these nicer suburbs gave us a rush. It was hard to imagine living out there, and the idea that girls who had this life would be interested in a bunch of project dudes seemed crazy to us.

But I guess we gave them a rush, too. We had that danger element. Tupac can tell you: girls love a thug. We'd pull up on them playing our music loud as they were walking home from school, showing off the fact that we may be roughnecks, but we had a car. Then we'd exchange numbers. And maybe, a few days later, we'd pick 'em up at school and take them for a Jamba Juice. Or, we'd meet at World on Wheels. You know, real player shit.

In 1998, my son Keith Jr. was born. At the time, having a kid was nowhere on my radar. My son's mom and I first started talking in 1997. She was from our projects, with pretty green eyes. Originally, I was supposed to get hooked up with her cousin, and she was going to be matched up with Branden. Branden was shy, though, so I used to talk for him and make up shit he said, Cyrano-style. Eventually, she and I started to hang out and have sex, and soon after that, she was pregnant.

I was scared to death. We weren't really in a relationship, and I was too damn immature to understand what I was facing. Even when I told my mom about the pregnancy, I didn't do it like a man and take responsibility. I was childish and whiny and feeling sorry for myself. When Keith Jr. was born, I wasn't there for the actual birth, but I visited him in the hospital. Seeing him, I kept waiting for some instant connection to kick in. As someone who didn't grow up with a dad around, I had this idea that I would be there for my kid, that I'd do things differently, but the truth was, I had no idea what that even meant or looked like. Keith Jr. might've been my baby, but I was still a kid myself.

After that, I stayed away from him for the first few months, but I came back around, and as I did, our connection grew. Eventually, his mother started dropping him with me while she went to school, and I'd hang with him the whole day, walking him through the projects, having him kick it with the homies. I didn't know what the fuck I was doing changing diapers or feeding him and shit, but I knew I liked having this little man around.

One day, I went to pick up Keith from his mother's house and saw a burn on his body in the shape of a clothes iron. His mother had fallen asleep, and he'd burned himself. It was an accident, but I was mad and didn't see it like that, so I took him to my mom's and refused to give him back. His mother showed up later with the police. An officer told me I had to return him, but he gave me a card to set up a custody hearing. That may be why, the next day, his mom took Keith Jr. and boarded a plane for Austin, Texas, to go live with her father.

As a foolish teenager, I actually did think I could be a better parent, or at least, given that my mother was clean and out of the projects, that I could put him in a better situation. But looking back, I see that that wasn't what wanting custody was really about. Maybe I wanted to be vindictive. Maybe we were playing the whole situation out like unprepared, immature teenagers do, with me blaming her for falling asleep and her blaming me for not being around, both of us not even aware of how Keith Jr. was suffering. Maybe I'm reading too deep into it and the truth is that neither of us knew what the fuck we were doing.

With Keith Jr. in Texas, it was difficult to keep that connection. A mother carries the child and will always have that bond, but a father has to develop and nurture and cultivate a relationship to establish it—so, Keith Jr. and I never really got there. In my head, I like to pretend I would've been an incredible father to him and raised him right and made all the best choices, but if I'm being honest with myself, I know that's not how it would've played out. I was a teenage gangster, in these streets, selling drugs and committing crimes. I was no role model, no father figure to emulate. So, Keith grew up in Texas without me. And though it's easy to stand on the sidelines here and criticize his mother for her mistakes, at the end of the day, he's still alive. And if he had grown up with me, surrounded by the things I was doing, inheriting the legacy I inherited, would he be? I just don't know.

BY THE TIME SENIOR YEAR started, I was eager to get back into school. Life after dropping out was fucking boring. And though I couldn't admit it to myself at the time, it was embarrassing. I was supposed to be one of the smart ones, one of the homies who got made fun of for liking school. And now these fools were going to be graduating high school while I sat on my ass at home? I couldn't have that. Not only did I want to get back, but I wanted to graduate with Branden, Rah Rah, and the rest of my class—which meant I would need to basically do two and a half years of school in one year.

So, from six in the morning until nine at night, I went to

school. I took zero and double-zero periods before school even started, then regular school, then night school from four to nine P.M. After nine, I would sit with Branden in this broke-ass white-and-burgundy Beretta with no engine doing homework as we sold drugs. We kept a cutting board and our dope in the trunk. If someone came and knocked on the window, we'd get out, take the money, pop the trunk, serve 'em the drugs, close the trunk up, and start homework again. That's called multitasking.

The audacity of even trying to pack two and a half years of high school into one showed that, despite all the attempts to snuff him out, the fire of my inner nerd was still lit. I'd had to bury it to survive my day-to-day, but if anything, this proved my gangster persona was just that, a persona. For some people who choose the streets, the fire goes completely out and never comes back. But if you watched me with school, or Branden with sports, you could see the spark of what we might've become if we had been allowed to get comfortable with ourselves and avoid the street bullshit. Because we weren't selling at school at the time, and I didn't feel I needed to prove to anyone what sort of influence or power I had, when I was in school, I had space to learn. I could just be Keith.

Of course, I couldn't do it on my own. I needed someone at the school who still believed in me, who still felt I was worth saving. And that person was our dean of students, Mrs. Lainey Foster. Back in the day, Mrs. Foster had been the teacher who got my mother to graduate high school when, thanks to the drugs and the trouble she'd been making in the neighborhood, no one thought she ever would. Mrs. Foster had been the one to kick me out of Jordan as a tenth-grader to teach me a lesson when she thought I was too arrogant and cocky and acted like I was running the school. But during my senior year, she was my rock. Whenever I was having a hard time, I could go to her office to do my work or talk through my problems with her. She was my liaison with the other teachers and everyone else. She knew my family. She knew my history. And I guess she saw past that fake gangster shit and knew that the real me needed and wanted that push to finish high school.

Even later in my life, Mrs. Foster never stopped believing in me. When I got out of prison and was struggling, she gave me a key to her house and told me if I ever needed a place to stay, I was always welcome there. To this day, I still have that key on my key ring.

With Mrs. Foster's help, I worked my ass off, and by the summer of senior year, I'd finished tenth, eleventh, and twelfth grade and had graduated with my friends in the Class of 1999. I even made it to senior prom. We didn't bring dates; we went as a crew. Before the prom, we all gathered at my mother's house to take pictures. Instead of posing with dates, we posed with money, flashing thousands of dollars, acting like it was pocket change.

We looked good, though. I was dressed in an all-beige suit with ostrich skin boots, a fedora, clear glasses, and jewelry. Branden was in an all-black suit, and Rah Rah in all-white, matching the Lincoln Town Car we rented. When we got to the Long Beach Hyatt, it wasn't just a high school dance; it was a fucking hood party. Girls were bringing kingpins from the Nickersons ten years older than them as dates and shit. I can't tell you what the dance floor looked like, or what the prom king and queen wore. That shit was so far off my radar, I didn't even

notice it. I noticed only what was in my world. My homies partying, kicking it, flashing bills, and singing Cash Money, No
Limit, and Tupac tracks as loud as we could.

FOR A FEW YEARS, OUR crew had been steadily making money.
We had the wholesale businesses in other cities, multiple spots
to cook in Jordan Downs, and our main house to sell out of.
And then one day in 1999, in the span of a couple of hours, we
lost it all.

The police raided all the properties where we had been
active, from Rah Rah's cousin's house to Branden's aunt's
house and everything else in between. It wasn't unusual for the
police to conduct raids on the mere suspicion of drug activity.
They were constantly breaking down doors and doing drug
sweeps, fishing for something. As we weren't dumb enough to
sell to an undercover, the best they could hope for was to catch
us in the act and put some charges on us after the fact. But
when they went through all our various drug and cookhouses,
none of us was there. And, ironically, the only place they actually found drugs was in the trunk of our broke-ass Beretta, but
because the car wasn't legally tied to any registration, they
couldn't link it or the drugs to any of us.

Nonetheless, it was a bad beat. We had no place to cook, no
place to sell, no specific address to lay our heads. We couldn't
buy new drugs, because all our money was gone. (Technically,
we could've gone to the police station and tried to claim it, but
no one was dumb enough to do that.) On top of that, everyone
saw we had just gotten raided, so people were staying away
because we were hot.

For a while, we tried to make it work. Branden and I went back to selling small time on the streets to the smokers, but those crumbs were making us only enough to cover our day-to-day expenses. I'd always been the one to source the dope, and because we couldn't get anyone to front us significant weight in Jordan Downs after the raid, I started buying from the Nickersons. It was truce times, and one of the big-time dealers there actually wanted to see us back on our feet, so he gave us the best deal we could find.

One day, I went over there on a bike and picked up a new package. As I was riding back to Jordan Downs through Fudge Town at around nine P.M., a police cruiser cut me off on the sidewalk. The cops jumped out for a stop-and-frisk, found the drugs in my backpack, and arrested me. Luckily, the dope wasn't cut up or cooked, so I told them that I just used, and because it was my first offense, they made me attend a course on drugs, with no jail time.

The problem was, the course was held in Bebop Bishop Bloods territory, and because they weren't part of the truce, I had to carry a gun, which seemed to defeat the whole purpose of getting off on probation. After doing that once, I found someone I could pay to sign in for me and say I had gone to all the classes. I brought that back to court, and that was it.

With all this upheaval, Branden and I realized that it was just too hard to keep our old crew together. Our styles were too different. Whereas Branden thrived off the energy of the group, I didn't like having a bunch of people around. Greg and Branden were still shipping drugs out to Iowa and other outposts, but we didn't have much of anything going on in Watts. There was no blowup, no big fight. We both needed money and, at that point, both realized we each had to do our own things to survive. So each of us linked up with a different big homie.

Big homies, OGs who were usually at least ten years older, acted like a combination of a father figure, big brother, and adviser. Because they'd seen the streets for a while, they had more experience and savvy. They taught us how to work diplomacy, how to handle your business and still remain on the streets. For Branden, that person was Caca. For me, Nardo and BE-K.

Nardo, a slim dude with dark brown skin who kept his hair faded, was quiet, really quiet. And serious, really *fucking* serious. He might get in a good mood around the right crew when he was chilling, but the man didn't play, and he didn't want to be in anyone else's business, either. You couldn't even say "Let me tell you something" to him. To him, any use of the word *tell* was too close to *snitch*. You might be able to use "I'll let you know" or "I'll put you up on game," but he was *not* with that word *tell*. And he made it a point never to know anyone else's business.

Nardo was known as "Fresh" in the eighties, and when I started using the name, completely unaware of its history, he came to me to let me know he didn't have a problem with it, but that I should know that the name had some meaning in the streets. After that, he took me under his wing, calling me "Lil' One" because of the association, lacing my boots, teaching me survival skills, and mentoring me. Nardo was one of those dudes who was about and for the neighborhood. If he had $100K, he'd probably give it all out to his people. He understood what investing in the community meant, which is why, to this day, he's one of the most respected OGs not just in Watts, but around the country.

BE-K was maybe ten years older than me, a tall, husky, dark-skinned dude with long braids. An older cat with a young spirit, he'd come up under Nardo in the late eighties, when the drug and gang wars were peaking. He'd had a different upbringing and a different mentality. Whereas, much like Nardo, I liked to keep a lower profile, BE-K was basically the first verse of the Lil Boosie song "Bankroll" personified: he wanted you to know he was having money, and lots of it, even if it wasn't true. And so, he would floss and always keep a fat roll on him, which he wasn't afraid of flashing. "If you're known for getting money," he told me, "people will come to you."

But lest you saw that money and thought about jacking him, he also kept a big-ass .357 with an eight-inch barrel on his person at all times, and he had a reputation for flashing that as well.

BE-K first came to talk to me while I was in the middle of a dice game in Jordan Downs with some of the big ballers from my community, dudes who'd been stacking money since the 1970s. I was playing with my last hundred, but these cats had enough that they could lose five thousand and not even think about it. I was hungry, scavenging for their money. Meanwhile, they were playing for fun.

Somehow, I managed to hang in and get hot, and within ten minutes, that one hundred dollars I'd started off with had grown to about two thousand. That's when BE-K, fresh out of prison, pulled up. When he saw me winning, he told me to get out right then. "You'll never win all their money," he said. "Take what you got and go do something for yourself."

I got out of the game and into his car, and we went shopping with the winnings. During our shopping spree, he mentioned he'd kept up with what was happening in the projects while he was in jail, and he said he wanted to get a spot where we could hustle together. So, we took the sixty-two dollars apiece we each had left after our shopping spree, bought a quarter piece of powder cocaine, cooked it up, and within forty-five days, we'd flipped it into half a kilo.

Our game wasn't sexy—we were selling three-dollar crack rocks out of a small one-bedroom. Most dealers don't want to deal with the low-budget clientele; they stick to the higher prices, selling at ten, twenty, or fifty dollars. But our business was effective. We realized there was a lot of small money out there, so we started cutting five-dollar rocks in half, selling them for three dollars, and that extra dollar profit started to add up quickly. Once we had enough money, we ditched our three-dollar hustle; got a bigger house in Jordan Downs, Unit 404; and put a team together combining some of each of our old crews. "The 404 Boys" were open for business.

We started diversifying right away. We had dudes going to downtown L.A., and then Ohio and Detroit and Vegas. Because they weren't getting profiled, a white woman in her fifties and her teenage daughter used to drive hundreds of pounds of weed all the way to Ohio for us. For an extra fee, I would sometimes travel to some of these cities and cook the drugs myself, using extended-stay hotels with their own kitchens, as I didn't trust local cookhouses.

But it wasn't just drug cooking and distribution. We were trying to get money in any way possible. Sometimes this meant robbing banks. Now, this wasn't the version of bank robberies you see in the movies. There were no rubber presidents' masks or nun costumes. We weren't going after oil paintings or gold bars. We weren't trying to get one last big score before we retired. Not everything is *Heat*.

We'd travel all the way down past Palm Springs, looking for sparsely populated towns with older banks close to the freeway. When we found one, we'd make a disturbance call at a building close to the bank and then time out how long it took the police to arrive. Anything forty-five seconds or under, and we'd pass. A minute or over, and we were in business. Most of the time, the guy going into the bank wouldn't even have a gun. He'd pull up his hood, pull down his hat, and hand the teller a note telling them to give him the money from the drawers. Or, you'd approach the bank manager, who had the keys to the ATM. On a good day, when it had just been replenished, you could get eighty thousand dollars with no ink packs.

We didn't worry about the money being clean or having nonconsecutive serial numbers or any of that shit. We weren't planning on investing in a mutual fund or claiming the money on our tax returns. With our share, we might go cop a used Lexus or Infiniti, or go to the casino in Compton, or buy a sack of drugs from the dope man to turn into product. No matter what, that money was staying on the black market.

Whether it was bank robbing or drug selling, at the end of the day, it was all just a hustle. Our goal was simple: get money any way you can. This is one of the hardest things for me to explain to white folks trying to pin this down in a way that translates to their world. You could be a drug dealer, but also rob banks, sell burgers, paint houses. These were not job titles. You weren't trying to build a career or move up a corporate ladder. At eight years old, I may've been piercing ears in exchange for Nintendo games, but it wasn't because I planned to go to cosmetology school. I was just trying to survive and make enough money to eat and get a little something for myself. That's it. It didn't go further than that.

As I got older, someone driving through the hood might see me, roll down the window, and ask if I wanted to get some money. And if I did, I'd get in the car—it didn't matter what we were doing. We might be going to rob a bank or a drug dealer; or lay concrete; or paint a house. The job wasn't the point. The hustle was the hustle was the hustle.

In our world, we never achieved kingpin status. Not with Branden or BE-K. We never saw twenty kilos of drugs or had to figure out how to hide duffel bags of money. We didn't have a direct connect from Colombia. It was never like that. Those were the dudes getting busted by federal probes and wiretaps and the FBI and shit. Our world was smaller—I don't think I ever cooked more than two kilos at once, or made more than fifty or sixty thousand in one rotation—but it was ours. What we did was establish our own connects, our own out-of-town operations, and get money for ourselves. We didn't just piggy-back off my cousins and the OGs who had been doing this shit since "Freeway" Rick Ross first hooked up with the CIA. We didn't want to be employees; we wanted to own our own businesses. And for us to start at fifteen, cooking drugs and moving them out of state on our own—that was unheard of, that was the thing that made us hood legends. We may not have had LeBron James money, but we had Kobe Bryant game.

In my time with Branden, our focus was moving product out of town. We had one dope house, but lines into many cities. With BE-K, it was a different model. We were running five dope houses in Jordan Downs, and we mostly sold locally.

From a visibility standpoint, it was a higher risk, but it gave our partnership clout. Our names rang out: BE-K and Fresh. He was the face of the operation, the one with the flash and pomp and circumstance. I was the engine, the one with the connect and the cooking skills. To help us clean cash, I set up a T-shirt shop in my mother's name. I bought expensive jewelry—a pinkie ring, diamond earrings, a necklace. We were known for closing down Unit 404 and throwing legendary neighborhood parties, paying for everything. DJ Mark, who used to work with Brand Nubian, would spin records, and we'd bring out cases of alcohol—Belvedere, Grey Goose, Rémy Martin, and Hennessy XO, which was my drink.

I used to sit out there, watching all these people drinking our liquor and dancing, and I'd feel like we were untouchable.

5

How Much a Dollar Cost

THE TROUBLE STARTED WITH A SIMPLE DRUG DEAL. IT WAS 2002, and I'd been with BE-K and the 404 crew for a few years now. At some point that fall, dudes from the Hoover Crips, in South Central, reached out to have me purchase and cook some dope for them. I was with it because I figured we could make money off the top, but BE-K had a different plan.

"Fuck 'em," he said. "Let's just take their money."

I wasn't into that. I was the one who did the deal, so any bullshit would come back around on me. I told BE-K that I could cut their drugs and we could make money without causing some unnecessary bullshit, and I thought he had agreed. Our homie B-Red was already buying a kilo, and he'd asked if we wanted to put in on it, too, so he could get a better price. We asked for nine ounces—four and a half for us, four and a half for the Hoovers.

Later on, when I knew B-Red would be dropping the drugs off, I was in the car with one of my little brothers, rolling back to the 404, when I spotted BE-K and the crew on the porch. I'm a big believer in reading the energy of a room as a way to detect trouble, and after noting BE-K's and everyone else's body language and feeling their vibe, I told my brother to drop me off and go home. Nothing about this felt right.

When B-Red's Ford Expedition rolled up, I walked over to the car to get our quarter bird, but he resisted, saying he needed to give it directly to BE-K. This struck me as strange. Every other time he'd dropped off the drugs, he'd just passed them to me. After all, I was the cook. That's when I knew there had been a conversation behind my back. Trickery was at hand. Once B-Red had handed BE-K the drugs, I asked BE-K directly for the Hoovers' half, so I could cook it up. He stepped up to the 404's porch, turned around, and looked down at me from a few steps above.

"Naw," he said. "We're just gonna take it."

Angry, I started to yell.

BE-K didn't say anything. He just pulled out his big-ass .357.

Upon seeing that, I walked up to face him on the porch. "If you're gonna pull it out," I said, "you better go all the way with it." But as I spoke, his boy Junior, a dude from the generation above me, blindsided me with a punch to the jaw from behind, and I dropped like a stone into a pond. When I bounced up, I was woozy from the shot, and it took a minute to get my bearings. When I finally did, I stood there staring at BE-K.

"So, this is how it's going to be, huh?" I asked. "This is how it's gonna go down?" And then I walked away.

My immediate plan was to go get one of my guns and shoot Junior. The way I was brought up in the game, if someone in your crew was going to inflict violence on you, he was supposed to show you enough respect to at least give you a chance to defend yourself. Junior's punch from behind wasn't just a punch. It was a lack of respect, which made it a much more serious offense.

At the time, I had a girl in Long Beach, and at night, I would stay either with her or at the 404. Back in Long Beach at my girlfriend's mom's house, I couldn't sleep. First and foremost, I felt betrayed and hurt by BE-K for pulling this scheme and putting me in this situation. But I could deal with only one offense at a time, and on some hierarchy-of-needs shit, Junior's actions demanded more immediate attention. Only after I had settled that could I address BE-K.

The next day, I went back to the 404. With BE-K and most of the crew standing on the porch, I asked where Junior was.

"Now's not a good time, Fresh," BE-K said.

I pulled up my shirt and showed him I wasn't carrying a gun. I'd decided that the more effective strategy would be to beat Junior's ass and embarrass him in front of everyone. I told BE-K as much.

"I just want to fight him heads-up."

BE-K tried to shake it off again, but a crowd of other people from the projects had started to gather, wondering what was happening, including Junior. When he came through, I stepped to him and told him I was going to whup his ass, but he pulled out one of my guns from his pants. Through buying and straight taking them from dudes, I'd acquired a bunch of guns, which I'd stashed throughout the house. And now here was Junior, sticking my own gun in my face.

"Ain't no fighting," he said.

"Oh, so this is how you want it to go down," I said. "You too scared to fight?"

After a minute, Junior walked away, tossing threats behind him. Not only had he hit me from behind, but he'd now also refused to fight me heads-up and had even stuck a gun in my face. Now I couldn't let it go. I could see only red.

That night, I used a sledgehammer to knock a hole in the wall in the abandoned factory behind the 404 and then another on the other side. One hole to ambush, one hole to exit. I sat in that building, among the rats and other animals, for two straight nights, waiting for Junior to show his face so I could get my revenge, but he never came through.

In the darkness of the factory, I started to think about the entire 404 situation. If I was being honest with myself, it hadn't felt right for a while. We'd started out as partners, but with BE-K's flash and our age difference, I had been feeling over-shadowed, like I wasn't really getting the credit I deserved. I was the momentum behind this whole enterprise—I was sourcing the drugs, cooking, enforcing when I needed to—but a lot of the time, it felt like I was just another dude in BE-K's crew. Before this, we'd had petty squabbles—about money, or girls—but to everyone else, we'd always tried to put up a united front. This shit wore on me. I felt used, like a fool.

I hadn't been right for a while, either. What had started as curiosity about cocaine when I was fifteen had, by now, turned into a serious habit. I had a taste for it, and once we had our own drug houses, I had an excuse to use: so I could stay up and sell my dope. When the clientele and the money started coming in, so did the girls, and then I was experiencing sex on coke and using it as an excuse to party or whatever. I just kept finding more and more reasons to get high.

Most people hid their coke habits, but that wasn't me. Because I was so open about it, I became a bad influence, as others around me started following my lead. But I always had to be the alpha, so that meant I was going to take it the farthest. By nineteen, I was snorting half ounces, keeping a bag on me at all times. It got to the point where everyone who knew me knew I was holding. "Man, bring it out your sock," they'd say when I rolled through. You couldn't even say my pupils were dilated, because whenever you looked at me, it looked like I just had big eyes. I was high all day every day.

Even after our crews split, Branden and I used to meet up late at night on the project baseball field to talk. One night, on that same field where we used to sleep as kids, we discussed our current situation. I told him about the problems I was having with BE-K. Branden, who knew me and knew what I was cool with and what I wasn't, didn't like this situation for me at all.

"Leave that shit, Fresh," he told me, as he had on multiple occasions. "Let's get the crew back together."

"Nah," I said, staring off, looking for the bats I used to see as a kid. "I've got my money tied up in that shit. I can't do it."

But, looking back, I don't know what I was talking about. What money? Certainly not enough that I couldn't just walk away. I don't know if there was some sort of father figure shit keeping me there, but I felt a blind sense of loyalty to BE–K. I knew on some level that I couldn't trust him. I just wasn't confident enough to make the move.

For as long as I could, I had buried these doubts and focused on the money. But when BE–K started fucking with that and my safety, it exposed just how fragile our relationship really was. And the doubts had turned into a rage I couldn't control.

The next day, the anger was still building. Fueled by both coke-induced and real paranoia, I went over to the Jordan High School bleachers. From the top, I could see all the 404 dudes outside the unit. I called one on my cell, watched him answer, and told him to put my little cousin on the phone. Once my cousin got on, I told him to get out of the house because I was coming. From the bleachers, I could see him laughing, clowning me as we were talking, before handing the phone back to the other dude. That was enough to set me off. All my insecurities, my anger, my sadness, and my feelings of betrayal became one big ball of rage. I took the gate behind the bleachers and shook it loose until it broke. Then I propped it against the wall like a ramp. After taking one more big snort of cocaine, I ran to the top of the ramp, took out a MAC-11 submachine gun, and started shooting up the 404.

Looking back now, I see that being so angry that I could shoot up a place where my friends and even some of my family members were staying seems crazy, but it was part of my conditioning. Gangs are groups of people coming together for a common cause—maybe that's money, or protection, or to move drugs—but as soon as you're not pulling your own weight, or you fall out of favor, or you see rivals within the gang mobilizing against you, you realize how expendable you are.

Gangs have short memories for compliments and long memories for insults, and if you get blinded by the family-and-loyalty narrative and don't learn from the people who came before you, you're going to lose every time. On the streets, self-preservation rules above everything else. There is a saying in Watts that the neighborhood's name is actually an acronym: We Are Taught To Survive. In that moment up on that wall, feeling the things I was feeling, on the drugs I was on, I thought my only chance at survival was to let all those motherfuckers in the 404 know I was not to be fucked with. And so, I put thirty rounds in the building.

No one was hit. That's one good thing about the projects: those brick walls are thick.

After I finished shooting, I immediately went to Branden's house and told him what I'd done. He stared at me and then walked away, into his back room. I heard him cursing to himself as he rummaged around. Because Branden was never afraid to tell you to your face that you'd fucked up, I got ready for him to come back and chew my ass out.

But when he came back out, he didn't yell. He just stood there holding his AK-47 and looking me in the face.

"Let's go back."

"No," I told him. "It's cool. Let's let it lie."

I had made my point. Not sure where else to go, I checked into a motel and lay on the bed thinking about how betrayed I felt. I'd brought three people with me over to the 404, and seeing them all siding with BE-K hurt my heart. Even after all that, I couldn't just turn away and leave. I still needed to see where I stood. So, the day after I shot it up, I went back to the 404.

Walking in the door, I put my gun on the table, went into the living room, snatched up the remote control, and turned on the music. I was trying to act like it was business as usual, like it might be any other day, but I had a plan. The gun I put on the table was empty. My loaded gun was still on me. If anyone tried to pick up the empty gun and turn it against me, I would have the drop. But no one did. My coming back had thrown them off. They weren't sure how to react to me. Everyone pretended it was cool, but you could tell they were eyeing me, trying to figure out my endgame. The tension was palpable.

A week later, they made their move. I was at a dice game without my gun, and I knew better. Just as I was asking another player, the homie Big Hogg, if I could hold his, I saw the expression on his face and knew there was trouble. When I turned around, Junior and two other dudes had guns out and pointed at me. I had no play. They could kill me right there. And honestly, I would've understood why. But as I waited for them to shoot, one of them, whom I'd grown up with, suggested they call BE-K first.

"We've got Fresh," he said when he got BE-K on the phone. "What you want us to do?"

I waited to get my sentence. But I didn't have to wait long. Even through the phone, I could hear BE-K yelling, "You motherfuckers best not touch him! And if you do, don't come back!"

Defeated, the three put away their guns and walked back to the 404. Somehow, I was still alive.

After the dice game, I went to a cookhouse only BE-K and I knew about and asked the woman who lived there to call BE-K. Once he got on the phone, I asked if we could meet. He agreed and said he'd come alone. I didn't believe him, so I went out to track his movements, but sure enough, he was true to his word. He came to the spot alone, and even brought along the original four and a half ounces from the Hoover gang crew as a peace offering, as well as some more to cook.

We didn't have a long, drawn-out conversation. There were no apologies. In the game, that's not how these things went down.

"Let's just get back to business," BE-K said. And so, we did.

Years later, BE-K would be murdered while I was in prison. That day, sitting in my cell, I cried.

ON FEBRUARY 24, 2003, MY daughter Keivionna was born. I'd been back with BE-K for a few months, but I was mostly staying with Keivionna's mother, Tiffany, in Long Beach. Unlike with Keith Jr., I felt more prepared for my daughter's birth. Now, that might sound objectively ludicrous, given my profession and my personal drug habit, but I was putting away money and living with Tiffany at the time. We even had a baby shower.

However, the night Tiffany went into labor, I was caught by surprise. We all were. A month before her due date, she started having contractions. I was at the 404, chopping drugs and getting high, when I heard the news. I called my mother's house, and my uncle agreed to come pick me up and drive me to Long Beach Memorial Hospital. The only problem was, Tiffany was having the baby at St. Mary's.

By the time I realized I was in the wrong place, my uncle had already left, so I had to catch a bus down Atlantic Avenue and then walk my ass to the right hospital. Because of this dumb mistake, I missed the birth of my daughter.

But once I made it to the room where Tiffany and Keivi were resting, I remember staring at my daughter and knowing instinctively something different was going to be expected of me now. Having a little girl awakened this sense of protectiveness I don't think I felt having a son. It's not to say that I had the tools at the time to be able to be a good role model for her; as a parent, I was as new with her as I had been with Keith Jr., but now I knew enough to know I wanted more for her. It wasn't much, but at least it was something.

With the birth of my daughter and all the shit that went down at the 404, I was spending a lot more time in Long Beach than Watts. I was much more in and out, and I didn't care as much about the money I had tied up in the operation. I might come through to put in work, but I would never sleep there anymore. The beef may've been squashed, but something had shifted.

Something changed in me after I shot up the 404. When I'd been with Branden and that crew, it had been all about hustling and selling drugs and making that money. And for the first few years with BE-K and them, it was the same. I had been the enforcer in the crew, and I wasn't afraid to shoot, but I did whatever made me the most money, and that had been cooking drugs and selling them. But now my survival instincts took over, and I went into full-time gangbanging mode. Because the truce was still on, and there was no big war with the Nickersons to fight, I was like a soldier with no mission looking to insert himself into other people's problems. Any knickknack shit, and I'm ready. Some small beef with Fudge Town? Fuck it, let's go. Some young boys shooting at cars around the way? Fuck it, let's *go*.

I wasn't just looking for problems; I *was* the problem.

I'D KNOWN THE RECORD STORE was a drug front for a while. I'd been watching all the businesses in the strip mall at the MLK Shopping Center and had noticed that almost all the other stores used a bank service to pick up their money, but the record store never did. Instead, twice a week, someone would come out of the shop with a bag of cash. That week, it hadn't happened yet, so, when my little brother Kevin came to me asking for some money, I had the same fraternal feeling Bo had once had for me when he first taught me to cook.

"Fuck giving you money," I told him. "I'll show you how to get money."

That night, I grabbed my gun, and we jumped in the car and headed to the record shop. Purposely, to avoid other customers, I got there right as they were closing. At the time, I could see five people working in the store, cleaning up. In fact, they'd already locked the door, but I knocked on the glass. "Can I come in?" I asked. "I just want to get a shirt."

When they let me in, I walked around, grabbed a few items, and then headed to the counter. Once there, I showed the woman at the register my gun and said, "I want all the money. Put it in the same bag with the clothes."

She did what I told her, but while she was grabbing the money, I saw a security guard making the rounds outside look inquisitively into the store. Thinking quickly, I told the girl behind the counter to walk me to the door. To make it seem more casual, I took my phone out and pretended to be trying to get her phone number, but the guard must've seen the terror on the young woman's face, because when we opened the door, he grabbed his radio. As soon as he did, I pulled out my pistol.

"Just do your eight hours and go home, bro," I told him.

He dropped the radio, and I hustled out to my brother's car. When I got in, I told him, "Take me back to the projects." As we were driving away, I threw the bag with the cash at him. "*That's* how you make money."

I was too cocky, too high on drugs and my own power. I'd gotten away with so much that I felt there was no way in hell anyone would rat on me if I made a move. But, a few days later, I got word from someone in my community who worked at the store: they had me on tape. Though I'd asked for the security camera CDs, I didn't realize they backed up automatically to a hard drive, and thanks to the security guard, there was no chance my crime would go unreported, even at a drug front. I was wanted for robbery, and because I had told that young woman to walk three steps with me to the door, I also now had a kidnapping charge. I assumed the combination of those charges meant I'd be looking at a life sentence. At twenty-two years old, I couldn't handle that. So, for the next two months, I went on the run.

Now, this wasn't like some white banker going on the run. I didn't have the money to change my name and move to the islands—or even to leave South Central. I was Black and lived in L.A. The statistical likelihood that I would be pulled over by the cops was almost guaranteed. And the ones who patrolled

Watts knew me. The LAPD gang unit kept baseball cards with our pictures and stats on the back, including our aliases, if we were known to carry weapons or sell drugs—all that stuff. But don't get it twisted: we knew them, too.

We knew their shifts, when they were working overtime, who partnered with whom, who would get out of the car to chase you, and who would leave you alone when it was raining. They were their own gang looking to outshine one another at our expense, and they played dirty—especially one I'll call Mr. Gang Unit. Mr. Gang Unit was a cocky white detective in his thirties, a real arrogant fucker. At the time I knew him, he was fucking at least two women in the community, so he knew all sorts of things, and he tried to use that information in any way he could, spreading disinformation within the gangs and putting snitch jackets on random people to try to isolate them from the rest of the group. He was grimy.

I'd always figured prison would be inevitable, part of my growth. I watched other people in my community go to prison all the time; I figured it was a part of strengthening your reputation, as if surviving prison were just another notch on your belt. The problem was, I wasn't ready to go, and I certainly didn't want to give someone like Mr. Gang Unit the satisfaction of being the one to bring me in. And so, I ran.

For most of this time, I stayed in other projects, like the Nickersons or Imperial Court, shacking up with women I knew or with trusted friends. Because it was truce times, this was okay, but sometimes I had to go all the way out to the projects in Pacoima, about thirty-five miles north of Watts, which were controlled by the Pirus. I would creep into a building in the middle of the night, praying I wouldn't see anybody, my gun on me at all times, knowing that, worse than the cops, if I was found by any Pirus on their home turf, I was dead anyway. To make things even more complicated, all this moving around and staying with random women didn't exactly play in my favor with Tiffany. One night, she called my phone while I was asleep, and another woman answered.

When I got on, she said, "I understand the situation, but if you can be with that bitch, then you can be at home with me and your daughter."

She was right, so I told her I'd come to Long Beach. On the way, I stopped back by Jordan Downs. My sister had wanted to get rid of a car, so I figured I'd drive it out to Long Beach, see my daughter, and then burn it so my sister could collect the insurance money. Before leaving, I broke one of the car windows and left the glass lying there, so my sister could report the car stolen. Then I drove it out and parked it around the corner from where my daughter was staying. After pouring gasoline inside the car, I lit a cigar and threw it in. But the cigar must not have been fully lit.

Cursing, I got closer to the car and tossed in a lit match, and as I did, an enormous backdraft rushed through the open window and gave me third-degree burns on my face and chest. I can't tell you what it felt like, because I have no memory. My body was in shock. Later, the doctor would tell me that if I had been breathing in rather than out at that exact moment, I would've been killed instantly.

Even though I knew the hospital would report a burn victim to the cops, my injuries were so bad that I had no choice but to go there. When we arrived, I told Tiffany to fill out my information but to put me down as "Eddie Wright," a name borrowed from an uncle of mine who had died a decade earlier. But when the nurse came in to see me and put my wristband on, I looked down and saw "Keith Corbin" on it. In the stress of the moment, Tiffany had forgotten to change my name.

Knowing the police would be on their way, I waited for the doctor to leave my room, snatched up as many ointments and tools as I could, and walked out, back to Long Beach. While I was there, I tried to deal with the burns myself, applying lotions and IcyHot—anything I could think of to heal the skin and deal with the pain—but no matter what I used, it felt like I was on fire. My skin was white as fuck—but not in the way that would help me avoid jail time.

I was in serious agony and knew I needed to go back to the hospital. But when I walked outside to smoke a cigarette and think about my next move, I noticed an unmarked car parked on the road with a big antenna on the back. When I looked the other way, I saw another, similar car. I called one of my homies from Grape Street, told him the cops were watching the house, and asked him to come get me. When he got there, I got in the car, and he drove away and made a right turn, passing an alley behind the house. As we passed, we saw a car come out of the alley and pull out behind us. My buddy panicked and made a right and then another right, and suddenly, we were right back in front of the house, surrounded.

Officers crashed down on the windshield with their guns drawn, yelling, "Don't move! Put your hands up! Don't move!"

The Long Beach Police officers pulled me out and put me against the wall. I heard them make a call: "We have Corbin here, but we think it's his brother."

"Hold him," a voice on the other line said. "I'll be right there."

The voice sounded familiar. And sure enough, ten minutes later, an unmarked police car from Watts rolled up. It was Mr. Gang Unit.

"I got you, Fresh," he told me, a big smile on his face. "You're gonna be locked up for a while."

I tried to be stoic and not give him the satisfaction. I told him that if he had me, to just take me in and stop talking about it. But the worst part was, I knew he was right.

PART TWO

Corbin; his eldest daughter, Keivionna; and
Corbin's mother, Lydia, in the visitor center at
Calipatria State Prison.

6

Collect Calls

NO ONE TELLS YOU ABOUT THE SMELL. YOU HEAR A LOT ABOUT jail on the outside, but never that. It's distinct, like feet and mold and other things left wet that'll never fully dry. It smells like too many grown men in too small a space eating too much shitty food. And because the air recirculates, it never changes. Walking out of jail is like walking out of a smokehouse. People can smell the jail on you.

When I was arrested in Long Beach, I was charged with firearm possession, use of a firearm to commit a crime, five counts of armed robbery by force or fear (one for each person in the store at the time), and forcibly moving someone against their will. I ended up in Downtown Los Angeles, in L.A. County Jail. Because I was being tried in Compton, I'd have to get on this big gray bus every day and head east on the 105 to go to court. A split second after passing the Wilmington exit, you could look over the top of the Imperial Courts projects and see my mom's yard. On multiple occasions, I remember seeing her in her yard watering her grass, living her life. Man, I hated that.

But what I hated more was the County Jail. People worry about going to prison, but the County Jail is ten times more dangerous. There is no structure. It's a fucking free-for-all. And unlike in the rest of the world, being white in L.A. County Jail is not a privilege. Once white dudes get to prison or jail in other parts of California, they've got the white supremacists and the Nazis and various motorcycle gangs to link up with. But if you are white and in L.A. County, you'd better mind your business and pray, because you have no leverage and no protection.

Then again, everyone entering County Jail has to have their guard up. Just before the gray bus pulls into the underground drop-off area, it's like the quiet before the storm, or that moment of silence before an army goes into battle. Because, as anyone who has been there before knows, you've got to get your mind right to handle County. And the worst part is, the people in County are always changing, so you never know what you're about to enter into. As soon as they take you off the bus and walk you through the double doors, it's on.

The first thing the L.A. County sheriffs do is try to intimidate you. They herd you like cattle into this forty-by-forty room and start yelling and throwing people down. Once everyone is uncuffed, they slam the door and leave. You don't get any information; you can't ask any questions. You just wait. And it could be like this for five hours—standing, packed in sardine-tight. Some people are coming down off drugs, so they might be lying down on the floor or throwing up. And you can smell everyone.

Eventually, they move you into the next cubicle, and there, they strip you naked and have you turn, face the wall with your hands on it, and—in front of five to ten deputies—make you squat down, cough, bend over, spread your cheeks, and cough again. Then you see a counselor, who asks you if you're having suicidal thoughts. After that, a doctor; then fingerprints and a group shower with one hundred other naked motherfuckers; and then you get your County blues. It's like being on a conveyor belt in a meat processing plant.

After you're processed, they take you up to a room that might be ten by twenty, with twenty other dudes in there, packed to the gills, where you wait until they find a place to house you. And because there's so much overcrowding, this part of the process can take up to four days. No beds. Just you sitting with your back to the wall, looking through the little window in the door to see who might walk past, occasionally getting tossed a peanut butter and jelly sack lunch or a boiled egg and bread for breakfast. Depending on whom you're with, this could be the hardest four days of your life.

Imagine being at war with a bunch of other gangs in South Central and then getting dropped into a cell with all of them for several days with no walls between you. You have to be on alert the entire fucking time. It's like if a zoo gathered all its animals and opened the gates. Sure, the bears and the lions are gonna eat first, but even some of the giraffes and the birds will find a way to adapt and go from being prey to predator.

When the guards come for you next, you've got to be ready. They'll pop the doors open and tell you to shut the fuck up, because if you miss your name, they'll keep you there for another night. When they do call your name and inmate number, they hand you a little green card and walk you into the main jail. At this point, you're relieved to be leaving this unpredictable mindfuck. But you still can't relax. You're on your way to the jungle.

First off, it's loud. Oh my god, it's loud. You smell smoke in the air; and the smell of alcohol, like you've just walked into a brewery, because everyone is making some kind of booze. County Jail has maybe nine floors, and your card will tell you which one you're on, whether it's 2000, 3000, 4000, etc. Usually, they try to group you by where your people already are, so if you tell them you're with a gang, they'll put you on a floor with that gang. It may sound smart in the moment, but later, when it's time to come home and get your life together, that admission could fuck you up, because that's admissible in court, and your sentence might now include gang enhancements (additional years added for known gang activity), injunctions, and all kinds of other shit. Immediately, you're faced with a no-win situation: do you take the chance of going through County on your own, being okay wherever they put you, or do you get put with your people and have a better chance at survival in the short term, even if it might fuck you up in the long run?

My first time in County, I chose the former. I was gonna

take my chances. But, being a first-timer, I didn't know all sorts of shit. And one of the big ones was the mural.

Wherever you're going in County, there are murals on the walls. Some of them are of fallen officers, some are of famous people, but there is one person who has more murals than all the rest combined: John Fucking Wayne, the Duke. John Wayne wasn't just my Granny's favorite; he was the idol of every deputy sheriff in County. And if you happened to accidentally lean on the Duke or even just touch him, they would beat your ass to the ground right in front of everybody.

On the outside, the way to understand gang culture and territory is literally to read the writing on the wall and see who's tagging what. Well, it's no different in County: the writing's on the wall. And the sheriffs aren't exactly a bunch of subtle English major motherfuckers, so the meaning was right in front of us for all to see: their idol was a racist actor who got famous as a cowboy inflicting frontier justice in old Westerns depicting a time when white people were considered superior and slavery still existed. Yep, noted.

Anyway, once you entered your floor, you'd find it was broken up into four sections: Able, Banker, Charlie, Denver. Each one had two tiers, with maybe twelve cells per tier and forty-eight cells in each section. Each cell was painted blue and held four to six beds, though, if it was full—and it was always full—there were usually another two mattresses on the floor. The bars were painted dark blue, so you didn't see the muck and dirt and grime.

My first time in, my cell was number twelve, so I had to walk all the way down the tier. At the zoo, when you walk by the giraffes and the zebras, they go about their business, but when you pass by the predators, they come up to the fence. It's the same in jail. I walked by some cells and saw dudes lying down on bunks or opening letters, not paying no mind—but the predators? They were on the door. They wanted to know who was coming in. As I walked past their cells, I started downloading images in my mind of everybody I saw on the bars, everyone calling out, "Where you from, homie?"

I said nothing. That was always my plan. Even my first time, I knew to leave them guessing. Don't confirm anything, don't respond. Just look at them and keep walking. When I got to my cell, I sat there waiting. I knew it wouldn't be long. I was waiting for the Rooster.

Guards in a prison will usually bargain with the inmate they feel is the most aggressive, try to use him to keep everyone else in check. You know how a rooster puffs up and does all this shit with their feathers to show off? Well, the Rooster is the inmate who most eagerly tries to exert dominance. And the fact that I didn't reveal who I was meant that the Rooster would have to come find me. These fuckers can't stand not knowing.

My goal was always to make them tip their hand first. After all, in the end, despite all that puffing up and crowing, a rooster is just a dumb bird that can't really fly. While I was unpacking, the guards let the Rooster out of his cell, and he showed up at my bars asking, "Aye homie, where you from?"

Before I answered, I wanted to see if I could flip it and ask him the same. Most of the time, these dudes are so proud to bang their hood that you can assess if they're going to be a threat or an ally. This information was vital.

If he was going to be a friend, I'd politely tell him, "I'm

from Grape Street Watts, homie," and start engaging in conversation. If he was going to be a foe, I'd act differently. I knew that once I told him where I was from, it was going to be a problem, so I decided I wouldn't reveal it. I might just say, "Why you wanna know? I don't even know you, homie."

He might get mad and go crazy at the bars, but I couldn't reveal myself as an enemy until I was on the other side, able to defend myself. I couldn't be scared; I needed to be tactical. This shit was important. It would set the tone for my entire stay.

IT WAS IN COUNTY WHERE I first started to cook.

Unsurprisingly, the food they serve you in County is terrible. Three times a day, an inmate comes by, shoves a meal on a tray through the food slot in your cell door, and picks it up a few hours later. The menu was not exactly varied. One day it might be "Eraserheads" (pasta with hot dogs cut up on top), or these long hot links everyone called "donkey dicks," or beans with more cut-up hot dogs, or a public school–style hamburger with a flour-kissed stale brown bun and a patty cooked long past medium well, or slimy chicken sandwiches scorching hot from the microwave.

Because all the food is processed, canned, bagged shit, and it's always the same, dudes will go to extreme lengths just to try something new. With all the shitty slop we were eating, you couldn't help but be nostalgic for the meals from back home. I used to think about my Granny's fried chicken. She always cooked it in the cast-iron skillet, and as she fried that chicken thigh, it would get a dark ring on the bottom and have this perfect crunch as you bit through the salty, flaky skin and got to the moist meat inside. I thought about other things, too: finding perfectly braised and caramelized onions blending together with creamy mashed potatoes and crispy, sizzling meat in Granny's beef and potato burritos; even her sausage, chicken, crab leg, and shrimp gumbo, which I'd stopped eating years ago, after I ate so much one New Year's Eve, I started throwing up.

Everyone chased those food memories in jail. So, early on, I watched and soaked up what other folks were doing. I watched the Asians making kimchi from the occasional vegetable they'd give us at lunch. I saw Latin dudes making tamales by grinding down Fritos from the commissary, adding hot water, smashing the Fritos down to dust, adding more water, spreading the paste into a square on the Frito bag, taking roast beef or cheese or whatever, rolling everything up, and standing it up to dry. When the Frito mixture dried up again, you'd have a pretty damn good tamale.

My personal favorite was the spread. A spread was just like it sounds: a variety of foods you'd put together to try to trigger your taste buds. Put another way, it was basically figuring out how to make foods that tasted gross on their own taste pretty damn good when you mixed them all up. On some level, I was trying to recapture the perfect textures I used to get eating my Granny's chili beans and rice. I'd always loved how the rice absorbed the flavors of the chili bean gravy and how the cheese and broken-up saltine crackers sprinkled over the top gave it a salted creaminess as well as a crunch. But if you wanted to achieve something even halfway comparable to my Granny's dishes in jail, you had no choice but to experiment. You could get there only through trial and error, finding the right foods in the commissary to purchase and mix together in your cell.

When I first got in, I would make cooked noodles and maybe add some tuna or mackerel, but that was too mushy. The next time, looking to combat the mushiness, I'd add pork rinds for crunch, or some pickle for acid and texture. Once I realized that played, I started craving some smoke in it, so I'd cut up a summer sausage and throw that in as well. Eventually, that bowl of mushy noodles would have a layered texture and taste. A little heat from the chili lime flavor packet with the noodles, some smoke from the sausage, a little seafood from the mackerel (smoke and seafood: there's a reason paellas work), the bite of pickle to give it that shock of vinegar to cut through the fat, the crisp flavor off the pork rinds to give it more texture—it might've looked nasty and sounded gross, but when you ate it, the flavor was there because you were using the same dials as a chef: salt, acidity, texture, flavor, heat, and sweetness. I was finding my palate and figuring out balance through experimentation. I got better and better the more I learned and the more reference points I had. I might eat one spread and realize my taste buds were asking for something else or telling me to add or eliminate a flavor, so each time I ate it, I tried to tweak it until I got the best fucking spread you'd ever tried.

Just like with the drugs, I wanted my spreads to stand out. In the thriving jail economy, if you were known for making decent food, you could trade on that talent. So, I looked for ways to separate myself. If everyone was using chili lime, I wanted to try garlic and onion powder. If folks were throwing Ritz crackers in there for crunch, I'd use fried tortillas. Or maybe I'd make a rice bowl and add the mackerel in first, before

I added the hot water, so it would steam up and the fish flavor would season the rice.

Considering we were locked up for twenty-three hours and forty-five minutes a day—the other fifteen minutes were for a cold-ass shower or some physical exercise—experimentation with food was a way to pass the time and keep your mind off everything else while you tried to fight your case. Because that shit felt insurmountable.

ON THE DAYS I WAS due in court, they'd wake us up at three A.M., put us on a bus by four, and keep us in a cell at the courthouse from six thirty A.M. until the last dude was done with the judge at six P.M. On those days, we wouldn't get back to County until nine. This alone is a big reason it's crucial to make bail. County will break you down mentally. If the DA really wanted to force you to take a deal, they'd subject you to this routine four or five days in a row, waking you at three A.M. and making you go through the entire process, only to tell you at the very end of the day that they made a mistake and you weren't actually supposed to be in court that day.

Meanwhile, every day you were at court, it was a risk to your life. There are thousands of dudes from Compton, Watts, Lynwood, South Gate, and Carson going to court in Compton each day. During "court movement," which is basically what they call moving your ass from jail to the courthouse, you are assigned to cells according to what court you're going to. So, Compton might be in cells 201 and 202. But it's not well organized, and there are two doors between you and the guards. A lot of times, I'd see groups of dudes from other gangs purposely slip into the wrong cells to beat someone's ass and then, when the guards finally came, act confused about what cell they were supposed to be in and move on out, betting on the fact that whoever just got their ass beat would keep it to themselves.

On top of that, you'd have to be ready to deal with the unpredictable moods of dudes getting sentenced to prison time all day long. So, you might be hanging in your cell, minding your business, about to get released that day, and some nineteen-year-old with nothing to lose after getting life with no parole will come back to the cell angry as hell, hear you're supposed to get out, and decide to beat your ass strictly out of envy for your situation. Now, not only have you just gotten your ass whupped, but you might also have gotten a new charge off the fight and be forced to stick around. And this shit does not get better the more you do it. It happens every single day.

They take the fight out of you, and by the end of a week, you're ready to say, "What are you offering? Five years? Give it here"—just to get out of County, go to the pen, do the time, and come home. They have all the leverage. But if you can make bail, it's a completely different story. You can fight the case for two to three years, tie the court up, make them spend money, and the DA might decide you are costing too many resources and either cut a more favorable deal or drop the charges.

I didn't have the money for bail or my own private attorney, so I started my case with a public defender. He showed me the transcripts from witness interviews and the police report on my case, and from the jump, I could see a lot of exaggerations and lies, but when I tried to talk to him about strategy, he wouldn't engage. His sole focus seemed to be on getting me to take a plea deal as quickly and cleanly as possible. He had no interest in actually defending me, or at least improving my situation, so I fired him and requested a state-appointed attorney. Thankfully, the lawyer I got was a Black man who genuinely seemed to be there to help his people. He encouraged me to go through my paperwork and point out the inconsistencies. By diligently scouring the videotape and testimony and talking it through, we managed to get them to drop the charges of armed robbery, use of a firearm, and forcibly moving someone against their will. By the end, I was left with just four counts of robbery by force.

The endgame of County Jail is to make you so uncomfortable that you will do anything to leave it. I was someone who already had people in there, a state-appointed lawyer who genuinely wanted to help, and enough knowledge of the legal system to at least have a strategy, and County still almost broke me. Every aspect of the place is designed to wear you down. From the mind-fucking court process, to the shitty food, to the inhumane confinement, to the racist murals on the walls, to the tyrannical guards who can fuck your whole world up because it's actually against their interests not to.

I felt this firsthand. At one point during my initial bid, I'd been moved out from L.A. County Jail to another county facility called Wayside. I didn't want to be there. It was too far for my family to travel to, so I was even more alone. I wanted to go back to L.A. County, so I played it like I needed to talk to a shrink. The guard knew I was bullshitting, but there was nothing he could do about it. He was annoyed, though, and punished me by cuffing my hands behind my back instead of in front, like he did with the other inmates sitting next to me waiting for transfers.

It was painful and uncomfortable—I was sitting on a bench and couldn't lean back—so I asked the guard, "Can you move my handcuffs to the front like everyone else?" He told me no. This pissed me off, so when he left, I slipped my arms under my butt and slid my feet through the cuffs. When he came back and saw they were in the front, he got so mad, he wrote me up for an attempted escape charge. In the moment, I didn't care. I just wanted to get the fuck back to County. The problem was when they pulled my file to assess and assign me to a prison to carry out my sentence, they saw this escape charge pinned to my file and, instead of seven years in a Level 2 facility with a lower custody level, more freedom, and dorms, I was now going to a Level 4 facility, the highest security, mostly filled with inmates doing serious bids and on death row.

With the stroke of a pen, this guard had changed the course of my prison life forever.

7

I Got the Keys

WHEN THE STATE COMES FOR YOU, IT'S LIKE A KIDNAPPING. THEY come in the middle of the night, wearing all black. While everyone else is sleeping, they pop your door, grab you, cuff you up, and walk your ass to a bus.

Unlike the sheriffs running the jails, the prison guards deal with you with a little more respect—their tone isn't as aggressive, and they are willing to communicate directly with you—which, in a sense, is their way of asserting even more authority. They don't need to yell; they've got control of you in other ways. Now, at the time, I didn't realize this. I was scared but trying to be tough, and when I get that fight-or-flight feeling, my instinct is naturally to fight. So, on the bus, when they told us to be quiet, I got loud. This was a mistake.

They pulled the bus over to the side of the road, took me off, and made it very clear to me that they would make it seem like I was resisting and leave my ass right there, and they weren't talking about alive. That scared me even more. Shit, at that moment, I wanted my momma. The whole rest of the long-ass ride to the state reception center, I was dead quiet, which I figured was better than dead.

A lot of people don't know about reception centers, the stop between County and prison. Reception centers are essentially shipping ports for prisoners. Think of the Port of Long Beach. Everything arriving into Long Beach by boat comes through the port, where it's kept on the docks until they figure out its destination and what truck to load it on to take it there.

Processing at the reception center is more or less the same as at County, but faster: they know you're coming, so they've got a bed for you. They ask if you're in a gang, make you see the psychiatrist and get a TB shot, and make sure you've got a clean bill of health before they put you in with the general population. This is where I first found out I wasn't going to be in dorms with the rest, that I was going to be housed in a cell. I was confused—I saw people with more time than me in those dorms—and it made me scared, panicky, and claustrophobic as I looked around my cellblock and saw all those gates, cages, and barbed wire with signs showing images of people being electrocuted.

From the moment I got off the bus, the contrast to County became real. Everyone at the reception center was quiet, taking in the seriousness of their situation. As someone whose senses are heightened in chaos and crisis, who came up in the constant commotion of the projects, I was thrown off. Normally, you associate quiet with tranquility, but this wasn't that. I moved my way past the cells and saw the shadow of a face in every window slit. I was already at a disadvantage. Everyone knew what I looked like coming in, but I didn't know who they were. In prison, I didn't have to try to figure out who the predators were: because of their cases, activities, and criminal history, everyone in a cell was deemed unfit for gen pop. They were all predators. No one was showing their hand, but I sensed the danger really fast. The dorms may've been like being in the jungle during the day, but the cells were the jungle at night. In that moment, I felt as vulnerable as I ever had.

Reception centers are a strange version of limbo—while you're there, you don't get phone calls or anything; basically, all you can do is write letters. And if you don't get mail, you can get jealous over the smallest thing. You see others getting letters every day, and you start to question your relationships with people, question your family. You forget that life on the streets doesn't stop just because you're locked up with nothing to do, so you start wondering why the fuck your homies and family can't take a moment of their time to say "what's up" and ask how you're doing. You forget how busy you were on the street, how many excuses you had for not writing your homies who were locked up. When this happens, you might start writing hate mail, further alienating yourself from those on the outside. It turns into a psychological war.

You can be in reception for up to a year, but I got my transfer slip after ninety days. In the fall of 2004, right before I was transferred, I met with the counselor, and they started asking me questions.

"How old were you when you were first arrested?"

"Are you affiliated with a gang?"

"What level of school did you complete?"

"Have you ever served in the armed forces?"

Something I didn't know the first time I got to prison was that my answers to these boring-ass questions were actually tallied up as points against me. This was where the "attempted escape" from County really hurt. My final tally was sixty points. Fifty-nine points or fewer, and I'd have been in the lower-security Level 3. But now I was in Level 4, which meant I was going to Calipatria State Prison, in Imperial County, California. (Look, if you want to get technical, they sent me to another prison, called Centinela, for six months before Calipatria, but I'm trying to tell a story here and save you from the boring logistical shit. Just know Centinela sucked, too.)

I'd never heard of Calipatria, but when I asked around the yard, it came back that it was one of the worst prisons in the whole system, home to a bunch of paperwork gangs (gangs that operate strictly in prisons) and to many of the inmate shot callers in the California penal system.

Calipatria's claim to fame is that it's the "lowest prison in the Western Hemisphere," because it's nearly two hundred feet below sea level, but I'm not sure that's really a claim to fame. Its real claim to fame is probably the so-called death fence surrounding the facility. Installed in 1993, the fence instantly shoots four thousand volts through anyone who touches it. Calipatria sits on over a thousand acres near the Mexican border, not far from the Salton Sea, a toxic lake filled with pesticides from nearby farms, which also make the entire facility smell like cow shit, especially in the summer, when it gets up to 120 degrees.

The prison itself looks like a combination of a small municipal airport and a college campus . . . if that college had cut its entire landscaping budget twenty years ago. The part of the prison I was in features five big buildings in a semicircle around a half-oval yard split down the middle by a barbed wire fence. There are five guard towers staffed by dudes with semiautomatic rifles and two more external ones. The prison is designed to house 2,300 prisoners, but when I was there in 2005, it had over 4,000, which meant that some of the lower-level prisoners slept on mattresses brought into the chapel, the gym, and the common areas. They even built fifty-bed camps outdoors.

Back in the 1960s, over 60 percent of the inmates in American prisons were white. But after the "war on drugs," everything flipped. At the end of the 1980s, minorities were five times as likely to get arrested for drugs. By 2005, they made up 60 percent of the state and federal prison population in the United States and nearly two-thirds of male inmates in California. Couple that with the passage of the "three strikes law" in the nineties, and you could understand why these prisons were crowded as hell. So, the idea of any sort of nuance when it came to whom you would associate with in prison went out the fucking window. Back in the day, when the prison populations were smaller, there were also more interracial gangs, which formed around region or city loyalties. But not anymore. Now, it didn't matter your progressive political views or your multicultural background or who your stepdad was—Blacks hung out with Blacks, Latinos with Latinos, and whites with whites.

The prison couldn't officially approve of segregation, but there were ways around that. In *Enforcing the Convict Code: Violence and Prison Culture,* the author, Rebecca Trammell, cites a study of California prison reception centers in 2008, which found that guards made the inmates say their race and then asked if they would be willing to bunk with other races. If an inmate said yes, he was "asked again until the inmate figured out the correct answer was no." For the prison, this was the bluntest and easiest way to tamp down violence.

Among the prisoners, once we were inside, we took it one step further and broke ourselves down into "cars." A car is your prison family, your tribe, the people you ride with. Your car is determined by your race, where you're from, and your gang. A car can be two people or a hundred, but there's always a driver, someone steering the car, deciding which way to go. That person "has the keys." When I got to Calipatria, the driver was my homie Cisco, a lifer from Grape Street who was about twenty years older than me. (He ran with my mom back in the day.) As soon as I got there, he got me moved into his building, solidifying my rep. Though we had about fifteen to twenty people in our car, because Compton and Watts—"the Hub" and "the Dub"—usually roll together in prison, there were forty to fifty dudes in total from our two hoods. We rolled deep.

An important distinction between Level 4 and the other levels was that, in the fours, the paperwork gangs had everything locked down. They were lifers, and the prison was now their home, so they weren't looking to disrespect or mess up what they had going on in there for some shit happening on the outside. Anything that went down on the streets stayed on the streets. You could be a Bounty Hunter Blood; you could've shot my brother or, hell, shot me—that would have to remain on the outside.

That's not to say violence didn't occur. It certainly did. But mostly it was a result of what you did *in* prison. Even so, I never felt safe while I was there. Not one day. Not even the day of my release: you're not safe or even *out* until you're sitting on your couch at home. And you'd better not tell anyone your release date, because prisoners can use that information against you, start testing you, knowing full well you don't want to do anything that might jeopardize your getting out. That whole "misery loves company" line? That shit should be on posters on the walls of prisons, because there are plenty of dudes who aren't going home who would love to catch you up and make you one of them. You can go in that motherfucker with thirty days and, just by protecting yourself (and hurting someone really bad in the process), wind up never getting out, Now the thirty days is out the window. Now you're in for life.

In a way, prison is like Tetris. You can see what's happened in the past and where things need to fit, where your strengths and vulnerabilities are, but you never know the next pieces coming until they're already there. You're dealing with the guards, the different races, the different tribes within the races, the regulations, stress from what's happening on the streets— all of it. And even when it seems all good, that shit can change in one day. There could be peace on the yard, with things running smoothly and all the key holders in communication, but then a new bus shows up, and some white boy skinhead from Pelican Bay comes in and supersedes the white boy you've been talking to, and now everything is thrown off.

This was why, inside, I became a master at recognizing

patterns and routines. Every day, we'd go to the yard and, for the first ten or fifteen minutes, I'd stand there and take in the energy. The first part of my routine was to watch everyone else's routines. Ninety-five percent of the time, I'd see the same things. You know which dudes are gonna be doing calisthenics over by the pull-up and dip bars, and which OGs will be at the card tables playing dominoes and chess, and which inmates will be working the gardening and maintenance jobs, and which will be at the commissary. But 5 percent of the time, things are off. Like, *Why are all the Muslim Brothers working out in front of Building 3 today? Normally, they're over by Building 5.* And then you realize, *Oh, they're waiting for some poor dude to walk out of Building 3 so they can stab him up.*

In a yard full of predators, recognizing the signs of an attack is how you avoid becoming prey.

8

I Seen a Man Die

WHEN I GOT IN, I RECONNECTED WITH MY HOMIE KILLA BOB, WHO about ten years before had gotten locked up for murder at age sixteen. Bob and I had a deep history. When we were teens, he came to me for a gun after getting into it with an older dude in Jordan Downs, and I'd been there with him when he shot the dude. So, when I saw him again for the first time in a decade, there was a flood of emotions.

I carried a lot of regret for how it had all gone down, but Bob seemed okay with me, and it was good to kick it again. But I noticed that because the dude had been in there since he was a teenager, he was still immature as hell, and a loose cannon. And soon enough, he started running his mouth about a high-ranking member of United Blood Nation, one of the largest paper gangs in California. He actually wrote on some kite (a passed note) how this guy was a snitch, and the UBN basically did *CSI*-level handwriting analysis of birthday cards everyone had signed, and they figured out it was him. It was only a year into my time at Calipatria, but before this, Cisco, my driver, had been moved off the yard, and I'd been given the keys. This was my crew now, Bob included. So, the UBN, one of the most dangerous prison gangs in the country, came to me telling me they wanted us to stab our own homie as a disciplinary measure, or they would. I wasn't going to let anyone force my hand, so I declined.

That same day, when we got out to the yard, all these UBN lifers, about twenty of them, came over to six of us. You could see that some had knives and were ready to go to war. I was scared as hell, but I knew I had to stand my ground. I talked to Peabody. A founder of the UBN, Peabody was one of the most powerful dudes within the entire California state penitentiary system.

I told him the evidence they had against Bob wasn't enough for us to take action. "My homie says he didn't do it," I said. "And what you've got isn't enough to convince me otherwise."

Now, I knew for a fact my homie was guilty as fuck, but that wasn't the point. We'd handle that on our own. It was the principle of the thing—I wasn't going to let someone else tell me how to deal with my own people. On top of that, if my people saw me following orders from another car, they could lose their faith in my ability to drive ours.

There was a pause, and in that moment, I could feel how close shit was to jumping off. But then Peabody stepped forward and spoke. "Do you really stand by your homie?"

I said I did, and he nodded and said that was all he needed to hear. He then turned around and spoke to his car. "We're letting this shit go. From now on, business as usual." And then he walked away.

My homies were all relieved, but I didn't buy it. Something was off. I knew Peabody's history, and it felt like we'd gotten off too easy, so I went back up to him. "Yo, Peabody," I said. "I know your game. Be straight up with me—you trying to tell us everything is cool so you can turn around and jump us?"

He stared at me with a smile and shook his head. "Youngster, you're a sharp motherfucker," he said. "But nah, we're cool. Anyone else got something to say about this, you let me know, and I'll deal with it on my end."

It was baptism by fire in the art of prison negotiation, politicking, and diplomacy. These cats had been in there for twenty or thirty years. While they knew all the angles, I was going by feel. If I'd gotten aggressive, and we'd argued back and forth, we'd have probably all been dead. And if I had done what they asked, they would've felt like they owned my car and not given us the proper respect. So, I had to remain cool and level-headed, but be assertive and admit no wrong.

Of course, when we left the yard, we had to discipline Bob. For the sake of the car, I had put my word to a lie to cover for him. Besides, he had almost gotten us all killed over shit talk in a passed note. Externally, I had to have his back. Internally, I had to show the others that shit like that wouldn't fly. I learned really quickly that I wasn't making decisions only for myself anymore. I had to think on behalf of my car. I had people under my care.

IN LATE 2005, NOT LONG after I was moved to C Yard, I was hanging in my cell when I heard a guard in the tower get on the intercom and announce to the whole building, "Corbin, Cell Thirty-two, you need to call home."

This was strange. We were on lockdown then because a huge riot had broken out between the Mexicans and the prison guards that had resulted in one of the Mexicans getting shot in the head right in front of us. (To this day, the image of that dude bleeding out fucks me up.) While on lockdown, you weren't allowed to make or receive calls, so my first thought was that someone was trying to set me up by making it look like I was getting special privileges from the guards while everyone else was locked up.

When the guard came to the door, I raised my hands up and said, "What's up?"

"You got a phone call."

"What?"

He explained that my people had called me up. "You need to call home."

Once I better understood the circumstances, I knew that whatever news I was about to get wasn't going to be good. And everyone else knew it, too. As I followed the guard past the ten cells between mine and the phone, nobody made eye contact with me or came to their window.

I called my mother's house, and my older sister, Nedra, my dad's daughter, answered. That had never happened before. I could hear lots of voices in the background as she said to the room, "Here's Keith right now; he's on the phone."

The phone was passed to my mother: "Kevin was shot. Five or six times," she said. She went on to explain how he was DOA when he first arrived at the hospital, but that they'd brought him back to life. I didn't hear any of that, or anything else past "Kevin was shot." I slammed the phone down and turned to walk away, but just as impulsively, I picked it back up and dialed home again.

This time, my daddy got on the phone and kept telling me, "He all right, he all right," but I don't remember the conversation. It must've gone on for some time, though, because the guy in the tower actually had the fucking audacity to tell me to wrap it up, even though he knew it was bad news.

I hung up the phone and walked back to my cell. My cellmate asked what was going on, and I just told him, "Man, I don't wanna be bothered right now." Then I lay on my bunk with my head under the covers. I could not talk about it. I put it in the file cabinet in my mind and locked that shit away. It was the only way I knew how to cope.

Even so, this shit hit me hard. Kevin was my only full-blood brother. Ever since he was born, we ran together, played together, and walked to and from school together. I used to protect him. I was his Truett. He had been an incredible athlete since he was young. An amazing baseball player, left-handed, in the batting cages all day, he had basically been adopted by his Little League coach, and that family had helped set him on an athletic path. He wasn't in the game. He never had been. And I respected that so much, because we'd grown up in the same damn place, looking out the same damn window, and my eye had never gone past the gangsters on the sidewalk outside. But his had. He wanted more than that, and he never let the streets conquer him like they conquered me. Just a few years before, he had earned a scholarship to play football at West Virginia State. We were all so proud.

This particular incident had happened while he was home on break. One of his friends, from Los Angeles Southwest College, was throwing a party. My mother told him not to go because her intuition told her there'd be trouble. But Kevin made his way there anyway. Because of his association and his resemblance to me and Branden, some girl at the party must've called back to the Nickersons and said, "Fresh's brother, BL's cousin, is up in here." They must've had a description of what he was wearing, because when he came out, a guy in a car outside rolled down his window, called out my brother's name. And when Kevin looked over, they shot him five times, everywhere from his nuts to his upper torso.

Hearing that I'd nearly lost him—my full-blood brother, someone I'd tried to protect my whole life—I basically blacked out. It was one thing for Truett to get killed. As hard as that had been for me, part of me had to accept that he was in the game and there was always that potential. But for my brother Kevin, who had avoided all the bullshit and was making a new way for himself playing football across the fucking country, to get shot down like that due to his association with me, I didn't know how to process that.

Part of the problem was that this kept happening. After the accidental shooting of a powerful Blood in 2002, the Rodney King–era truce between the Bounty Hunter Bloods and Grape Street had finally ended. This had led to retaliation, and just like that, Watts was a war zone again. In early 2005, another of my original crew, Lil Moe-C, was shot and killed. BE-K was killed. And a Nickerson dude we'd been cool with during the truce shot Branden in his face. (He survived.)

This was how it was now. Before the truce, the gang war between the Nickersons and Grape Street was a pretty conventional turf war. During the truce, however, everyone intermixed on every level. Both sides knew the layout of each other's projects, where the dope houses were, where the guns were, and who stayed where. We were friends, but more than that, family connections were being established. Grape Street dudes were having kids with Nickerson women, and vice versa. Because the truce lasted as long as it did, those relationships had a chance to go deep. Roots were established. So, when the war kicked back off, it was no longer just a gang war. It was a family feud. And that intimacy, having people on both sides of the conflict, made it that much more brutal. There's nothing uglier than the brother-versus-brother mentality of a civil war. My younger brother Kevin had a daughter with the same woman who later had a son by the dude who shot Branden. So, when that dude shot Branden, it wasn't just a Blood shooting a Crip. It was family shooting family.

BECAUSE OF THE PERSONAL NATURE of the war at that time, I have no doubt prison saved my life. If I hadn't been in prison, I'd have been either shot and killed already or serving a life sentence for retaliating after all these killings. I was probably in the best place I could be to come out of it alive. Even if, at the time, you couldn't tell me that.

Most people in prison take up some sort of improvement plan as a way to make the time pass. The majority of these revolve around exercise. Dudes get "prison big." But that's standard. As for me, I began to read. First, mainly urban tales, stories about the streets, the gangster autobiographies: *Blue Rage, Black Redemption; Monster;* Sister Souljah's *No Disrespect* and her first novel, *The Coldest Winter Ever.* I read all the Teri Woods books—*True to the Game, Dutch, Deadly Reigns,* etc. But all the books, no matter who wrote them, started to sound the same. Different city, different time, but the same damn elements. I'd read one chapter and see how the four or five teenage characters were introduced, and I wouldn't have to read the rest, because I could tell you how it was all going to play out: who was gonna snitch, who was gonna get killed, who was going to jail, and who was going to be the one to walk away, "get out."

That was it. Our stories always ended at the "out." Our literature was mirroring the expectations society had for us. To the larger society, the "out" alone should've been enough of a happy ending for us. They couldn't comprehend that that alone wasn't the prize. I always wondered why that was all we got. When I read these books, I wanted to see what happened to the dude beyond that. Did he struggle climbing the corporate ladder? Did he get a good rate on his mortgage? Did he have trouble finding an interior designer who shared his vision for the living room?

Why don't we get to have stupid problems?

Once I tired of those stories, I started reading biographies, focusing on leaders I'd learned about in school: Napoléon, Hitler, Genghis Khan, folks who were ambitious or crazy enough to try to take over the whole world. I read philosophy. And I did my own Bible study. It wasn't necessarily the straight religious aspect as much as trying to really understand the Scripture. Dudes could quote Scripture all day, but that was just memorizing some shit. How many actually knew what the hell any of the shit they were saying meant? So, I would go through the Bible, look up the references, make sure I understood them. But there was also this fire inside me that wanted a closer connection with my higher power. In the Bible, it says, "For you are all children of light, children of the day. We are not of the night or of the darkness."

I was tired of being about that darkness. With the mess I was in, I had a desire to do something different, and looking for some help, I tried to find it with the Lord. So, I started reading and praying and finding my way back there.

I also started playing chess, learning the game first by watching the OGs in the yard. Chess suited my mind. I liked the strategy. I liked the way you could set your opponent up, have them thinking you were doing one type of defense or offense, and by the time they realized they were wrong, you'd have their king. Checkmate.

Prison worked like that, too. Survival depended on strategy, but being too obvious about your moves was a sure sign they wouldn't work. This was why nighttime in prison was when the real moves were made. If you wanted to sharpen your knife, you did it when everyone was asleep, so people wouldn't hear the metal scraping against the floor. If you wanted to pass a message, you'd go fishing in the night, putting your message on a string with an anchor and sliding it into someone else's cell. Maybe the Mexicans were talking to one another, and you'd hear them suddenly switch to Spanish. Or the Blacks would start speaking Swahili. Or doing sign language through the windows. It was all about getting information past your opponents. Just like with chess, if you were gonna play, you needed to become a student of the game. And inside, I knew the chessboard. I knew the moves. I knew the danger. And because of that, I knew the consequences, too.

God help me.

9

Free Game

BACK IN THE 1970S, A DUDE FROM WATTS NAMED JOE HUNTER went through the prison food line and asked for an extra piece of chicken.

The thing to know about Joe Hunter was Joe Hunter was big, huge as a motherfucker. And if you were a big, huge motherfucker like Joe Hunter was, you needed extra protein. So, Joe Hunter went through the line and asked for that extra chicken, and, big, huge motherfucker that he was, Joe Hunter got it.

Then, one day, for whatever reason—despite Joe Hunter's being a big, huge motherfucker, or maybe *because* Joe Hunter was a big, huge motherfucker—the prison guard decided he didn't want Joe Hunter to have that extra protein. So, he took the chicken off Joe Hunter's plate and made a scene throwing it away right in front of him. This did not sit well with a mother-fucker as big and huge as Joe Hunter. So, Joe Hunter decided to take it upon himself to knock that prison guard out cold right where he stood, over the trash barrel where he'd dumped the protein that was supposed to be in Joe Hunter's body helping him stay big and huge and motherfucker-like.

Forty years later, they still talk about the time Joe Hunter knocked a CO out over a piece of chicken.

IN THE OUTSIDE WORLD, KITCHEN jobs don't mean much of any-thing, but in prison, a job in the kitchen is prestigious. Coveted. It's like a spot on the Supreme Court. You get in only if some-one else dies or leaves. And the confirmation process is compli-cated. Because the head chef in a prison kitchen is a civilian, to get in there you need to have either a certain level of clearance or connections. They don't let just anybody associate with free staff.

I didn't have the clearance. When I got in my first kitchen, in Calipatria in early 2007, I was a hothead who had just been in the hole for four months on another yard for attacking a snitch—but I did have connections. To get a job in the prison kitchen, it worked like this: First, you needed someone to leave. Maybe they got sent to the hole or transferred or did something stupid in the kitchen and got caught and lost their job. Second, you needed to be the same race as the person who had left. The way it was set up, every major race was represented and, within those races, every major gang or organization with power. So, if you were Black, this meant the Bloods, Crips, paperwork gangs, and sometimes the Muslim Brotherhood.

Now, of course, the job is supposed to be set up like a lottery. If it were being run straight and someone left, a name would be randomly selected, and that person would get the job. But with so much racial tension in prison, true random selection would've sown chaos, and that wouldn't be good for anyone, so everything was tightly controlled.

If a Blood left a job, a Blood would get that job. The only time this changed significantly was in the aftermath of a race war. Then there would be an evolution in the power structure. So, if, for example, the Blacks and whites on C Yard went to war, both groups would be sent to different yards. This meant that all the jobs those Black and white inmates had held could now be filled by Latinos. It also meant you might have a hundred new Black guys and white guys in other yards. This kind of change can disrupt the balance and the way business goes down, leading to wars—and wars were to be avoided whenever possible.

In the kitchens, it was especially important that the jobs making and distributing the food (the cooks and the line crew) were evenly spread among Blacks, whites, and Latinos. If the kitchen was all one race, they would have too much power, and the other races wouldn't trust the food. So, by keeping it even, you ensured that your people had enough representation to keep an eye on the others and make sure the food was safe. The same sort of thing went for working maintenance, gardening, or any of the other yard jobs. If it was all one race, they would be the only ones using shovels to bury weapons, and thus the only ones armed if a race war went down during yard time. The office, too: if you needed services or help, you had to go through your people in that office, or you couldn't be sure things would get done. The system was all about checks and balances.

In the event of a kitchen vacancy, assuming you were the required race (in my case, Black) and in the right group within that race (in my case, a Crip), and you had enough pull for your people to advocate for you, the Black kitchen staff would then reach out to their Black representative in the office, and the guy in the office would then do what he needed to do to send a job ducket to that inmate to let him know he was now hired in the kitchen. It was a network within a network, some real Boss Tweed patronage shit.

Given that I'm a chef now, you could look at my job in the prison kitchen as destined and assume that the reason I chose the kitchen was that I always loved food, that I was looking for comfort and familiarity, that kitchens reminded me of my Granny. But the truth was, I would've taken any fucking job to get out of that cell.

In the kitchen, you were a dockworker, a dishwasher, a cook, or a server on the line. Each job had a "lead," and the lead was usually paid the most. But seeing how the highest-paid cook in the kitchen got nineteen cents an hour, naturally you looked for other perks. The cooks controlled the food they made. After they'd finished serving all the inmates, they decided exactly what was done with the extra food, and they distributed that however they wanted. Dudes on the line controlled everything left there. So, if there were extra fruit cocktails sitting out, those guys would take them and divide them up among themselves. And the dockworkers got all the shit coming off the truck.

I was a dockworker when I first came in. I'd start work at 3:45 A.M. unloading ingredients and premade meals off the trucks that came from Central Kitchen. That might seem like a bad time to start, but it was exactly what I wanted. I was always looking to hustle. When I first got the job, I paid attention to everything. All the details mattered. I needed to know exactly how much food the yard needed to feed the inmates. How many cans of jelly did we go through before more came in? How much peanut butter? I memorized the breakfast schedule so I knew when we were using more or less of certain ingredients.

In fact, I still know it:

Saturday was eggs.

Sunday was Grand Slam (sausage, eggs, potatoes).

Monday was S.O.S. ("shit on a shingle," aka creamed beef on toast).

Tuesday was eggs, beans, and tortillas.

Wednesday was hot cereal.

Thursday was pancakes.

Friday was a cold-ass pastry.

Once I had the real numbers, I waited for my shot. I was low man on the totem pole in there, so I wasn't going to make any moves without approval, but when the dude I worked with got caught trying to sneak some jelly out, I went up to him and told him, "Man, I'm the new guy. They're not even gonna be looking at me, because they don't think I'd be involved so soon. I can get the shit out for you, and if I get caught, it's on me."

He looked at me for a long while. "All right."

I got the jelly out and passed it along, and the next day, he started telling me about the operation he had going. And that quick, I became a partner.

His operation worked like this:

Say they gave us twelve cans of grape jelly, but we needed only six. I would hold the other six back, and we'd divide them among the kitchen workers to keep people from crying. So, maybe we'd give out four and keep two. The stuff I kept I'd sell, or use to make other things (for example, alcohol). Now, this was dangerous of course, because if the inmates on the yard found out I was holding back things and selling them what was already technically theirs, they'd have gotten rightfully pissed. You could get stabbed for that.

But there were other ways to make your crew appreciate putting you up for a kitchen gig. I worked off-loading the trucks, but I'd also help out cooking in the kitchen. So, if I knew my homies from Building 5 were coming in for breakfast, I might make a special batch of raspberry, chocolate chip, or peanut butter banana pancakes and tell my buddy on the line to give my buddies those specific pancakes when they came through. Or we'd take whatever meat was left over, and I'd make some special burritos and bring them back to the cellblock when I left. Dudes loved that, because it reminded them of the streets and took their minds off prison, even if for only a moment.

But sometimes I'd make something special in the kitchen and pass it along to some random dude I didn't usually even deal with. You should've seen how getting something different from the same old bullshit puffed a dude up and made his day. It fed the stomach, but it also fed the ego. And now I'd made a friend. This dude and I still might not talk, but I had just done the rarest thing in prison—looked out for someone without asking for anything in return. And I figured, why not? It made me feel good and, hell, that small, random act of kindness might save my life one day.

While in the kitchen, I had no food-based epiphany. When you're warming up oatmeal and watching dudes make shit on a shingle, it doesn't exactly awaken you to the glory of food. At the time, I was mostly thinking about trying to be the Crip Suge Knight. I wanted a record label, I wanted artists, and I wanted a Camaro with a Welch's Grape purple paint job and a logo reading "Watts Grape."

Working in that kitchen, though, sharpened my creative side. It made me more adaptable. Later on, when I started cooking professionally, I could count on the ingenuity I learned in prison to help when I didn't have all the components for a recipe. Some prison cooks might have just given up on it, but not me. I'd start substituting, and inventing, and trying new things. I saw what was around me and created from it. I didn't have a fear of failure.

With my natural entrepreneurial, creative spirit and those extra ingredients I held back, I started my own moonshine business. In prison, we called it "white lightning." First, I'd get some apples or oranges, or the fruit cocktail, and put it in a bag and let it ferment. Then I'd add some edges of bread to get some yeast in the mix, let that sit for two days, then add anything containing sugar—syrup, candy, chocolate, whatever. The purpose was to create a flavor and a color, so you might throw in orange Starburst or green Skittles, or use packets of Kool-Aid.

To get it to boil, I'd put my booze in a gallon container, set the container in a bag on a stool in my cell, and drop in two "stingers"—you make stingers by taking nail clippers apart and attaching each of the metal sections to positive and negative wires of an electric cord. Then I'd add salt to get it to ionize, and then—boom! The alcohol would start to boil. I'd fasten the bag closed so that when the mixture boiled, the alcohol vaporized. But with nowhere to go, it would condense inside the bag and drip down the interior sides. Once I'd collected all the alcohol in the bag, I'd cut a hole in the corner and let it drip into a cup. In some ways, it was the opposite of the way I'd cooked dope—I was trying to extract purity rather than stretch it. Either way, my skills were on point. I could sell a sixteen-ounce tumbler of lightning for fifty dollars, which was damn near top of market. Everyone knew I had top-dollar shit.

10

This Is America

EVEN MORE SO THAN IN THE PROJECTS, THE UNDERGROUND economy inside a prison is the prison's beating heart. Because what the state provides is not sufficient, you have to grease palms and provide for yourself with better than they can provide for you. Which brings me back to the institution.

What is the purpose of prison exactly? The state claims that prison is there for rehabilitation, but there is nothing in the U.S. prison system that leads to rehabilitation. Most of the time, it's the opposite. I had watched kids go into prison for a mistaken identity conviction, or something petty like snatching a purse, and when they came home, they were ready like a motherfucker to commit acts of violence. Why? Because while they were inside, some instinct got switched on, and they did what they had to do to survive. The system is designed to swallow prey whole and spit them out as shells of men. Or, it turns those prey into predators. But it sure as shit doesn't rehabilitate. That's all on you. But unless you have your own epiphany, or achieve growth by making a change in your life on your own, prison won't get you there. It isn't even trying.

Even things that seem rehabilitation oriented, like trade schools and courses, are run by the inmates themselves and set up mostly to further establish the underground economy. On our level, it's all about trades and favors, but from the state's perspective, it's economics.

This shit isn't new. America was built, and continues to grow, on the backs of cheap or free labor. It's my understanding that what motivated Abraham Lincoln to free the slaves during the Civil War was not just benevolence, but also the knowledge that doing so would cripple the southern states' economies and make them easier to defeat. But after the "good guys" won, and the Constitution changed, they were like, "Shit, what are we going to do for labor now?" So, in a sense, prisons became the "cheap" version of the "free" labor the slaves were doing beforehand.

Just look at what happens inside. Almost all the work opportunities are privately funded contracts the state enters into with companies who don't mind generating wealth and money off inmates making nine cents an hour. The companies get to put "Made in the USA" on their tags, and the state gets to say they're keeping us out of trouble and teaching us job skills. People know that inmates make license plates, but we do a hell of a lot more. California inmates process meat, milk, eggs, and bread. We make juice boxes. We make furniture and lockers and library book carts and diplomas for colleges. We make gun containers and shooting targets. We make dentures and prosthetics. We work in call centers. Shit, female prisoners in South Carolina were making lingerie for Victoria's Secret.

Ironically, once you're inside, you still want those jobs. Because a prison job is not about what you're doing for the state; it's about the opportunity to support yourself through the freedoms the job grants you. And as I said before, the underground economy in prison is so damn big, it should have its own GDP.

Obviously, every yard had several dudes making booze. Any food you wanted, you could get for a price. Prisoners are probably the most resourceful, creative cooks in America. They could take a hot pot and remove the thermostat to make it go even hotter, to the point where it could toast bread. If you got your hands on a big old grease can, you could turn it into a fryer. Or, if you really weren't fucking around, you could use your actual bunk to cook. You'd take a milk carton and a piece of a blanket, roll it up really tight and put it in the carton so the top of the material was sticking out like a wick, set the carton up on stacked books, and light the blanket scrap on fire until the flame was right under the metal of the bunk. Now you had yourself a griddle—at least until the fire alarm went off.

Just like on the outside, I had my go-to spots for all the things I needed. I'd go to the dude in Building 5, second tier, Cell 32, for chili chimichangas. On my way out to the yard, I'd stop downstairs by Cell 11 and grab some prison-style Reese's peanut butter cups (crushed-up cookies, peanut butter, and syrup shaped into one-ounce pill cups with a melted Hershey bar over the top). If I wanted new clothes, I'd hit up my homies in laundry, and they'd come through with a fresh pair of blue pants, a powder blue shirt, new drawers, and socks. If I wanted a TV or a radio or a crockpot or some clippers, I'd talk to my boys in Property, who kept entire caches of contraband shit locked up.

And it wasn't just goods, but services, too. Lots of inmates have hustles as tattoo artists and barbers, but some are even more specialized. There were inmates who'd gotten so good at the legal system, from having exhausted all remedies on their court cases, that you could pay them by the hour in food or money essentially to become your jailhouse lawyer and file the right paperwork for you. You could have your family send money meant for you to an OG who no longer owed the state restitution, so the prison wouldn't dip into it and take 55 percent of what they'd sent. That OG could take a cut, but you'd still get more of your money than you would have otherwise. And if you knew the right person in the Program Office, you could pay to get into the building you wanted to be in, or get the job you wanted.

But just like on the outside, the biggest, most lucrative sector of the prison underground economy was drugs. Every race had their own drug operation. Among the Mexicans and the whites, there was a stricter hierarchy, with someone at the top controlling the business. But just like in the streets, for us Blacks in prison, we had no specific hierarchy. You had to figure it out for yourself. I had been off drugs for almost a year when I went through reception, but when I got to Calipatria, I started using cocaine again, and selling crystal and heroin. We had all sorts of strategies to move drugs. In Level 2 and 3 yards, where security was laxer, people would literally pull up to the side of the prison and throw a backpack of drugs over the gate. But you couldn't do that in Level 4, so we had to become more creative.

One of my homies used to have his girl visit and put drugs in little colored balloons—red, green, purple, etc. She'd then buy a pack of Skittles at the commissary, go to the bathroom, pour out the Skittles, and put the drug-filled balloons in the wrapper. Then, in the visiting room, while they were talking, he'd be popping candy-colored drug balloons to throw up later, when he got back to his cell.

We also had a guard on the take. We used to give him between five hundred and seven hundred dollars to wrap up whatever we wanted in a fourteen-inch flour tortilla, like a burrito, and carry it in his lunch pail. It could be ounces of weed, grams of coke or crystal, cellphones—anything that fit in there. It was a risk for him, but depending on how fast we moved the drugs, he could make an extra seven thousand dollars a month on top of his salary.

On the whole, most guards are dirty in some way. I'd guess that 90 percent of the guards at the prisons I was in broke the prison's bylaws in some manner. It wasn't that they were all running drugs, but they might sell outside food or take one inmate's alcohol and gift it to someone else.

Figuring out which guards to ask about bringing in drugs and other, more serious contraband was complicated. First, you had to cultivate a level of trust. A lot of inmates thought that wooing female guards was a better strategy, but to me, that was shortsighted, because it involved emotions, and emotions are volatile. With the male guards, they knew it was just about business from the beginning. There was no confusion.

In order to test which guards might be open for business, you needed to push boundaries on your privileges, see if you could get them to break smaller jail rules and show some favoritism toward you and then create situations in which you defended them to everybody. You knew it wasn't going to be some guard from the "goon squad," the "elite" investigative unit within the guards. The goon squad thought of themselves as more hard-core than typical guards, wearing different colors and trying to act all tough and shit. Given how hated they were, you didn't want any privileges with a member of the goon squad. It was like it was on the streets: it was fine if you knew the name of the beat cop in your part of the hood and you guys were on speaking terms, but another thing altogether if you were known to be cool with Denzel in *Training Day*. Hell no.

This sort of rapport was even easier with the civilians who worked for the prison. They tended to be more sympathetic to your plight. Usually, with them, you'd start with something small, like asking them to get you cigarettes. Then, once they'd done it a few times, you could build up the asks. The civilian cooks we worked with in the kitchen at Calipatria were a brother-sister team, and they brought in drugs for us. They were at it until 2017, when an inmate's confiscated phone revealed the operation.

I remember reading about those arrests and being surprised that their operation had gone on that long—and feeling slightly guilty for any part I'd played involving them back in the day. But that was the nature of the game in prison; those were the stakes. And like it or not, almost everyone played.

THOUGH WE WORKED WITH WHITE and Mexican guys in the kitchen and learned some things from one another—for example, I had never tried chorizo before prison—this wasn't *American History X*: we mostly hung with our own. But that's not to say I didn't have respect for some of them as men. I remember one white dude in the kitchen got into it with a Black dockworker over his allotment of jelly. Now, the white boys had a rule in prison: You weren't allowed to fight any Blacks one-on-one. It was going to be either a full-on war or nothing. But because this one white dude felt disrespected, he took it upon himself to stand up and challenge my boy head-on without any support from his own people, fully knowing that, win or lose, there would be repercussions on his end.

From our perspective, we were cool setting it up, because we figured the white boy was going to get his ass beat. But damn, if the white boy didn't beat my homie's ass. Bad, too. After that, I gave him his allotment of jelly. He might've been on that white-supremacy shit, but as a man, he stood up for himself knowing it would have consequences. (And it did. Not long after, he was jumped by his own people.) When a man puts everything on the line to get what's his, how can you not respect that?

In 2007, two weeks into working in the kitchen, I came to know an older Muslim by the name of Tobias Tubbs, aka Shaq. He became my mentor. Shaq was serving life without the possibility of parole and had been around. He mentored both

Bloods and Crips, and he owned the kitchen, whether he was in there or not. When you worked in Shaq's kitchen, you made sure it was in order, because if you didn't, you were going to hear a whole swarm of shit from him. He was a force of nature.

Other than Shaq, my two closest homies in the kitchen were QT and Tiny Wood Rat. QT was about ten years older than me, a dark-skinned, athletically built dude with a mini-Afro who was serving a life sentence for murder. Given that he was from South Central and was an East Coast Crip, it didn't take long for us to realize we had a lot of people in common and—well, the company you keep speaks to the type of person you are. So, I knew QT was real. And real recognizes real, I guess.

Like my Pa Pa, Tiny Wood Rat was a red motherfucker, the type who'd crimson up in his cheeks if he got angry or was working out too hard. And because he was always working out, Tiny was red a *lot*. He was only five foot five, but all biceps, triceps, and traps, built like Mike Tyson, probably about 210 pounds. He was a Kitchen Crip from Watts, and the name "Tiny" came from the gang, not from his size. There were multiple "Wood Rats" in the Kitchen Crip family, so after the original, you might have Lil' Wood Rat. Then someone in the next generation would be Baby Wood Rat, then Tiny, Infant, Newborn, and so on.

When Shaq wasn't there, Tiny was the lead cook and ran the kitchen. I can still picture the layout. When you walked in from the chow hall, you saw a steam line to the left, where we'd send the food out the window to the inmates, with two big-ass eight-foot griddles behind it. Behind those sat twelve ovens stacked three by two, back-to-back. To the left of the ovens was the dish-washing area and the bread room. To its right, there was an office with a big-ass glass window where the COs and free staff sat. That ran all along the wall until you got to the door leading out to the loading docks, which sat kitty-corner from the walk-in fridge.

The kitchen was a cocktail of aromas, but one of those gross, layered cocktails, because each section had its own distinct odor, and none of them was very good. The fridges smelled like spoiled food and mold; the griddles, grease and oil; and because we cooked so many things with water, the oven had that burnt-radiator stink like old steam and heat.

Tiny Wood Rat and I used to get in around four A.M. to get the food ready before QT and the others came in around six. We served breakfast to the population at seven. We'd have music on—T.I., Jeezy, Rihanna, Chris Brown, and others popular at the time—and be joking and laughing. Then, once the dining hall cleared out, Tiny, QT, and I would do workouts in the kitchen. Some days, it would be a thousand burpees, or we'd take hotel pans, load them up, put them inside laundry bags tied to mop sticks, and do bench presses on crates. Other days, we'd do a thousand push-ups or bench-press the tables. And every day, we'd go in the bread pantry and box, using gloves QT had made out of denim and padding from chairs.

After the workout, Tiny and I would prepare a meal, and we'd all sit down and chop it up. This was also a chance for me to be creative. Sometimes, I'd do things like take the liquid from the roast beef and cook it up as a beef broth with caramelized onions, add toasted bread and cheese, and make a prison French onion soup. Or I'd make banana pancakes from scratch with grilled ham or sauteed chicken on the side, plus a jug of lemonade or orange juice. At the time, as I was preparing these dishes, I'd joke that when I got out, I was gonna open a restaurant taking prison foods and making them mainstream. And considering that, by then, I'd perfected the spreads I'd first started making in County, the other inmates might've believed me. But our conversations weren't about just food. We talked about everything: politics; if someone got a letter; if someone had a new girl or had lost their girl; shit we'd done on the streets; shit we'd seen other people do on the streets.

I loved those conversations, not only for the moments of normalcy they allowed me to feel, but also because I loved learning the different ways other people thought. That shit goes back to my youth and my obsession with finding an identity through learning as much as I could about the way other people identified themselves. I wasn't interested only in what dudes were doing, but also in how they were *thinking* about what they were doing. Someone might tell a story about maximizing their profits selling drugs, but if I just took the drugs out of the story, I'd learn a process for maximizing profit, period. I ate that shit up. And over a year, as we did that every day, we bonded over those conversations and over our routines together and became incredibly close. It didn't matter that, on the outside, Tiny Wood Rat and QT would have been my sworn enemies; the bond was that strong. We had one another's backs.

But the limits of that closeness were tested one late-January day in 2008.

We'd just been released for the yard. When I walked out, I saw that all the East Coasters were already grouped in front of my building. At first, with the way they were standing, it felt like it was about to be a hit. I saw QT and three other OG East

Coasters and greeted them like I normally did, but they were all looking at me strange. Finally, QT grabbed me.

"Yo, Fresh, let me holler at you."

We walked to the side, and he started talking.

"So, your homies and my homies had a big-ass party, but there was a shootout inside the club." He looked at me again. "You hear anything about that?"

"Nah," I said. "That's crazy."

"Yeah," he said, slowly. "Well . . . your cousin BL you always talk about? I think he was there, and he got killed."

I looked at QT. "Nah. Hell nah."

Outside my brain, the yard grew quiet. The sounds were muted, muffled, almost as if I had just dunked my head underwater. I couldn't believe it. I couldn't fathom it. Not Branden. He'd been shot three years earlier, through his cheek, and survived.

Just then, Killa Bob walked up. I told him what QT had told me. Immediately, his eyes welled up with tears, but he shook his head, too.

"Hell no. Can't be true."

"Why don't you just call home?" QT asked me. Then, quieter, he said, "I just wanted you to hear it from me because, no matter what, I don't want it to change our relationship."

I walked inside to the pay phone as fast as I could. Two years before, I'd made a similar walk, in this same building, to these same phones, to call home to find out about Kevin. If Branden had really gotten shot, wouldn't someone have called me? I needed to know it wasn't true. I called my mom. When she picked up, she started to say something, but I was already talking over her.

"Is it true? Is it true? Where Branden at? Get Branden. Where he at? Is it true?"

When I finally stopped, my mother told me the story.

Branden was at that party, and when the shooting started, he'd actually gotten out. But when he realized his kid's mother was still inside, he went back, and as he came out, an East Coaster shot him in the head. Branden Bullard—my cousin, my phantom twin, my best friend—had died. He was twenty-five.

I dropped the phone, sat down on a nearby bench, and cried. Just then, the chaplain tapped my shoulder. A couple of guards were with him. On the advice of my family, they were going to confine me to my quarters. Everyone was worried about what I might do.

At the time, I couldn't know that Branden's murder would kick off one of the biggest gang wars in L.A. in a decade, a war between QT's East Coasters and Grape Street that would leave nine dead in less than two months and get so bad that the LAPD chief would call a special meeting with the FBI, DEA, ATF, and ICE just to address it. I couldn't know that this would fuck me up—not just the grief and the anger, but the things it would set in motion for my life.

All I knew was that Branden was dead.

11

Lord Knows

AT THE TIME HE WAS KILLED, BRANDEN WAS RUNNING THE PROJECTS; he was the general. But for some time, our relationship had been strained. I wrote him angry letters from prison, cussing him out because he wasn't communicating enough or taking care of me as I expected he would, given all we'd gone through together. And he wrote back, saying I didn't understand all the pressure he was dealing with trying to keep our name on top with all these dudes out there trying to kill him. Like typical twenty-somethings, we were both focused on our own selfish shit, talking past each other in our letters, each of us voicing his grievances but not hearing the other side.

So, when he died, it fucked me up that the last letters we'd written each other were critical and hurtful and that I never got a chance to forgive him or ask for forgiveness myself. Even before I went to prison, he'd been hurt when I didn't want to get our cliques back together. He felt I'd abandoned him. Prison only perpetuated our anger with each other. Knowing he's resting without fully understanding how much I loved and cared about him is something I still deal with every day.

As much as anyone else in our lives, Branden and I had raised each other. Because we didn't have other men in our lives to show us the path, we'd pulled from each other's strengths and modeled behaviors. We made our own path. So, when I lost Branden, I felt I'd lost a part of myself. Without him as my mirror, I didn't know who I was.

My family had worked out a deal with the prison to send the tape of Branden's funeral service to Calipatria and allow me and my choice of a few homies to hold our own service in the chapel for him and view the film. But when it came time to hold the service, I didn't think there was any way I could watch the tape and not go back to the yard and be violent, so I didn't go through with it. To this day, I've never watched it.

Knowing that trouble could break out between us and East Coast if I had gone back to the yard right away, the guards confined me to my cell for three days. During that time, QT made a point of checking on me, coming by my cell with food from the kitchen and telling me people wanted to know how I was doing. Because of this, when I was finally released to go back to work, it was easier to walk into the kitchen and be around him. Still, I closed myself off from the other East Coasters, communicating only with the dudes with whom I'd formed a strong relationship.

After Branden was killed, though it was business as usual in the kitchen, our boxing sessions seemed to take on a new and different intensity. I don't know if we felt like those were our opportunities to act on the anger and grief that had nowhere else to go. I'd hit QT thinking about his people killing my cousin, and he'd hit me back thinking about all his friends who had been killed in retaliation. It was a way for us to be in control of an uncontrollable situation and still keep our friendship intact. We felt the war inside us, and this was the safest way to fight it.

FOR THE NEXT FEW MONTHS, things were kept in check. Then a white boy Crip showed up in the yard.

Normally, everyone sticks to their race, and things remain straightforward. But in rare circumstances, you'll get a crossover: A Black who grew up in a Mexican neighborhood and repped the Norteños will want to maintain his gang affiliation in prison. Or, in this case, a white boy from Sacramento will want to stick with the Crip set he repped up north. If a Black dude crossed lines, we didn't really give a shit. We might not fuck with him, but we were not going to kill him. But the white boys in prison, because their numbers were smaller and they needed every warm body they could get, racist or otherwise, considered it a grave offense if you sided with anyone else. You *would* get killed.

When this white boy Crip came into C Yard and wanted to stay a Crip, all the white gangs—the Aryan Brotherhood, the skinheads, the 8-8s—got pissed. We didn't really think they'd do anything, but one day, as two guards walked the handcuffed white Crip to the counselor's office, a white boy porter cleaning the hallway stabbed him up in front of the guards. After that, the yard was buzzing. Many of the OGs weren't willing to go to war over a white boy, but a lot of us younger Blacks saw the act as blatant disrespect, because Black or not, he was repping Black.

So, QT, Tiny Wood Rat, and I rallied all the youngsters, both Bloods and Crips, and we waited for our moment. A few days later, it went down. Once the youngsters were let out of school and into the yard, we gathered and stabbed up a white boy as he ran around the track, kicking off a massive race riot. When it was over, many of us spent the next six months in solitary, fighting cases stemming from that riot.

One by one, we were released, now into B Yard. Because so many Blacks had been removed from C, it now belonged to the Mexicans. We were all starting over. Without our jobs or a central race-based problem to unite us, it was inevitable that the tensions between East Coast and Grape Street would reignite. We were two of the biggest Black gangs in prison, and on the streets, we were still very much at war.

Sure enough, one day, war broke out. Two of my homies from Watts got into it on the basketball court with an extremely influential dude from East Coast over a bullshit foul call. After they jumped him, and a bigger fight broke out, another riot seemed inevitable. Knowing this, the guards locked us down for three days. During that time, there were lots of conversations and kites going back and forth. All the tension everyone had kept bottled up since Branden was killed seemed like it was finally going to explode.

QT and I were in constant contact, and initially, we felt there was no way we could keep this from happening. I remember talking to him on our contraband cellphones late one night.

"Fresh, it's gonna go down," he said.

"Man, I hate to end with you on the other side of the line," I said, "but it's just the way shit go."

QT agreed. "I feel you," he said. "But if it's gotta go down, it's gotta go down."

After we hung up, I fell asleep and dreamt I was falling into a deep pool of water.

The next day, two Grape Street homies, Cockeye and Killa Bob, happened to be in the yard when the East Coasters finally got released. Because they were working their jobs, they were separated from the Grape Street car, making them vulnerable. Knowing they were out on the yard with no one else, I started yelling and banging on the wall for a guard. When he finally came by, I tried to level with him.

"Look, man, I need to get out to the yard," I said. "My people are out there by themselves, and I need to be with them."

This guard was one of the cooler, more reasonable ones; you could have a real conversation with him. Still, he gave me a look. "Man, Corbin, sit down. You're supposed to go home soon. Let them handle their own shit."

He was right. I had only ninety days left. But I couldn't let my homies go down like that. I started shaking the bars. "I gotta get to the yard! I gotta get to the yard!"

Seeing how for real I was, the guard sighed. "All right. This is what I'm going to do. You feeling sick?"

Immediately I caught on. "Yeah, I'm feeling sick," I said. "I need to go to the nurse."

"I'll write you a pass, and if you come back, you come back. If you don't, you don't."

As soon as I got that pass, I went out to the yard as quickly as I could. QT and two more OGs from East Coast were surrounding Cockeye and Killa Bob by the benches. Later, QT would tell me that if I hadn't come out just then, they were going to stab them up. But when I got there, and QT saw me, he walked past my homies.

"Fresh," he said. "I'm glad you came out."

There, on the yard, we started to piece together a solution to prevent our two sides from going to war. Our first idea was to try to get the youngsters to realize that, if we did this, it would mean ceding control of another yard to the other races. But that wasn't going to do it for the young boys. They wanted personal satisfaction. QT and I understood that. We'd gotten that sort of release during our boxing matches back in C Yard's kitchen. And with that in mind, we decided to do the same for our two sides.

Instead of a full-fledged war on the yard, we had our guys line up and call each other out. We set up two fights a day until everybody had gotten around to each other. To do it, we had to get permission from the guards, so QT and his boy Tiny Psych and Cockeye and I talked to our COs and explained that the only way to keep the yard from blowing up was to have these boxing matches. Amazingly, they agreed. So, for eight days straight, every morning right after breakfast, the Building 1 CO would let two East Coasters come to Building 5 and let two Grape Street dudes out. And, one by one, they'd get locked into a rotunda and fight until one tapped or was knocked out.

After the eight days, the yard returned to normal. There's no way that would've happened if QT and I hadn't created that bond in the kitchen. We were proud of that.

ON MARCH 24, 2010, I was released from Calipatria State Prison. I had been in prison for six years, five months, and twenty-two days. I was twenty-nine years old. The day I left, Receive and Release called for me, and I went out the same way I'd come in. My family had sent me a fresh outfit, so I was able to change into the new clothes. Then I picked up my property and waited for transport to take me to the Greyhound bus station in Imperial County. (At the time, family members were not allowed to pick inmates up directly from prison.)

It wasn't until I got to the highway on the other side of the gate, and the barbed wire and fences were out of view, that it dawned on me that I was out. But even as I greeted my family at the bus station—my daughter, her mother, two of my brothers, and one of my homies—I still felt a sense of disbelief. Even in the car with my family, as we drove back to Watts, I found myself looking out the window a few times, just to see if the prison was in my rear. I couldn't actually process the fact that I was free.

The trauma of being in prison doesn't go away for a long time. You're still sleeping and moving like you're locked up. And freedom actually feels uncomfortable. In prison, everything is about permission. You get used to being "allowed" to do things. You're allowed to take a shower. You're allowed to go to the yard, to eat, to use the phone. So when you're finally out, it's extremely difficult to just get up and do things in the house without saying, "Is it cool if I take a shower?" or "Is it cool if I get something to drink?" or "Is it cool if I turn on the TV?"

Your family is sitting there being like, "Yeah, it's your house. Do what you want."

But that takes some getting used to. Same thing for going to the bathroom. You're used to doing it out in the middle of your cell with others around, so you start leaving the door open, flushing multiple times per trip—and again, your family is like, "What's wrong with you? Just close the fucking door."

There were other things, too. Driving was incredibly foreign. Trying to merge into traffic after seven years away—you lose your sense of how that works. The first time I tried it, I was so uncomfortable, I had to pull over and let someone else drive. Also, food didn't sit well. The food in jail might be bullshit, but it's still healthier than most fast food. And after seven years of not eating that shit, my body didn't know how to handle it. Rather than eat it, I found myself making spreads at my house.

But more than all that, the world was fucking different. There was social media and iPhones and shit. I remember getting handed a Samsung Galaxy and getting so frustrated with it, I just went out and bought a flip phone. But the literal world, too. Development had finally come to South Central. Downtown Long Beach had a promenade and a Ferris wheel. For some reason, white people were intentionally getting closer to our hood.

As for my own setup, I came home thinking I would go back to hustling. I asked my mother to help me open a new T-shirt shop, and with her business license, I started one right

across the street from the old shop at 103rd and Grape. It was
easy. We put in a glass case counter and some wall panels with
hooks, and then I went to the Fashion District in Downtown
L.A. and bought bulk shirts wholesale to stock the place. From
there, we also acquired the shop next door and were planning to
build that into an ice-cream parlor. My dad worked for the city
and knew plumbing, so I had him put bathrooms in, dig
trenches—all that.

This was a front, of course. What I really wanted to do was
get back in the dope game. It helped that, as soon as I got home,
my younger brother Gerald had fifteen pounds of weed for me,
and Rah Rah got me a phone and helped me get a car. Some of
the drug networks I'd opened up were still running, and they
had enough respect to let me back in, so I started selling weed
and coke from a car hidden behind the shop and shipping narcotics from the store.

But I was different. When I was younger, part of my power
lay in my recklessness. Before, it was "Fuck the police," sell
dope, carry guns, bang bang. I didn't think about anything, and
I didn't much care for anything outside my hustle. And when
you're like that, you are a scary motherfucker to deal with. But
when I came back, I was like a high-impact NFL running back
returning to the field from an injury. Doing everything on
instinct, by reaction, went out the window. Now I was more
self-conscious, maybe even timid. You don't want another
injury, so you lose the thing that made you who you were.

It was more than that, though. The deaths of Branden and
BE-K had changed me. When I got back to the streets, less than
10 percent of the dudes in my generation were still there and
none of my core crew. Of the eleven dudes who'd originally

lived in Rah Rah's cousin's house with me when we were fifteen, six were dead, and most of the rest were either in prison or gone. These had been my homies for life, so it wasn't like I could just replace them with new friends. Also, I wasn't trying to fit in with the youngsters in the generation below me. Yet, even as I felt myself mentally disconnecting from this life, I threw myself all the way back in.

I had to be cautious, though. A lot had transitioned over the nearly seven years I'd been gone. There had been internal and external wars, and I knew just how treacherous the streets could be if I moved too fast. I was spending most of my time at the shop one block from Jordan Downs, but for the first ninety days, I didn't go there. Instead of walking my ass into something, I posted up in my location, where I could see everything coming my way.

This may have felt safer, but because of the consistent flow of dudes coming to see me and hang out, it also gave my shop a reputation as the Grape Street headquarters. The younger generation realized I had clout with the Nickersons from our time together during the truce, so I became a spokesman of sorts, the big homie who could go there and talk to Nickerson dudes in my generation. And because Branden had been killed, older people in my community were fearful that my return would mean a whole lot more violence—and they expressed their fears to the police, who needed to watch for only a few days to see that I was getting phone calls from younger gangsters, who were also coming by my shop. After I was caught on tape handing a bag to some youngsters before some shootings went down, my parole was upgraded to gang parole, and I was fitted with an ankle monitor. My parole officer—the same dude Branden had

had—liked to point out that Branden was shot and killed the day he got his own ankle monitor removed.

EVERYTHING SEEMED TO BE HAPPENING both too fast and too slow for me. I saw other people from my hood making money, dudes who hadn't been shit when I went to prison, and I thought I needed to get on that level immediately. But at the same time, I had lost a step. The natural instincts I had acquired from years on the streets, I no longer had. I didn't know the key players, I didn't know the wars, I didn't know the territories. I had lost my sense of when to run from the police and when to stand my ground. And with two strikes against me, I didn't want to risk packing a pistol. The game had evolved, and I didn't have the fluency to see what I needed to do to evolve with it.

I saw how true this was that November. I was driving along with my little brother when, out of nowhere, three cops were on the car, one on each side and one on the hood, all with guns drawn. Because I was still using, I always had cocaine on me, so they threw me in the back of a squad car, and that was that. In some ways, this was inevitable. At that time, I was the worst version of myself, with all the arrogance of my pre-prison years and none of the street sense.

Sitting in that car, I was even more fearful than I was the first time I was arrested. This time, it wasn't fear of the unknown, of whether I could deal with prison or any of that. No, this time I was scared because I *knew* how unfair the system was. I *knew* how unjust the courts were, I *understood* what "strikes" meant. I *knew* about enhancements and how these public defenders played.

I was charged with possession of narcotics with intent to sell (which made no sense, because I had a straw in the bag), but I knew too much now to be surprised. I got sentenced to two years with half time, which meant I'd have to do one year in Folsom State Prison.

I'd been free for only eight months.

ASIDE FROM BEING FAMOUS BECAUSE Johnny Cash recorded a live album there, Folsom is known for being old as hell. It opened in 1880 and looks like a gloomy, dark castle in the woods. It's also famous because, while most prisons go up only two tiers, Folsom has five steep-ass tiers almost four stories high, and lots of prisoners have been thrown over the sides to their deaths.

Being in Folsom is like playing a part in a real-life horror film, like the prison version of *Nightmare on Elm Street*. It's too damn spooky. And the year I spent there was my hardest year in prison. If you go in there with a seven-year sentence, your release date is nowhere near top of mind, so you can actually program, get into your routines, and live your life. But with only a year, you're babysitting that date the whole time. From the beginning, the countdown is on—which makes it so much more stressful. On top of that, you don't build up any privileges. You don't have the time to establish yourself. So, while I did run my car and call the shots, I didn't have enough time to put in for any jobs, or school—nothing.

I finally got out again in November 2011. Just like at

Calipatria, as you get close to your date, your family can send you clothes for your release. Up there, I also had a choice: either I could take an eight-hour Greyhound bus back to L.A. or I could fly. I opted to purchase a plane ticket out of Sacramento airport. What I didn't realize was that the guards had to watch you get on the plane. So, though I was technically a free man, the prison guards insisted on walking me all the way through the airport handcuffed, and they didn't take the cuffs off me until my flight was boarding. It was as if they were determined not to give me back my dignity until the last possible moment. Meanwhile, the other passengers waiting at the gate saw these guards take handcuffs off me before I boarded along with them. It was embarrassing as hell. And let's just say, for the entire flight to LAX, there wasn't a lot of chitchat with the passengers around me.

ONE DAY IN 2011, NOT long after I got out, I was driving through Watts with my eight-year-old daughter, Keivionna, in the back of the car, trying to be on some dad shit, taking her to get something to eat. We were coming up Wilmington and had stopped at the light on 103rd. I was asking her what she wanted to order when I heard a steady tapping noise.

I turned my head and saw a Bounty Hunter Blood from the Nickersons with the motherfucking barrel of his gun against my window.

"Come on, Fresh," he said. "You know better than to have your kids in your car," he said. Then he turned around and walked off.

I was shook. He could've just shot, but because he came

from behind my car, he saw my daughter in there. He must've figured it wasn't worth it to kill me then. But his message was clear: "Sooner or later, you know we'll get at you. So, why you endangering your kids?"

From then on, and still to this day, my children do not ride in my car with me.

While living in Long Beach, trying to take it slow and figure out my options, Keivi came home one day and told me something that affected me even more than that gun tapping on the window. She was nine at the time, and hanging with her friends at the Del Amo swap meet, when a dude I had been in Calipatria with approached her and asked, "Ain't you Fresh's daughter?" He'd seen her picture in my cell a bunch and remembered her, and to prove he knew me, he proceeded to tell her all kinds of stories about my activities and the way my name rang out in the streets. This confused her. From the time she was born, whenever I walked into my house, I switched hats. I was just her dad, and even though she knew I was doing time in prison, she didn't know what was really going on in my world. My house was my safe haven; street dudes couldn't just come over and watch a game or a fight. I kept that shit in the streets.

When Keivi asked me if I was a gangster, I responded with "No, I'm your father" and tried to let it slide, but it hit me that, because she was getting older, this was only the beginning. I couldn't shield her from my true past forever. And almost immediately, I went from being proud of my reputation in the street to being ashamed of it. I thought, if I died that day, how confused she might be at the funeral, hearing all these dudes testifying to how hard Fresh was.

This was the push I needed to really get serious about

pivoting away from all the gangster shit. Not long after that, I applied and got into the Los Angeles Violence Intervention Training Academy, or LAVITA, so I could train to be a community intervention worker. There, I got certified as a gang counselor, an interventionist, and a cease-fire mediator.

The training covered a variety of topics, from bringing two gangs to the table to negotiate truces and cease-fires to even just buying time and managing rumor control after a shooting, so the anger could subside and the chances of retaliation be lessened. It also involved becoming the communicator between the police and the community, to keep things calm while the cops did their job. Frankly, this was a huge step for me, coming from where I was coming from, and was the hardest part of the job: I was not excited at the idea of working with the police. At the time, I rationalized it as a way to get some money, keep the police off my back, and also be true to changing my narrative.

The day I graduated from the program, we had a big-ass party in Jordan Downs to celebrate. People were proud of me, and I was feeling good about myself. Everyone was relaxing. Then, all of a sudden, something popped off with the youngsters, and they all started congregating at the edge of the building, by the street. I went over there to try to use my training to settle shit down and find out the facts, just as I had been taught to do, when the cops showed up. All the young'uns took off, and while they ran away, someone tossed a gun into the bushes. I stayed put. After all, I was there doing what I was supposed to be doing. But because I didn't run, and despite trying to use what I'd learned in a program working *with* the damn police, they pinned the gun on me and took me back to jail in June 2012.

An experience like that should've set me back permanently.

It was the most cynical shit that could happen, the answer any street dude could give as to why you don't fuck with the police. *See?* I could hear them saying. *This is what happens. This is what you get.*

And sadly, they were kind of right. Even so, I didn't want to give up. Fuck the police. I had to keep trying for my daughter. As for my case, we took our time with it, read the police report. We knew it was going to be the police's word against that of a two-time felon and that I wouldn't be able to get off without someone else coming and claiming the gun was theirs, but I was prepared. They tried to give me two more years at Folsom, but I knew I couldn't handle that much time at that spooky, haunted hellhole, so I did everything I could to bring that down. I was taking a life skills course at the time, so I went to the judge and asked him if he'd allow me six months to finish before he sentenced me. To bolster my case, I brought letters from the chaplain and the captain of the County Jail, and the judge granted me that. Then, once in County, I became a facilitator, teaching life skills with the 360 Program. Thanks to my role, I had total freedom to move about the jail and even taught a class in which we painted flowers and other designs alongside those big-ass murals of John Wayne. Because, you know, fuck that dude.

When they finally transferred me to do the rest of my sentence at Folsom, I had ten months left. Originally, my plan was to keep my head down, stay out of trouble, and grind that shit out. But then I found out that the motherfucker who'd killed my brother Truett nineteen years earlier was also locked up at Folsom.

I first heard this while I was hanging in the yard with some other Watts dudes from Front Street.

"Yo, Fresh. You know the nigga who killed your brother is here, right?"

At first, I was suspicious and figured it was a setup. After all, if it was true, it meant that these Front Street dudes had known they were locked up with a man who'd killed their homie and hadn't done anything the whole time. I stayed quiet, took in the information, and went back to my cell. The next day, I caught up with the dude coming out of the chapel.

"Yo, how you doing?" I said to him. I introduced myself as Fresh from Grape, so it was clear to him I wasn't associated with Front Street.

The man shook my hand. He was born again, a Christian now, and so, when he introduced himself, he used his real name. That wasn't the name I knew, so I tried another tack.

"Man, I understand you're doing your church thing and all that now, but you from Watts. What they call you, homie?"

Tentatively, he told me his street name, but he assured me he didn't go by that anymore, not since he'd found the Lord. I wished him well and went on my way. When I got back to my cell, I called my brother Bo's daughter and told her the two names the dude had given me. My niece was still in the streets and knew everyone in that neighborhood.

Almost immediately, she replied, "Yeah, that's him. That's the guy who shot my uncle."

I hung up. That was all I needed to hear. I may have had only six months left, but I didn't respect the date. I wasn't about to pass up the opportunity to finally get revenge on the man who'd destroyed the last vestiges of my childhood nineteen years before, who'd taken my role model from me.

I just needed to track down a knife.

A few days later, I caught back up with him. He was on his way to Bible study, walking with the Good Book in his hand, but it didn't matter to me that he'd found Jesus. He could've found Jesus standing next to him, and I still would've hurt him.

When he passed by, I stabbed him. Afterward, there was a brief scuffle, and the guards locked the yard down, but that was that.

No one saw what went down, and they never found the knife. As a Level 4 dude operating in a Level 3 prison, I saw the place—its many blind spots, the freedom of movement—as a chessboard, one on which I was already three steps ahead. To his credit, the dude didn't say shit about what happened. Whether it was Jesus or the streets that kept his mouth shut, I will never know. He got stitched up and transferred to another building in Folsom, and I never saw him again.

Though the environment was less threatening, I still wasn't okay sticking around Folsom any longer than I had to. After three months, I finally couldn't take sitting with them ghosts no more. I went to the psychiatrist and told them the walls were closing in on me and the place was making me lose my mind, so they transferred me to Corcoran, in Kings County, where they kept Charles Manson. Compared to all the other prisons' living arrangements, the dorm I lived in there was totally kick back. It was the type of place I should've gone during my first bid, if that County guard hadn't changed the trajectory of my prison life. Compared to everything else I'd been through in prison over the last ten years, those last few months in Corcoran felt like a breeze.

PART THREE

The author (in white shirt) and several members of the
LocoL team. *Left to right:* Imani Earl, Carnisha Coleman,
and Marlon Friend.

12

Perfect Timing

WHEN I GOT OUT OF PRISON IN 2014, I WAS OVER IT. OVER PRISON. Over anything involving police. And over their gang intervention training, that's for damn sure.

But if I wanted to get over hustling, I was going to need a job. The only jobs I knew that would hire ex-cons with no college degree or experience were labor jobs—jobs digging shit, building shit, carrying shit, loading and unloading shit. So, my younger brother Bam and I set out to find one of those. But no one would take us. Then we heard that the Chevron oil refinery in El Segundo was hiring, so we went to the agency filling those jobs, but they turned us down, too.

It all seemed futile, but I had noticed something. These oil refinery gigs required certain types of certification. If you could get in, they would train and pay to get you these, but our problem was we couldn't get in. So, I decided we should invest in ourselves and get the certifications first, to make it easier for someone to say yes to us because, financially, we would be a smarter hire. Over the next few months, Bam and I got our certs for as many things as we could afford: driving forklifts, first responders to chemical spills. We took a Refinery Safety Overview class. We got Confined Space certified, OSHA certified. And when we resubmitted applications to the agency, we got placed for a two-month gig at the same Chevron that had originally turned us away.

My job was to oversee the work being done on the equipment, make sure the employees were following all the safety protocols and that the machines' paperwork and permits were in order. At nineteen dollars an hour plus overtime, I liked the pay, but the job was boring as hell. You have to understand, I was thirty-four years old, and this was my first real job. I thought I was grinding selling three-dollar crack rocks to smokers on a street corner, but this was a different kind of grind—the monotonous version. Nevertheless, it felt good to have honest paying work.

After the initial assignment, I got hired back to do another job, this time for three months. Before we began to work in earnest, the woman running the oil refinery, Tameka, asked everyone to write a goal letter for themselves. In mine, I wrote that I'd never worked for anyone but myself in my life, but my goal was to one day have *her* position. And why wouldn't I want that? She was making seventy thousand per assignment.

After reading my letter, Tameka called me into her office. I didn't think much of the conversation, but it must've stuck with her, because after the three-month turnaround, she made a list of people she wanted to take right into the next shift and continue working, and I was one of them. Even better, she offered me a double promotion, skipping me over shift lead and right to a general foreman's position on the grounds crew, which would take my salary up to between ten and twelve thousand a month. I couldn't believe it. I didn't know anyone who'd come out of jail and gone from not even being able to get a job to making a hundred grand a year legit.

A week later, they asked me for my ID, given that I would be driving company equipment. It was all standard procedure, and I didn't think anything of it—until the next day, when a security guard came to find me at my post.

"Come with me," he said.

With no warning, he walked me to the gate, had me clock out, took my badge, and told me I was being terminated.

I called the agency. They said Chevron had started doing background checks and that anyone who had a felony record wasn't allowed to work. The worst part, though? The background check was done just for new hires and for foreman level and above. If I had stayed at the level I was at, I would've kept my job. Shit, I might *still* be working there. Ironically, my hard work and determination got me terminated.

It was like the backward version of the American Dream.

In mere minutes, I was out in the parking lot. For a long time, I sat there staring off at nothing. I was devastated. And angry. And confused. And feeling hopeless. There was so much on my shoulders.

I'd had my second daughter, Cali, with Tiffany a few months earlier. Tiffany's pregnancy was incredibly difficult. She was always nauseated, vomiting until there was nothing left to throw up. Instead of gaining weight, she lost so much that she looked like a skeleton. Because she was dehydrated and malnourished, she was constantly going from her house in Long Beach to the hospital for IVs. Her aches were so bad that she'd spend most of the day soaking in the tub. Tiffany and I were separated then, and I was living with my mother, but I tried to be around to help her when I could.

Even before Cali was born, because I had been there to witness Tiffany's struggles, I was emotionally invested in a way I hadn't been with either of my two previous kids. When Cali finally arrived, it felt like a triumph. After all, she'd been fighting to stay alive, and we'd been fighting along with her, so when I first heard her cry, a calmness came over me. She was early and underweight, and for the first few days, I couldn't hold her, but I was happy just to sit next to the incubator and watch her chest rise and fall, rise and fall.

Of course, I was also scared. Neither of my other kids had been in the NICU, so I didn't know what to expect. I'd thought only as far as making sure Tiffany and Cali were alive through the pregnancy; I hadn't thought beyond that. And because I fell in love with Cali from the beginning, I was determined to be a better father.

Don't get it twisted—I still had no idea how to do that. At the time, I thought being a good father was about only two things: being a provider and not going back to prison. But given what had just happened at the oil refinery, I didn't see how I could do the providing in any meaningful way without putting myself in danger of being reincarcerated.

For the next two weeks, I fought myself over what I should do. Part of me thought, *Look at the evidence! You've had two legit jobs, and both got taken away on some bullshit. They're not trying to let you succeed legit.* Because of that, I was thinking maybe my only path *was* the dope game. It was what I knew, what I was good at. And the streets don't need to run background checks.

To have a little bit of income, I'd been using my connections to move some weed, but being a fence wasn't going to make me serious money. I could easily have reached out to my connects and gotten back in for real, but I'd need to make a move soon. The drug game is like a fast-moving stream: the longer you've been out of the water, the harder the current becomes to read.

I WAS IN MY CAR driving back to Watts from Long Beach when I answered the phone.

"Boy," my mother said. "You better get over to a Hundred and Third and Anzac right now, because they're opening a restaurant and they're hiring."

"A Hundred and Third and Anzac?"

"That's right."

It was the same address as our old clothing store, the one I ran with my mother before I went to prison. It felt like a sign.

"What are they calling it?"

My mother paused, looking. "I think they're calling it LocoL."

LocoL was conceived at one of those fancy-ass international chef conferences when Daniel Patterson, a white fine-dining chef with a few NorCal restaurants, heard the Korean American L.A. chef Roy Choi, who had trained at the Culinary Institute of America and made his name launching America's food truck revolution with Kogi, give a speech about chefs needing to pay attention to people in the hood.

Roy was already known for his involvement in low-income L.A. communities, but to see a chef like Daniel in Watts was a surprise. He'd made his name making high-end food at a tiny restaurant called Coi in San Francisco, but was also known for his nonprofit, the Cooking Project, which taught at-risk youth basic cooking skills. Working with the kids, he saw how learning to cook changed their perceptions of food and improved their physical and mental health. But more important, he saw how unequal the access to good food was, and he wanted to change that. After hearing Roy's speech, Daniel called him and together they started to build out their idea.

Roy and Daniel wanted to create restaurants in low-income neighborhoods, employing people from those hoods to serve fresh, "creative" fast food made with nourishing local ingredients. And it would be affordable. There would be six-dollar bowls of ginger chili lime noodles, four-dollar cheeseburgers and BBQ turkey sandwiches, two-dollar carnitas "foldies" (LocoL's version of the taco) and chicken or veggie "nugs." For a dollar, you could get an agua fresca or one of six different sides, including beef and onion gravy and "messy greens." It would be healthier, but never framed as "healthy." It would be cool, but not cool in the way that signaled gentrification and white folks in fancy jogging clothes. And they thought they would build them all over the country, starting in Watts. Roy would be the marketing guy, the branding, the face of LocoL. Being from L.A., he'd be able to understand the dynamics more intuitively, handle the media, and get the word out, while Daniel would primarily handle the food and the kitchen.

Of course, I didn't know any of this at the time. I didn't know who either of these motherfuckers was. Dudes in prison weren't exactly reading *Bon Appétit*, and our world in Watts was closed off from the trends of the white world. I didn't know what a "foodie" was; I didn't know what Eater was or anything about "list culture"; and I sure as shit didn't know that chefs "attracted a following." Who follows somebody around the country because they cook food? If we were going to talk top chefs, I'd assume you meant Pablo, El Chapo, Noriega, Freeway Rick, and Big Meech.

All I knew was that I needed a job and that someone in my neighborhood was hiring. I drove straight over to Anzac and 103rd, where folks were handing out applications, and filled one out; I even did an interview right there. It was pretty basic shit: "Do you want a job? Are you willing to work? Do you have any experience?" After the interview, they offered me a line cook position on the spot at fourteen dollars an hour, and I accepted it. Given that they seemed to be giving jobs away, I started taking applications over to our people in Jordan Downs. Because of this, it became a family affair. LocoL hired me, my mom, my brother, my uncle, and a few more homies from the neighborhood. We basically had a family business inside the building that used to house our old family business.

I was excited to get a job, but I was coming off potentially making ten grand a month in my oil gig, so this was still a blow for me. But a few days later, LocoL called back and offered me a position as kitchen manager, with a salary of sixty thousand a year. This was huge. It made me feel like the oil refinery wasn't where I was supposed to be. It was here, in my neighborhood, working among my people.

At the time I got the job, they were still building out the location, but I needed money right away, so I hit up the general contractor, Prophet Walker. Prophet was from Watts and had done time, but he was a smart, successful dude who had built himself a nice reputation in the construction world. A lot of people in the neighborhood were being put on the job, doing small things like securing the site or sleeping over in the building to make sure no one stole the copper. As part of that, Prophet put me on as a laborer, and for the next month, I did all the little jobs to help get LocoL ready for opening—painting, cleaning, installing equipment.

Aside from earning me money, this also allowed me the opportunity to be around Roy and Daniel as they came through to check on the progress. They were an odd pair—an Asian dude with tattoos and a skateboard vibe and a more upscale-looking, skinny white guy. Either way, they looked foreign as hell hanging out in Watts.

As a street dude, I'm not comfortable going up to someone and introducing myself the first time we're around each other. It may be normal in mainstream society, but in my culture, it's corny. That's not how we do it. It's more about vibing in the same space as someone, especially someone coming into my neighborhood. They may've been giving me a job, but this was my territory, so I wasn't going to defer to anyone just because they had money. In my hood, deference is a sign of weakness.

Eventually, though, the longer I got to be around both Daniel and Roy, the more I felt a level of comfort and respect. One night during the build-out, they both stayed late at the restaurant. As they were leaving—Roy was going to drive Daniel back into the city—I accompanied them out to the street where they were parked.

Daniel must have realized what I was doing: "Do you really feel like you need to walk us to the car?"

"Yeah," I said. "Because if I wasn't working for you guys, and I seen a rich Asian and a rich white boy walking through, I'd have y'all facedown in the dirt taking your wallets. And because I'm not the only one around here who thinks like me, I'm going to walk y'all to your car. Shit, I want to protect my interests."

We all laughed in the moment, but I was as serious as a heart attack.

WHEN THE SPACE WAS FINALLY ready to go, the partners in LocoL sat us all down on the strange block-shaped chairs they'd picked out for the dining room and introduced themselves. Daniel talked about the concept behind LocoL as fast food with a chef-driven alternative ideology.

I quickly learned that there were basically zero transferable skills from my time in the prison kitchen to LocoL. This wasn't reheating precooked food and holding boxing matches in the pantry. This was for real. And I had no real kitchen experience whatsoever. Outside the three people Daniel and Roy had brought in to help run the various parts of the kitchen, none of us did.

Looking back, I don't think the public grasped just what our presence there as employees meant for LocoL. Roy and Daniel had taken a chance on people who had no previous job history, who had been hustling on the streets, who had been incarcerated. And they should absolutely be commended for that. No one was doing that in any real way at the time—offering steady money, salaries. But the flipside was *we had no previous job history, had been hustling on the streets, or had been incarcerated*. Even under the best of circumstances, it was going to take months for all of us to acclimate to working for serious chefs in a serious restaurant.

We had about a week.

Despite the short time line and my inexperience, I was excited about the manager position. I knew I was good at that, especially because a lot of the people I would be managing in LocoL already knew and respected me, already saw me as a leader in the streets.

But being a manager in a Daniel Patterson kitchen goes beyond just leadership. You're expected to know how to do, and be able to show others how to do, everything: prep, cooking, operations, management, quality control, etc. It was like being a teacher in a classroom when you were barely a chapter ahead of your students in the book. And considering my skill level at the time, I'm not even sure I'd *gotten* the book.

I was so overwhelmed that first week that I pulled Daniel

aside in the back parking lot and told him that I quit. I was battling my addiction, unhappy with losing my job at the refinery, and trying to figure out how to not just work but lead in an environment that was completely foreign to me. My team knew me only from the streets, where my instincts had been gold, but here they saw me failing and so my immediate instinct was to bail.

Fuck this, I thought. And that's what I told Daniel.

He laughed and said, "Resignation not accepted. Give it a little more time. You'll be fine."

If he had listened to me, I would've been gone. But I guess I wanted to follow this new path just a little more than the old one. So I stayed.

But it wasn't easy. When it came to actual kitchen skills, I'm not going to play with you: I didn't know how to do shit. We would get a delivery of whole beef clods (I didn't know what the fuck a beef clod was), and I was expected to cut them up and braise them (I didn't know how to braise). I had no knife skills—I mean, I knew how to stab a nigga, but that didn't help. I didn't know how to hold a knife, or how dangerous a dull knife was. I didn't know that if you pressed your hand on the top of the knife blade, it would eventually cut into your skin. And once I was done doing a bad job cutting the meat, with my hand all fucked up, I'd crowd the pieces into the tilt skillet too tightly and end up steaming the meat without ever getting a proper sear on it.

I remember we once had a ratatouille special. Other than an animated movie with a rat, I didn't know what ratatouille was; all I knew was I had to make it. I remember, during the cooking process, I had the heat up way too high, and the sugars in the tomatoes scorched. From making prison moonshine, I knew that fruits had sugar in them, but tomatoes? What the fuck was that about?

And wait, you're trying to tell me a tomato is a *fruit*?

In those first few weeks, Daniel was in the kitchen working side by side with us every day. But it was about more than just teaching us recipes. We needed to learn how to use the equipment, clean, organize, order, rotate inventory, keep up with a prep schedule. And that was before we even got into how shit should taste.

It was a lot for everyone, and sometimes it showed. Daniel's perfectionist fine-dining tendencies and my authority issues would clash. We'd both get mad and neither would back down. When we argued, it was like a collision of two immovable objects. He came from the old-school cook mentality of intense discipline, of "yes, chef" no matter what. And I came from the no school. The Watts why-the-fuck-you-yelling-at-me-when-I-never-done-this-shit-before school. But this was the beginning of our path, and we were both still learning.

He was a hell of a cook, though. And not just fancy shit. His collard greens won approval even from the neighborhood grannies. They weren't like the collards I grew up with. My Granny would use smoked meat, but he replaced it with oil smoked over applewood chips, a technique he brought from Coi. He cooked onions with chile flakes in the smoked oil, then cooked the collards, then later added mustard greens and champagne vinegar, and finished it all with a little more smoked oil. They had a traditional taste, but they were vegan and wouldn't weigh you down.

I may've spent my entire life watching Granny cut, clean, and cook collard greens, but before getting in the kitchen at

LocoL, I'd never done it myself. I had no idea you needed to cook the greens for different amounts of time, so the first time I made them, my collards were barely done and my mustard greens were mush. Granny was probably turning over in her grave watching me fuck that dish up. But making those collards together with Daniel also gave me a chance to work on how to taste and season food, which was one of the foundational aspects of becoming a chef. At the end of every batch, we would adjust the salt, acid, and oil to get the balance just right.

The way we made collards wasn't the only thing that was new to me. When I was growing up, tradition was important. There was a right way and a wrong way to cook our food. But at LocoL, Daniel and Roy brought in influences and ingredients that no one in my community had grown up with. Miso. Ginger. Soy. Even tofu.

One of the most successful dishes was the foldie. By the time LocoL opened, Watts had become 70 percent Latino, and this was a nod to their culture. It was also a dish that tapped into Roy's experience making creative tacos. We took corn tortillas and quickly fried them to make them pliable. On top we put a slice of jack cheese and some bean puree, which was a mixture of beans, brown rice, lots of garlic, onions, and spices, all pulsed together. It tasted like the best refried beans you could imagine. Roy made charred tomatillo salsa, and it all went inside the tortilla, which we folded over and fried on the griddle until it was browned and crisp on the outside. Man, I could eat those all day.

Frankly, I should've been overwhelmed and intimidated by the sheer amount of shit I didn't know and was fucking up, but the truth was, I actually benefited from my ignorance. Had I been truly aware of all the many skills I was lacking, I might never have tried for the job in the first place.

Instead, I was motivated to find the same sort of kitchen sense I had developed while cooking work. At LocoL, we did everything in house. We made our own mayo, and I can't tell you how many of those I broke. (Raw egg yolk requires a different touch than cocaine.) I didn't know how to make dough for the buns, or let it rest, or keep a sourdough starter alive. Daniel was bringing high-end cooking techniques into a fast-food restaurant, and it was astonishing that any of us were able to keep up. He was fermenting barley. Sprouting grains. Making brown butter. It went so far beyond flipping burgers.

Beyond the challenge of mastering these new skills, I was having fun. This was a job, but we were still in the neighborhood chopping it up, and it just seemed like a trip. That project spirit was alive in that kitchen. Dudes might be getting high or drinking on the job. There were no background checks, no drug testing. Everyone thought it was cool—except Daniel and Roy.

LocoL opened on January 18, 2016, Martin Luther King, Jr., Day. The hype was staggering. This was the biggest thing to happen to Watts since Tommy Jacquette started the Watts Summer Festival in 1966. Folks started lining up at around seven A.M., and the line stretched down the street for four blocks. A DJ set up and played records. Football legend Jim Brown showed up in his Bentley to cut the ribbon. Tyrese came through in his silver Rolls-Royce. L.A. mayor Eric Garcetti was there. So was the police chief. And Roy's famous director buddy Jon Favreau. And Lena Dunham, from the rich white girl show on HBO.

It's hard to overstate how big a deal this was at the time.

LocoL was supposed to revolutionize fast food. René Redzepi, who created Noma—which, at the time I'm writing this, is still the number-one-ranked, most famous and celebrated restaurant in the world—was on the advisory board. We had the famous baker from San Francisco's Tartine Bakery giving us his recipe for our hamburger buns. Tony Konecny, the man behind a coffee company bought by Blue Bottle for a bunch of money, was roasting high-quality coffee for us at a discount so we could almost break even selling coffee for a dollar. A lot of rich white people seemed invested in our success.

Despite, or possibly because of, all that pressure, opening night was a shit show. But we didn't know any better. We were in the back making all of these mistakes while there were TV cameras and press everywhere and a line of people four blocks long waiting to order their food. Even though it was chaotic and dramatic, in a strange way, we embraced it. Most of us were coming from the projects, and that's what the projects were—a swirling cacophony of chaos and drama. When that's been your world for so long, you find comfort in the chaos. Plus, we didn't have any standards to measure it against, so we didn't know the degree to which we were fucking up. We saw food going out, we saw happy people eating, we saw them laughing and joking, and we figured it was all good.

It was a difference in thinking: For the professional chefs and management coming in from outside Watts, execution in a restaurant was do-or-die. Not for us. The only do-or-die thing for us was what was happening in the streets. And that shit was literal.

———

WITHIN A COUPLE OF WEEKS, I realized that the way I'd wielded authority on the streets and in the drug houses was not going to translate easily to restaurants.

Hierarchy was something I understood. On the streets, you were either the top dog giving orders or you were taking them. But as a manager in a kitchen, I was supposed to both give orders to the cooks and the house staff and be expected to take them from Daniel, Roy, and any other people above me. And because there were four other managers at my level (including my mother), as part of Daniel's level-the-playing-field operations strategy, when there was a decision to be made, we were each supposed to have equal say and come to some sort of consensus. Though I could see the intent behind it, it didn't make sense to me. Where I'm from, the streets don't have middle management.

It wasn't just the disagreements with other middle managers that were new for me. It was also hard for me to understand that I had to accept responsibility for the people fucking up under me. And trust me, we were fucking up *all* the damn time. Every day, there was some sort of chaos—people not showing up for work, grill cooks not preparing the burgers correctly, line cooks oversalting the messy greens, chili drying out on the steam table, tickets backing up in the kitchen. It was all kinds of shit.

If Daniel came through the kitchen and saw any of this happening, he would pull me outside and read me the riot act. From a kitchen perspective, this made sense. I was the one managing the people fucking up; their mistakes were my mistakes. But that's not how I saw it.

A lot of this had to do with ownership. In the drug game, if youngsters selling for me lost my drugs, I would still be responsible to pay the dope man, because the product was mine. But because the restaurant wasn't mine, it was harder for me to translate this. *Hey, I'm just an employee.* You're *the owner.* You *accept this shit.*

Despite the rocky moments, I gained respect for Daniel during our counseling sessions. One of the unique and noble aspects of the LocoL mission was employing Rita, a counselor who would be available to the staff by phone or on-site at certain times, for anything we might want to talk about. She was not a traditional therapist, but someone who worked with the body's reaction to trauma. She taught us breathing exercises and other shit for handling our feelings. I didn't think much of it at the time, but later I'd find it really useful for helping to control my anger.

At the beginning, everyone went to therapy—more out of curiosity than anything else. But because Black folks don't usually talk to counselors, don't tap into their feelings, don't want to admit they're emotionally stunted, interest in the counseling sessions soon tapered off.

Despite that, I still went to the group sessions they held every couple of weeks. We would sit around and tell our stories, and I discovered that Daniel and I had a lot in common. Even though he was white and privileged, and I was Black and not, we shared some struggles: Depression. Abandonment. Disrupted homes. Challenging authority. Anger. That "put it all on my shoulders" mentality.

After the counseling sessions, he and I started to hang out on our own time. We'd go to the bar after work and talk over drinks, or go out to eat together. He invited me to his house.

Over time, I stopped seeing him exclusively as the boss and more as a person. At first, he just looked like every other white guy I'd seen. He was a six-foot-tall, skinny guy in his late forties in a T-shirt, jeans, and sneakers. But as we hung out more, I could really *see* him. I noticed that he always looked like he'd just gotten out of the shower to run to the corner store for something. I noticed that he never wore T-shirts with logos, and when he did, he'd wear them inside out. I noticed that he didn't rock a watch or jewelry. I noticed he had a professorial vibe about him and was informed on all sorts of quirky shit, from avant-garde cooking techniques, to pop music, to labor policy. And Daniel started to come around to the fact that, even though I was an employee, it was extremely hard for me to be seen as an underling and not as an equal.

It wasn't all deep talks and shit, but it was talking. We were learning to see each other.

13

City 2 City

THE FIRST FEW MONTHS WERE CRAZY. WE WERE PACKED ALL THE time. Every publication wanted to write about us—and not just us, but me. My background was becoming a part of the LocoL story.

Management saw me as an example of what they had wanted to accomplish—to give a second chance to people who normally didn't get one. So, in much of the early publicity, I was put up front and made part of the narrative—an ex–gang member, born in these projects, incarcerated, now improving the neighborhood and himself in the process. That felt good, but it didn't feel totally honest. They didn't know it, but between the people I was associating with and the drugs I was still moving, I wasn't exactly the "ex"–gang member of that redemption narrative.

Looking back on it later, I saw that my personal story wasn't the only thing that wasn't quite ready for the spotlight. We had opened this thing, and we still didn't know what the fuck we were doing. It was like we were taxiing down the runway, about to take off, while still building the plane.

Speaking of planes, because we were on the cover of the magazines airlines put in the seatback pocket, we became an international foodie destination. We had white folks in from New Zealand, Germany, even Silver Lake. In all my years living there, I'd never seen this many non-undercover-cop white people purposely coming to Watts. I'm guessing it made them feel both virtuous and cool to support this great experiment—an affordable fast-food restaurant featuring celebrity chef–driven cuisine opened in a food desert employing folks from an underserved community. And so, they would come in once, take photos of the food and the restaurant, post those to social media, and then get back in their Ubers or rental cars and leave as quickly as they came—never to return.

But they were happily oblivious to what was actually going on there. They couldn't have known that the very corner where LocoL opened also happened to be one of the most infamous drug corners in America, especially for PCP. And they couldn't have known that this corner also happened to be incredibly dangerous, a border zone where Nickersons would cross over the tracks to ambush Grape Streets without having to go deeper into Jordan Downs.

Because of that issue, LocoL had in place an "ambassador" program from the beginning. The purpose of the program was to get Grape Street OGs like Nardo, Ant, and Deebo to stand outside the restaurant, meet and greet the white people, make sure they weren't robbed, and keep an eye on the streets. And they were valuable, too. Several times, we had to shut down the restaurant because one of these Grape Street Crips was able to spot suspicious behavior going on outside, like carsful of Nickersons circling the block.

On the surface, my job as kitchen manager was exactly what it sounded like: managing the kitchen. Beyond what I was responsible for inside the restaurant, I spent a lot of my time negotiating with the dudes from my generation over in the Nickersons, to claim LocoL as a safe haven. The gang truce was a distant memory, and many of the youngsters shooting at one another now had never lived in peacetime.

I tried to appeal to their realistic side. If they happened to kill a white civilian from some wealthy area, I told them, that would become national news. And if it became national news, old white people would start paying attention, and suddenly, everyone's operations and dealings would be fucked. Even at war, there was business to be done, and no one wanted to mess with their own money. The Nickersons from my generation agreed. And so, in all LocoL's time in Watts, we never had anyone shoot at the restaurant.

It was a lot, but I was invested. It didn't take long for me to buy into the idea of LocoL. I believed in the mission, the concept, what it was doing for the community, but I also wanted to make sure the owners didn't make decisions that would ultimately bite the restaurant in the ass. If the community turns against you in Watts, you're done. So, when the restaurant's project manager went about getting the curbs along one of the main streets in the neighborhood painted red and green, to restrict parking there, I had to let him know he needed to reverse that immediately, that he couldn't just come in and change the landscape of our neighborhood. And when I realized we were using an armored truck to pick up deposits from the restaurant, I nearly flipped the fuck out. I got on the phone with Roy and Daniel as quickly as I could.

"Man, y'all gotta stop that," I told them. "Y'all got the armored truck pulling up down here, making it look like we're making way more money than we are. Y'all are setting us up for a robbery."

Once I'd dealt with the external threats, I had to make sure everything internally was cool, too. This wasn't easy. Almost everyone at the restaurant was from my neighborhood, and everyone in my neighborhood had a history with everyone else. I was able to navigate these tensions, and keep everyone focused on the job, because I was respected in the streets, and I carried that authority over into the restaurant. If you disrupted LocoL, you disrespected me. At one time, we had two dudes working there who had a beef with each other—one's brother had allegedly killed the other's brother. Just a year before, these two dudes were shooting at each other in the streets. Now they were working side by side. Shit was heavy.

The first summer after opening, we participated in a job program for teenagers from Watts funded by the city. One day, this kid who was maybe eighteen years old pulled me aside.

"Yo, Fresh, man. I'm gonna have my people pick me up early today."

I asked him why.

"So I can get out of here before dark." He paused. "I'm from the Nickersons."

That blew my mind, especially because of the way he said it. There's a difference between someone saying "I *live in* the Nickersons" and "I'm *from* the Nickersons." The first is just a residence, but the second means you're representing that community. "I'm from the Nickersons" means "I'm with that bullshit."

Because he let me know, and didn't try to hide it, I respected him. He was putting it all on the line to come do a job and had taken a wild chance telling somebody like me he was from the Nickersons. He literally put his life in my hands in that moment. But I'm not a bully for the sake of being a bully. I respond with violence only when violence is brought before me.

"As long as you come in here to work, that's fine with me," I said. "I won't tell nobody. But, bro," I said, looking him in the face, "for your own sake, please don't tell nobody else."

So, after negotiating the safe zone around the restaurant, squashing personal feuds, concealing a sworn enemy, and checking in with my ambassadors to make sure no one was planning a robbery or trying to kill someone on our block, I'd get out my tasting spoons and decide whether the collard greens needed some champagne vinegar.

THERE WERE SO MANY THINGS to love about LocoL. The design was fantastic. In the front were three big-ass screened windows, and you could feel Watts flowing through the restaurant. You could hear music, people hollering and screaming. You could talk to your homies outside. You could even smell the sherm and the PCP. LocoL didn't feel afraid. Some new, "hip" restaurants, when they drop into neighborhoods, end up feeling like white islands in a sea of color, disconnected from the community around them. LocoL was not that. There were big, beautiful photos of Watts, taken by the rapper Evidence, on its walls, along with the phrase "We Are Here!" The way I read the "We" was "Watts." Watts was there in the building.

When it was all clicking, it was glorious. You could find Nardo in front in a black LocoL T-shirt, black jeans, and black sneakers, quiet and observant, manning the door, keeping an eye out for any issues, making sure customers were safe. You had Ant cleaning up trash, mopping the floor, and wiping down counters. My mother would be in a black skirt and tennis shoes, wandering from the office to the floor, greeting guests, shaking hands, taking pictures, spreading the Good News, occasionally even praying for someone in the middle of the food line. Past a wall filled with Polaroids of customers and employees, you'd find Andrew "Milk Chocolate" Miller, with his curly-haired white skater vibe and his Black swag, cooking twenty pounds of ground beef for the chili and six cases of collard greens in a tilt skillet, always cracking a steady stream of jokes. Running production in the back was Gwen from South L.A., the best cook and the only Latina not from Watts, rocking her pink lipstick, her hair pulled back in a ponytail. Kaitlynn, from Compton, was at the register, flashing her big, beautiful smile as she took orders from the customers. Past her, in the kitchen, you had Carnisha on the foldie grill, with her loud voice booming over Tupac coming through the speakers; Wayne, with his braids like O-Dog from *Menace II Society*, on the burger grill; quiet, mature Rob expo'ing, and my brother Marlon on the chicken and fries.

You'd hear orders being called out as tickets backed up, feel the energy from the crowd as customers bobbed their heads and sang along to the music. You'd see people who hadn't caught up in a while find each other in line and take their food out to the patio. All of it felt purposeful and real.

So did the way Daniel and Roy went about bringing LocoL to Watts. I'd been locked up, but my older homies told me they had been really respectful and thoughtful about coming in with their Black project manager, Vaughn Glover, to have real conversations with community leaders about the concept and how they were going to run LocoL. The intentions were good.

But you know what they say about good intentions.

For a while, the shine from LocoL radiated through all of us. In my thirty-five years of living in Watts, other than the truce, this was the first time I could remember positive news coming out of our community. And it wasn't about Roy and Daniel being our non-Black saviors. Much of it was about telling our stories. With Roy's approval, a filmmaker named Christopher Storer started taking documentary footage. I was on a panel at USC with Roy, talking about the LocoL mission. Hell, Bill Clinton even came by trying to wrangle primary votes for Hillary—until the folks of Watts let him know how they felt about the shitty welfare laws he passed while in office. But even the fact that Clinton thought to come down here and use us as a campaign stunt meant the world had to be watching and talking about what we were doing.

Meanwhile, I was still in the projects. My cocaine habit meant I was still getting high. And like my old T-shirt shop,

LocoL became the place to find me. My Grape Street homies would come hang out on the patio. But that exposure meant other gangs would know where to find me, too, so I kept my 9 mm close at work.

One day while we were working, the laundry people came and took away our dirty linens. A little later, they called Gwen and told her, "We think we found something you guys want back."

"Oh shit," I told her. "They've got my gun!"

Before I'd left the day before, I'd hid my gun in the laundry bag, so I wouldn't be traveling with it in the car. I had totally forgotten it was in there.

Despite being on parole from a federal penitentiary, my homegirl Gwen insisted on going to pick it up. When I protested, she wouldn't hear it.

"Fuck that. You my dog. I'm gonna go."

Looking back, I see I should've gone for the damn thing myself, but Gwen's willingness spoke to the relationship between us and what happens when a bunch of street niggas bring that love for each other into a business.

Gwen drove over to the laundry, picked up the gun, and brought it back.

"Maybe next time," she said, handing it to me, "don't put it in the fucking laundry."

ABOUT TWO MONTHS IN, ANDREW and Daniel asked me to come outside and have a talk. After LocoL's January debut in Watts, they were looking to open an Uptown Oakland location in May that would share space with another of Daniel's restaurants, plus a West Oakland commissary to supply all the Northern California restaurants. They asked me if I would ever consider a move to the Bay. I asked what they had in mind.

"Well, Fresh," Daniel said—early on, everyone called me by my street name—"our executive team works out of the Bay, and we'd like you on it."

I was excited but conflicted. On the one hand, it meant more money, more responsibility, and, for the first time in my life (outside prison), I could live in another part of California. On the other hand, I would be away from my family for most of the month and leaving the Watts restaurant just as I was starting to get into a rhythm. But, hey, at least this time I already had a couple of months' experience. And if Roy and Daniel had faith that I could do it, who was I to say I couldn't?

"Hell, yes," I said. "Let's do this!"

From the beginning, Roy and Daniel were all about growing. The way they talked about it, their goal was to open something like a thousand LocoLs across the country in five years. Now, I think that was a crazy exaggeration—not even McDonald's is opening two hundred restaurants a year in the United States—but they were always on the lookout for new spaces. Initially, they thought one of these would be in Nickerson Gardens. But considering that the first one was in Grape Street territory, that was gonna be a problem.

The fact that they'd opened the first LocoL near Jordan Downs wasn't intentional; it was coincidence. The original LocoL was supposed to be in the Tenderloin neighborhood in San Francisco, but that fell through, so they happened upon Watts because Roy knew Aqeela Sherrills from a business they ran together called Three Worlds Cafe. Aqeela grew up in my neighborhood. His mother, Miss Wajeha, would sell fried fish on Fridays out of a tent she set up in Jordan Downs. Aqeela was of the generation before mine and had been working in gang intervention since the early 1990s. He played a part in the 1992 truce, and we butted heads several times as I was coming up gangbanging during that decade. Like anyone with history in Jordan Downs, Aqeela's family and my family knew each other from way back, and I hung with some of his brothers, but he and I never vibed. Our approaches to the streets and Watts were just too different.

When Roy told Aqeela about LocoL falling through in San Francisco, Aqeela, who now owned the building where our store used to be on 103rd, offered it up as an alternative. Because Roy and Daniel were looking to set up in food deserts, Watts made sense. Aqeela acted as their tour guide, connect, and landlord within Watts, and that was good for job prospects in my neighborhood. Still, starting out in Grape Street Crips territory said something about who LocoL was with, whether its owners meant to or not.

Nevertheless, I reached out to those same Nickerson guys in my generation to take their temperature on the idea of opening a LocoL on their turf. Though they could see the advantages of creating jobs around their way, they figured the youngsters wouldn't go for it. We were back at war, after all. And I knew I sure as hell wasn't traveling to the Nickersons to train motherfuckers up on best practices.

We did make headway on a location over by Crenshaw High, thanks to Nipsey Hussle, a well-known rapper originally from Watts. Before he moved to the Slauson and Crenshaw area, he even went to Markham Middle School. Because Nipsey was part of the Rollin' 60s Crips, the biggest and most infamous gang in L.A. outside Grape Street, we'd gotten to know each other over the years. I set up a meeting for myself, Nipsey, my homie from Grape Street Montana, and Daniel to check out a building by Crenshaw High owned by Nipsey's cousin Fats.

Nipsey was going to get a percentage for branding, and because he was all about people in his community getting jobs, he was going to assist with hiring. We'd let them run and operate the restaurant. It seemed like a good deal for everyone, but before we could get it done, Fats was shot and killed. A year and a half later, Nipsey was killed as well.

Nipsey was one of the best, a street dude who gave a shit and didn't just talk about it. I still get emotional thinking about all that could have been done for South Central had he lived.

AS PART OF THE EXECUTIVE team, I had a lot of new responsibilities. I was still in charge of kitchen management and back-of-the-house duties on the operations side, but the most complicated of my new roles was acting as a kind of liaison when going into new Black communities.

Shortly after my promotion, an email came across my phone that I wasn't supposed to have been copied on. In it, Daniel, Roy, and Aqeela were discussing plans to open a LocoL in Newark, New Jersey. At one point, Daniel wrote, "There's a Grape Street in New Jersey. Do y'all think it would be a smart idea to bring Fresh with us?"

At the time, I didn't have any context, but the situation gave me pause. Had I been made a member of the executive team because of my talent or because, thanks to Grape Street's nationwide reach, I could get them in with intimidating people? Was I being seen as someone with a significant skill set and potential or as a prop for introductions to Black communities and a good look for PR?

In truth, the answer was probably both. And that was a smart business decision on their part, because I was uniquely positioned in the streets to help carry out the LocoL mission the right way; I'm recognizing that now. At the time, though, and further into my career, these questions would overshadow my confidence, marking my achievements with a mental asterisk. I wanted to be known for my talent, not my background. To put it in sports terms, I wanted to feel I got my spot because of my skills on the court, not just because I got the crowd's attention. No one wants to be the mascot.

I'D BEEN OUT OF PRISON for two years, but I didn't know real freedom until I moved to Oakland in 2016. At first, I crashed at Andrew's place, and then at the Waterfront Hotel, but eventually I settled in a two-bedroom apartment in Uptown, so that anyone coming up from Watts to train could stay in the second bedroom.

There was something about Oakland I'd always liked. Because it also has a rich Black history and culture, it felt like Watts's Bay Area cousin. And Uptown, with its art deco buildings, the iconic Fox and Paramount theaters, and murals, was electrifying to see in person. But for me, going anywhere outside L.A. always felt like entering a foreign land. I needed to find a way to center myself. So, the day I arrived, when Andrew picked me up from the airport, I made him drive straight to the Acorn projects in West Oakland.

In the same way you look for a familiar dish to act as your entry point when you sit down in a new restaurant, when I'm in any new hood, I look for the projects. That's where the people who speak my language are, the people I connect to. Andrew drove me there to help me find my entry point. I needed to see and feel the vibe of the place.

Coming from a place like Watts, where even your enemies know everything about you, it felt totally new, almost disorienting, to be just another face in the crowd. Up in the Bay, I had no long-standing beefs, no exes, no problems with random dudes because of something my homie had done to their cousin. That's not to say there wasn't some gang shit going on in East and West Oakland. I'm just saying the Bay's geographical divisions didn't apply to me. I didn't have to carry a gun. I could walk to the store with my shower shoes on, and no one would pay me no mind. If I wanted to go to the club, I didn't have to spend an hour looking through Instagram and checking social media to see if my enemies were there, calling around just to see what was up. My brain was used to constantly scanning for trouble, and while I could never turn that off, at least here I could turn it down. Oakland was a place for decompression. I felt lighter.

Being in Oakland opened me up to all sorts of new experiences, including going to a Whole Foods for the first time at age thirty-five. I remember walking in with Daniel. The first thing I noticed was the lack of security guards. There were no items in lockboxes, nothing hidden behind glass—just rows and rows of perfect fruits and vegetables, meats and fish and cheeses, each in its own little area with its own special, expert workers presiding over them, ready to tell you stories about where the foods were sourced and all that shit. They knew more about the fucking cheese's origin than I did my own father's.

As we walked through, I remember seeing an entire wall of glass containers filled with nuts, seeds, dried berries, and chocolates. Because they weren't locked up, I assumed they were free samples, so I shoved my hand inside the bin with the chocolate turtles, picked up a dozen of them, and started popping them in my mouth. As we walked the aisles, my mouth stuffed with chocolate, pecans, and caramel, I thought about Watts. It wasn't just that we didn't have Whole Foods; it was that the idea of a place like Whole Foods wasn't even in our frame of reference. That people would labor over and care about the minutiae of food (and pay a premium to get it) hadn't occurred to me before.

I wondered what Granny would've made of this. Everything she cooked she made with love and care—but she had to labor over cheap cuts of meat from the neckbone, cook things low and slow to tease out the flavors. You could taste the love *because* you could taste the time she had put into it. At Whole Foods, the food came pre-loved.

ON THE WORK FRONT, SHIT started heavy and stayed that way. We were pulling permits, ordering equipment, mapping out the kitchen, and hiring staff. Every day, it was one thing after another. I had a lot of the same duties managing the kitchen crews as we prepared to open, but on top of that, I was learning new skills. Daniel taught me how to evaluate spaces for their potential. He showed me how to walk the grid to see where equipment might go, how many staff would be needed to operate the kitchen, and how to put together a budget for labor costs. I learned how to design a menu and create a product list for food costs.

Because part of my job was to think about expansion (and urban relations), I ended up going on that trip to New Jersey to meet with Newark mayor Ras Baraka. The meeting itself was pretty nondescript; I didn't have a speaking role, so I stayed out of the way. Daniel wanted me to give my impression of the mayor. I saw him as a street dude like me who'd made his way up. What made a bigger impression on me, though, was the actual city of Newark.

Coming from Watts, I'd seen a lot of poverty, but Watts itself was vibrant. It may have been run down, but there was life happening all around—people barbecuing, gardening in their yards; little kids running around playing trash can basketball. But, from what I saw, that was not the case in Newark. Huge stretches of that city had been abandoned. We could drive ten blocks without seeing a single person—just street after street of empty, boarded-up, once-beautiful row houses, plywood over their windows, grass growing as tall as their gates. The city itself was choked off by highways, a concrete island surrounded by a sea of industrial activity, all aiming to feed the beast that is the New York metropolitan area. It seemed crazy to me that a place with its own sea- and airport would be so barren. Everything came through there, but nothing stayed.

Watts may be a food desert, but at least it's in California. Even without trying, you might accidentally find yourself with a lemon or orange tree in your backyard. But there were no accidental gardens in Newark—not as far as I could see. In one part of the city that we were considering for a LocoL, the liquor store acted as the only place for miles to buy anything to eat *or* drink. If you wanted something beyond fried chicken, fish, nachos, malt liquor, or soda, you were out of luck.

As desolate and neglected as Newark was, Manhattan was the opposite. The two were fewer than twenty miles apart, but when we took the train over, I felt like I was entering a different country. I remember coming out of the subway at Penn Station and FaceTiming my mother. "Look, Ma," I said, swinging the phone around to show her the energy and vibrancy of New York City. "Look where I am!"

We were in the city because Daniel wanted us to go to a bunch of top restaurants to make sure we saw how various kitchens worked. Our first stop was Chef David Chang's Momofuku. We were outside waiting in line for a few minutes when someone from the restaurant recognized Daniel, pulled us out, and, in a *Goodfellas* move, basically created a table for us. Chefs and managers came over and shook Daniel's hand, and instantly, we had drinks and more food than we could handle, all free. We sat at the counter and watched the cooks at work. They had the same kind of equipment we had, but their flow was a lot tighter. It created a new point of reference for what it meant to be a cook, and I thought about it a lot when I got back. Plus, the food was delicious.

After Momofuku, we went to a Portuguese place called Lupulo. While at the bar, I remember scouring the menu for something I recognized (and could afford) and seeing prosciutto; so I ordered that. A few minutes later, Daniel was recognized yet again. The chef/owner, George Mendes, came out, gave Daniel a hug, and asked me what I'd ordered; when he heard prosciutto, he immediately had his staff bring out slices of *ibérico* ham. When it arrived, he explained that this ham came from purebred, 100 percent black Iberian pigs fed a diet of acorns and chestnuts and aged for like three years. I'd never in my life tasted meat that rich and smooth before.

After Lupulo, we weren't done. We ended the night at the bar at the NoMad hotel, and there, it was the same—handshakes and hugs for Daniel, tables opening up miraculously, free food and drinks appearing out of nowhere.

At first, I didn't know what to make of this. I didn't know that the chef world was its own fraternity—it's hard to recognize something you don't even know exists—but I understood clout and connections. In my world, that meant walking past the line at a club in L.A. because your homie was working the door or getting hooked up with a free burger and fries because your homegirl was the cashier at McDonald's—shit like that. But this was on a whole other level.

At each of the places we went, Daniel would always point out how the kitchens were run. I didn't know what I was looking for or looking at, but he was patient with me. He would show me how some kitchens acted like conveyor belts, passing a dish along so that each person on the line could execute a specific task. Other kitchens worked with stations. I learned the hustle, the urgency. I saw cooks plating using tweezers and rulers. I saw cooks twisting and breaking live lobsters. I learned what a weird-ass geoduck was. It was a nonstop crash course in the culture of high-end restaurants. I didn't recognize the significance at the time, but those visits were providing me with the building blocks and the vocabulary to be able to start under-standing a true professional kitchen.

Though, once back in Oakland, I was hardly professional. I had more power and responsibility, but I was still acting like a youngster—from the way I was dressing, to my haircuts, to the way I interacted with the people I managed. Most of them were from neighborhoods in East and West Oakland that were just like mine. It felt good to be up in the Bay and still feel I was among my people, vibing with them just like I would have back in my own neighborhood. But I was still struggling with how to balance my street and professional lives. I would party with the kitchen crew just as I had with my Watts crew, blurring the lines with our after-work activities. I felt like Jacob wrestling with God in the Bible, but instead of turning into Israel, I was turning to drugs.

At that time, there was nowhere in the world I couldn't find cocaine; it had taken me all of a week to find a connect in Oak-land, over on Grand. At night, I would close the restaurant, pick up drugs, go back to the apartment, and party until four or five in the morning. Around five, I'd finally fall asleep—for maybe three hours. Then I'd jump out of bed, shower, and be at LocoL by eight thirty A.M.

Getting high felt different up in the Bay. Aside from work, it was all I did. Of course, I tried to hide it, but I couldn't have been doing a great job—I was always sweating, my nose was stuffed up, and my focus was scattered. I don't know if Daniel knew early on; at the time, he never brought it up, never threw it in my face or questioned me on it. He just kept urging me on, encouraging me. He believed in me. His belief kept me going. But the guilt of not truly giving him my all, of being so con-sumed by drugs, ate away at me.

DURING THIS TIME, I WAS coming back to L.A. twice a month to check on the Watts restaurant and see my family. And it was on one of these trips that the Bloods in the white Camaro came within a blown-up headrest of putting me down for good.

Later on the day of the shooting, I got word from one of my homies that a Mexican woman across the street from my aunt had cameras attached to her house and that they'd captured the whole thing. I remember going over to watch the tape on her television and having an out-of-body experience seeing that white Camaro circling the block. I could see that the dudes inside it were just youngsters. There had been a shooting at the Nickersons the night before, and these guys were probably looking for payback. The constant back-and-forth made it impossible for me to know for sure.

What I didn't expect to see on the video was OJ, another Grape Street homie who also worked at LocoL, walking up Anzac toward Century. I saw the young boys in the Camaro spot him and circle again to position themselves ahead of him on the block. Then, just as they got out of the car with their AKs to ambush him, we made a U-turn in my mom's car and came into the frame. As I watched them empty their weapons into the car, I also saw OJ break across the street and run through an alley to escape. I saw the youngsters get back in the car and drive away, likely convinced they'd dropped at least a couple of bodies.

Of course, the video didn't show what happened after we drove off. It didn't show us getting guns at my mother's house. It didn't show Montana joining me and Marlon. Or waiting outside the Compton Avenue liquor store for a Nickerson nigga to come through. I didn't really remember all that, either. I was on autopilot —with no thoughts, just muscle memory honed from decades of street warfare. But that day, when I saw the dude in the red hat whom I didn't end up shooting come out of the liquor store, and when I saw myself crack the car door open to fire at him, it was like I was disrupting a circuit in my brain.

I'd found peace and tranquility working at LocoL, yet, in that moment, I was willing to abandon it all. I'd found light, but I was compelled by the dark. It animated me so much that I dragged others into it. Others that I cared desperately about.

I remember now looking over my shoulder and seeing the faces of my brother Marlon and of Montana in the backseat. My brother was not a killer, and Montana had been making an effort to turn his life around, to put the street life in the past. And yet, they were showing me so much love in the moment that they were willing to throw everything away to go do this, to show they had my back. I hadn't seen the video yet, so I'd assumed at the time that the shooting was all on me, that the Bloods from the Nickersons had seen my face and wanted to put me in the ground, that they knew if they killed Fresh from Grape Street, it would be something to brag about. And now that they'd tried and missed, it was on me to clap back, regardless of who their real target had been. Not retaliating would have brought its own consequences. From then on, I'd be seen as soft, a coward. I could never ask anyone to do anything on my behalf. My whole rep was on the line.

For much of my life, retaliation wouldn't have been a question. When they came at us, we would go back at them twice as hard. They needed to know not to fuck with Fresh. But, in that moment, looking back at my brother and my homie, I decided to love them more.

"Fuck it. Let's go."

In the movie of my life, not retaliating for that shooting would be the turning point, the moment I chose "the good path." In that moment, I made a decision unlike any I'd ever made before. And who really knows why I decided to love my brother and my homie more and drive away? I wish my answer were clean and direct and pure. Had my time in Oakland given me a wider perspective on the futile nature of this gang war shit? Or maybe traveling around the country and being put in a serious role in the restaurant had given me hopes and dreams that went beyond the next day or week or month. The movie of my life would spell that shit out, right?

The truth is, I don't know why that was the moment things changed. This shit is never clean or simple. Even saying that God gave me the strength feels like an excuse, a cop-out. The truth is, I'd started this life halfway down a hole, and I'd been burying myself in it ever since. I don't know why this was the moment I decided I could crawl out of it.

I'd lived my entire life wearing the masks that would get me through to the next day—in the projects, in prison. That's where Fresh came in. In both those places, vulnerability was a liability. So, I did what I needed to do to survive. I cloaked myself in a predator's threads to avoid becoming prey. I embodied Fresh, not Keith. And the things that Fresh did and the things that Fresh was known for and the things that Fresh was comfortable with—all those things, Keith was fearful of. Keith always wanted a family; Keith always wanted an education, but given the climate he lived in, he had to create this Fresh character. Keith had to put up these walls surrounding him, so that to hurt him, you'd have to go through Fresh first. And you didn't fuck with Fresh. Fresh was with the violence. Fresh was with the hustling. Fresh was with the disrespect. Fresh didn't give a shit about prison time. Fresh was with all that.

In a freer place and time, I would happily have been Keith and seen how far I could run with that—dominate the debate team in high school and college, be a history professor or maybe a big-time litigator, and either way, get really fucking good at golf.

But that's not the life I'd lived. So, when I made the decision to be done with all this gangster shit for real, it wasn't like I could just give notice at Grape Street. Gangsters don't retire; they *get* retired, moved from the streets to ink on your body or tags on walls. I needed a different plan.

A few weeks later, I came back down to Watts. My big homie Nardo picked me up. As we drove through the projects, I was quiet. As I'd expected, there had been consequences to my decision not to retaliate. Seeing me as vulnerable, a few younger dudes from the neighborhood had tried to fuck with my weed-fencing hustle. And though they ended up only embarrassing themselves, it made me question my decision not to shoot back. On the streets, mercy was perceived as a weakness. These younger fools may've been the first to try to come at me, but they weren't going to be the last.

Of course, I didn't bring any of this up on that car ride with Nardo—we don't do that shit—but as we drove through, Nardo spoke.

"Man, whether you know it or not, you're carrying this neighborhood on your shoulders," he said. "You're an example for a lot of the homies over here trying to get away. Plus, you're employing our people and helping them take care of their families. You can't fuck up. Keep going."

I don't know if Nardo sensed my unease, but his little pep talk was just what I needed in that moment. He helped me see that though it would be complicated, there had to be a way for me to do my thing and keep my head up. I needed Keith to have the keys.

It's rare for a person to walk away from the streets and still be respected on them. But that's what I wanted—and I spent a lot of time thinking about what I could do to keep that respect while also distancing myself from the day-to-day.

There is no template for this shit. Everyone has to figure out their own path. During the ten years I was locked up, I lost a lot of people in my generation to death or prison. And, to me, those people were irreplaceable. So, in one sense, I wasn't walking away. My people were already gone.

On top of that, if you want to maintain respect in the organization, you can't be about the same shoot-'em-up bullshit as the young boys. Otherwise, they'll look at you like, *You can't give me no game. You're doing the same shit I'm doing.*

I thought my best path was to go from general to consigliere, from an active participant to a mentor-educator. I tried to teach the younger generation how to think, how to play street chess, how to survive. And when you take on a role like that, it doesn't come with the same sort of expectations. If you're coaching, you're not also expected to run onto the field and make the plays. If they were going to shoot, they would not ask me to roll with them. They would ask me for the best strategy to get home alive after they were done.

14

Takeover

AFTER THOSE FIRST CRAZY FEW MONTHS, BUSINESS AT LOCOL Watts slowed down considerably. Most of the foodie-tourist white folks who chased the new new had already made their one visit and weren't coming back. But we were still dependent on tourist traffic to make our numbers. The local scene wasn't gelling like we'd hoped. And if you know Watts, you can understand why.

Locating a business in Grape Street territory was a decision that, while good for me and my particular hood, had financial consequences for the business. Watts is made up of roughly forty thousand people. With gangs controlling each quadrant of the city, this means that only about ten thousand of those folks might actually feel safe coming to the restaurant. After all, people weren't going to cross gang lines and risk their lives to try a griddled tortilla foldie. Now, of those ten thousand, how many were kids? Or addicts with no income? Or people's moms on a fixed income? So, you had maybe two thousand people in the area who had the means to eat at LocoL. But of that two thousand, how many were going to spend their last few dollars trying some foods they weren't comfortable with?

The answer, as we quickly came to find out, was not fucking many.

This brought up a second issue: the food. Now, don't get it twisted; the food was objectively delicious. And it should've been. Daniel and Roy are two world-famous chefs at the top of their game. They have serious palates. The food was legit. And to their credit, they kept it affordable—probably more affordable than any other high-level restaurant ever started by two world-famous chefs. But that doesn't mean anything if the customer has no context.

You have to understand: in Watts, we grew up knowing only fast food, processed food, fried food, and whatever we were getting at home. I'm a chef and more willing to experiment than most, and I didn't even try sushi until I was in my thirties. All this is to say, you gain regulars at a restaurant by putting your customers at ease, giving them something they recognize and feel comfortable with. People in the hood aren't asking you to condescend to them, but they want you to meet them somewhere in the middle. Otherwise, they'll look around the restaurant, be happy for the people from their neighborhood with jobs there, and move on down to McDonald's to feed their whole family for ten bucks. I know because I've seen it happen over and over and over again.

If you want to bottle all the issues with the menu into one example, look no further than the original burger. The burger, like almost all the food at LocoL, faced twin challenges: it needed to stay cheap, but also be made with good ingredients. I understood that shit intuitively because it was like cooking coke: they were looking to stretch the product. Daniel might have had ten pounds of ground beef, but he needed sixteen pounds of product, so he started stretching the meat with fine, pulsed grains and tofu. Plus, he added seaweed, white soy, and something called garum (a fermented fish sauce) to give it the umami flavor. Now, Daniel being Daniel, he got the garum from René Redzepi at Noma in Copenhagen. And the bun recipe came from Chad Robertson at Tartine Bakery in San Francisco. The burger was finished with Monterey Jack cheese, a Koreanesque special sauce, and a burnt-scallion green relish.

When I first tried LocoL's original burger, I liked it—but I knew that, for people coming in there expecting a burger with a similar style and flavor to those at Watts's legendary Hawkins House of Burgers, this wasn't going to be it. For one, the scallion relish made everyone think we were putting collard greens on our burgers. Two, though Daniel did a hell of a job with the ratio, so you wouldn't really taste the grains, the texture from the mixture made the mouthfeel softer than that for a normal burger. Three, to keep up with production and get rid of human error, we salted the meat ahead of time, portioned it out, and froze it. So, the meat was actually curing while it waited to be cooked. Because of that, no matter how long we grilled it, when you bit into it, it looked medium rare. And folks around my way don't eat medium-rare meat.

Up in Oakland, we had almost the exact opposite issue. The Uptown location was not in a food desert, but in an upscale neighborhood with lots of other restaurants around. The foodie hipsters who frequented the area weren't fazed by Daniel's burger. In fact, the LocoL menu was almost *too* basic for Oakland. And because it was a business district, we might have a lunch rush every day, but dinnertime would be dead.

Again, our expansion had been reactive. Roy and Daniel opened in Uptown not because that was where a restaurant was most needed, but because Daniel had a space available there. After seeing Watts lose money, they figured that putting a LocoL in a nicer hood would be more profitable and help balance out Watts's losses. But looking back now, I see that opening one thing to help another can give off an air of desperation. Like dogs, customers can smell that fear on you. And it didn't help when a lily-white dude named Pete Wells, from *The New York Times*, who reviewed restaurants almost exclusively in his own city, decided to make an exception and fly three thousand miles across the country just to go in on us.

To be honest, I wasn't mad at the review Wells wrote. (I mean, I didn't know or care who the fuck he was.) He was careful to avoid talking shit about the employees (though he did have a few cracks about "bullet-proof windows" that didn't go unnoticed), and he even made some good points. The chicken nuggets *were* dry. The veggie burger sometimes *did* taste gummy. And I could see how our being in Uptown, among all those other restaurants, did make us fair game for criticism. Still . . . why? Why do it? What was the point?

Jonathan Gold, the OG *Los Angeles Times* food writer (RIP), asked that question later that week in his column: "The question wasn't how Locol's $5 Fried Chicken Burg might compare to the vastly better $9 fried chicken sandwiches at Night + Market Song or Oakland's own Bakesale Betty. It was why the New York Times was using its main restaurant column to gripe about bland turkey chili in an Oakland burger stand whose mandate was to feed a community with limited access to good, nutritious food."

Either way, all of L.A. and Oakland seemed to come to our defense . . . online. Even the outraged response to Wells's review mirrored the problems we were having: folks would much rather yell on social media about the injustice of the review than come show love and support by spending money at our damn restaurant.

But we kept trying. On March 31, 2017, we opened the West Oakland shop, which was supposed to serve as a bakery and our commissary kitchen for Northern California. Unlike Uptown, West Oakland was a tougher neighborhood, with almost no dining options, so I was hoping we'd make some noise there. Plus, because baking was a focus, we were able to experiment with new bread-based recipes.

After I got pizza lessons and a solid marinara recipe from the *pizzaiolo* at Oakland's Boot and Shoe Service pizzeria, we started offering hand-stretched and tossed whole cheese, pepperoni, and barbecue chicken pizzas for nine dollars. We were doing sweet-and-savory empanadas, and cinnamon rolls. We were selling the plain "bunzz" from Tartine's recipe for a dollar, a small chili for three dollars, and agua fresca or green juice for two. If you had a family of four, you could get a whole pizza, a salad, and four bunzz for twenty dollars. The shit we were doing and the prices we were doing it at were crazy.

But it still didn't click. There was no foot traffic, and almost instantly we had troubles with Ghost Town, the gang who controlled the territory around LocoL. Unlike in Watts, no one had properly checked in with them before we'd opened our doors.

Midway through 2017, Roy and Daniel called a meeting in the back of the commissary in West Oakland with me, Andrew, and Bambu, our head of marketing and front of house (who also happens to be a dope Filipino American rapper and activist). They told us they were pulling out of the day-to-day and turning the operation over to us. Major decisions would still need to be made by them, but daily operations were now in our hands. The way they explained it: LocoL was designed to be run by the locals.

Once again, I felt excited and scared. It was all on us now. Andrew, Bambu, and I took to calling ourselves the Three Horsemen. Andrew headed up the kitchen, Bambu controlled the marketing, and I was director of operations. Still, we were getting the keys to a house that needed a lot of work. None of our restaurants was profitable. We'd opened two more before we'd even figured out how to get sustained support for the first one.

There's a quote: "Ships don't sink because of the water around them, but because of the water inside." Well, the LocoL ship had been taking on water. But now that it was truly our baby, and now that I was at the point where I had at least foundational cooking skills, I was determined to figure it out. I went back to Watts and, with Daniel, Roy, and Andrew's cosign, helped reconstruct the menu there. My goal was to simplify. I wanted this LocoL to be less "chef-driven" and more "Watts-driven." That meant losing the burnt-scallion relish and the garum- and grain-filled burger and doing a traditional, diner-style cheeseburger. I added the pizza I'd learned to make up in Oakland, and I paid homage to L.A. with some bomb-ass chicken and waffles.

The key to the waffles was brown butter. I'd learned to make it at LocoL by cooking the butter until the water burned off and then the milk solids fried in the fat until they browned. The difference between regular butter and brown butter was like the difference between a seared steak and tartare. Once I captured that flavor, I started putting it in everything. I made the waffles from scratch using that brown butter to give them lightness, nuttiness, and a toasted aroma, and I made a syrup from 100 percent maple, homemade caramel, and more brown butter. This was one of the first dishes I'd actually made myself, and it gave me a rush to see folks in the restaurant eating and enjoying it.

Our catering gigs were a chance to tap into the creativity I'd used in prison with my spreads, except now I had real skills and ingredients. Our catering director, Justin, campaigned for me to do things off-menu, and I started riffing on what I'd learned at LocoL. Sometimes I'd text ideas to Daniel and he'd make suggestions, but other times I'd just freestyle on my own. It was the beginning of how we'd create together in the kitchen. I started making my own cheese sauce from scratch and doing a cauliflower mash with mushroom gravy. I felt alive cooking my own food. I loved tinkering with recipes, changing ingredients and flavors to see what happened.

With the revamped menus, our numbers improved—but it still wasn't enough. In June 2017, we shut down the Uptown Oakland LocoL and put our new menu in the West Oakland branch. Once Uptown closed, Bambu stayed up there, and I moved back down to Watts.

GOING BACK WAS STRANGE.

At the restaurant, I was flailing, trying all sorts of last-ditch moves to revive the place. I even employed two women from the Imperial Courts projects, as a way to open the restaurant up to another neighborhood. A few Imperial dudes used to come through on my word that it was a safe haven and that nothing would happen, but that was the extent of it. The other neighborhoods never came through.

Outside the restaurant, I was uncomfortable. I was out of tune with what was going on in my neighborhood. I didn't know where the war was at. I had flown back down for a few funerals while I was in Oakland, but I didn't know who the players were anymore or the cards they were playing. I didn't know the temperature of the situation—was it on the rise or on the low? I didn't know which blocks were getting shot up. And I'd almost gotten killed, right by my aunt's house. That stoked my paranoia.

I didn't have a set address; I was floating. Sometimes I'd stay at my mother's house in Watts, or Tiffany's house in Long Beach, or Roy's spot at the LINE hotel in Koreatown. I had access to a car, but I had nowhere to go. Because I was basically homeless and snorting coke, I spent a lot of time up all night.

Many nights, I would drive the Pacific Coast Highway and

go from beach to beach, stopping at Manhattan, Laguna, and others along the way. I used to snort as I was driving and then pull into a beach parking lot, take off my shoes, roll up my pants, and walk up to where the waves crashed over my feet and stare out into the ocean. I kept a big blanket in my car, in case I wanted to sleep for a few hours before the sun came up. When I was lying on a beach, I didn't feel homeless. I was chasing the same feeling I'd had as a kid, when I stared up at the night sky from the project field and pretended I was in the woods camping.

But by the time it was light out and people started coming around, reality would sneak back in. Then I'd get back in my car and head to work. I used to stop at one of those little bodegas and buy a toothbrush and a bottle of water to brush my teeth with before I went back into the restaurant; or I'd go by my momma's house and get a quick shower in. The cycle was brutal.

I needed cocaine to stay high through the night, and then, in order to keep from crashing during the day, I'd get high again before work. At some point, the combination of drugs and fatigue would kick in and, for self-preservation, my body would shut down. The scariest part was, I didn't know when that would happen. Would I be driving? Cooking at a hot grill? When would my switch turn off? Even so, I tried to keep my use from everyone. I had too much pride to let people know I was struggling, to let anyone in Watts know that Fresh wasn't killing it.

But I didn't know who I was anymore. I wasn't Fresh. I couldn't read the streets like a book. People weren't talking about me in hushed tones. And how could I be Keith when

Keith's identity was so wrapped up in LocoL and that was failing, too? Yet, despite all this self-doubt, the worst part was that I'd catch a glimpse of myself in the car mirror—bugged, blood-shot eyes; sweaty brow; drifting from beach to beach—and *still* think I looked good.

There is no confidence like cocaine confidence.

15

The Setup

BY THE SUMMER OF 2017, WATTS LOCOL WAS GOING THROUGH drastic changes. Previously, Aqeela had really been just the landlord and didn't have much say in the day-to-day operations, but as the Watts restaurant continued to be unprofitable, Roy brought him into the fold to shape things up and get costs down. One of the first people Aqeela suggested we fire was my mother. And because I was director of operations, it was my role to let her go. As you can imagine, this didn't go well.

But Aqeela wasn't done there. He started letting a lot of my people go—my uncle, Montana. To be fair, salaried employees throughout LocoL were being fired, but even with all the lay-offs, even with all the schedule stretching, LocoL still wasn't making any money. We just didn't have a customer base. And with me now back down in Watts, Aqeela and I were bumping heads all the time. There was too much shared history, too much tension between us going back decades.

We were never going to see eye to eye. And because Roy and Aqeela were close, and Daniel and I were close, neither of us was willing give up his place at the table.

And then I slipped up.

One early fall weekend in 2017, Chef Eric Greenspan was doing a "Clash of the Hatch" food truck challenge. I was sup-posed to represent LocoL and cook up a recipe using south-western chiles, serve it at the event, then do interviews and other shit to promote LocoL. But I'd done so much cocaine the night before and into that morning and even the afternoon that I didn't show up. I didn't call. I didn't tell anyone anything. I just missed the entire event.

And when I did that, I forfeited my place at the table. If Aqeela had been looking for an opening to make the case that I should be let go, I had just handed it to him. And the worst part was, he was right. I fucked up. This *was* a fireable offense.

At first, they suspended me for two weeks with pay. When the two weeks were over, I went to look at the work schedule and couldn't find my name. When I tried to log on to my email and Google Drive and found I couldn't access either, I knew I'd been laid off.

At the time, I had no perspective, no wisdom. I'd been doing drugs and stewing in my feelings for the better part of two weeks, and I had just lost the one thing I'd been leaning on to help me exit the streets. On top of that, my paranoia had convinced me that Aqeela had taken the job away from me because of our past, not because I had sabotaged myself.

In this frame of mind, I made a decision: if I wasn't going to be working at LocoL, LocoL wasn't going to be working, period. I got dressed, drove over to the restaurant, made all the employees leave, closed and locked the doors, and told everyone the restaurant wasn't opening. And when they saw it wasn't Keith the director of operations speaking, but Fresh the big homie from Grape Street, there was no argument. They just left. Delivery trucks pulled up, but I told them to take the deliveries back to the warehouse because the "restaurant was no longer in service." Then I sat outside on the patio and waited for something to happen.

All the politics bubbling under the surface at LocoL were exposed in that moment. All the legit, aboveboard business jargon was gone. In my mind, this was about who had more suction in the streets. If it was Aqeela, then he could come prove it by making me reopen. And we both knew that wasn't going to happen.

As I waited there on the patio, I got a call on my cell. It was my big homie Caca calling from prison. At first, he tried to play it off like he was just checking in on me.

"What's going on, brother?"

If he was playing that game, I would, too.

"Nothing," I said. "What's up with you? Why you calling me? Someone call you?"

"Man, it ain't even like that." Finally, he got to it: "But I did talk to old Aqeela."

He went on to tell me he and Aqeela were going into

business together on some weed-growing licenses and that he wanted me to make peace so I could also get in on the business. I loved Caca, but I didn't want Aqeela to think he could just get some dude to call me and I would back down.

"Man, fuck Aqeela. I respect you, Caca, but you need to stay out of this."

But Caca wasn't through. "Yo, Fresh," he said. "You see how upset you just got not getting your check? Think about the people you might be stopping from getting theirs."

He was right, of course. I *was* fucking with other people's livelihoods. My former co-workers, people I had hired and managed, were crying outside, worried about their jobs. What I'd done wasn't just crazy, but selfish.

After I talked to Caca, I got on the phone with Bambu and Andrew to let them know I would reopen the restaurant, but I wanted to make it clear it was not for Aqeela. It was because they'd asked me to and because I wanted to keep my people in Watts getting paid. By noon, the restaurant was back open, and it was business as usual. Well, for a day.

The next night, robbers came in and took the safe. From the security camera tape, it was impossible to see who had done it, but Aqeela tried to convince Daniel and Roy it was me. I knew how it looked. The day after I got fired, the restaurant got hit.

But, really? Rob the store I just got fired from? The next night? You think I'm that stupid? C'mon now.

When I talked to Aqeela, he hinted that if I just copped to the robbery, maybe he'd be able to get me my job back. If I blamed it on the drugs and everything . . . But that only made me more upset.

"Who you think you're talking to, man? Have you lost your motherfucking mind?"

We hung up with the situation unresolved. I was out of a job, but I sure as hell wasn't going to claim a robbery I didn't do. Looking back, I realize that while I didn't commit the robbery, my public tantrum and power play had signaled to the community that I was no longer involved with LocoL. And with both Montana and me both gone, they might as well have put a flashing sign up front saying, "Rob Me."

LOCOL MANAGED TO HOLD ON, in some capacity, for another ten months, even opening a small outpost in a San Jose Whole Foods in January 2018. But by August, Watts, the first and last location standing, had closed.

In less than three years, this grand experiment, this food revolution, was all over. At the time, my insecurities colored the way I thought of LocoL and its end. Outside of Pete Wells, the food media had loved us. *Food & Wine*'s Kate Krader said we were the "Best New Restaurant of 2016," and Jonathan Gold named us the *L.A. Times* "Restaurant of the Year" in 2017. We got press everywhere, and most of it was good. But I always had the sense that they were saying this shit because it was a feel-good story. LocoL had a mission. It went into food deserts and gave minorities jobs in their communities. And it was fucking cool. That combination is a drug the media can't resist.

And yet, even at its peak, the restaurant wasn't profitable. The second location confused people, because it didn't seem like part of our mission. For a long time after it closed, I con-stantly thought about the "woulda, shoulda, coulda" opportunities with LocoL, about what it might've been if it had been set up as a nonprofit from the jump. Investors might have gotten on board not to turn a profit, but with the idea that it needed only to sustain and reinvest in itself, that making it a revolution and trying to turn a profit at the same time were conflicting goals. Instead, we were always trying to speak in two languages when we hadn't even become fluent in the one.

It's easy to look back on all of the mistakes made during LocoL's run and consider it some sort of failure. I can do the same thing with myself. I was abusing cocaine and alcohol and blurring the lines between the streets and the workplace. At the time, I wasn't in any position to absorb and appreciate all the opportunities LocoL gave me. I wasn't ready. But, for the sake of my future, I now chose to see my past in a different way.

LocoL changed my life. And even better than that, it changed so many other people's lives. There was Gwen, who was still living in a halfway house when she started working with us. After LocoL closed she came to work at Alta as chef de cuisine, and then in 2020 she moved to Texas. She's now the chef at a restaurant there, running a kitchen and hiring and training people under her.

LocoL was the first real job for Carnisha after prison. She used her experience to get an even better job, and now owns a house and multiple businesses, and throws Sunday Kid's Day Parties in my projects. Montana is in the music industry, managing musicians and dealing with executives, and two twin dishwashers, who used to work alternating shifts in Watts, recently opened a franchise of Mr. Fries.

In Oakland, I hired a man named Cory, who'd just come home from prison after twenty-two years with a renewed appreciation for life outside. I saw his work ethic and started training him to be manager. After LocoL closed, Daniel hired him to work in his fine-dining restaurants. Cory quickly became one of the best servers, then pivoted and started his own cleaning business. After his first contracts to clean Daniel's Oakland restaurants, he grew his business and now hires others from the same organization that helped him get a job after prison.

From a business perspective, LocoL wasn't a success, but how many restaurants are? Most people open restaurants because they love food or see a business opportunity, but what Roy and Daniel had done went so much deeper than that. They planted seeds in the minds of people who'd nearly given up, who'd seen the regular world fail them time and time again, and they showed them that their previous failures didn't dictate their futures. They created generations of LocoL alums who have been able to take their experience, build on it, and hire more and more people like them. LocoL's business plan might've been flawed, but its mission wasn't. LocoL saved my life.

Now, how can I look at all that and call it a failure?

PART FOUR

Corbin with Chef Daniel Patterson at Alta.

16

Dedication

I KNEW WHAT I WAS DOING.

I knew that first I'd hear it fizzle and then I'd watch it foam.

I knew when to break up the mixture and set the beaker in the hot water.

I knew to wait until the cocaine had melted down into oil and risen to the top of the baking soda and water.

I knew that once everything melted, I would whisk and whisk until the water, oil, and baking soda all came together like pancake batter.

I knew when to move the beaker over to the sink, the way to

tilt it as cold water ran over the outside, and how to angle my fingers so cold water dribbled down into the beaker and got the mixture to harden until pieces started to float.

I knew when the crack was ready.

And I knew that, after I finished the cook, I had twenty minutes to get to the Long Beach airport to catch a flight back to Oakland if I was going to make my shift at the restaurant that day.

A YEAR EARLIER, AFTER GETTING fired from LocoL, I didn't know what I was doing. I thought I was done. And honestly, I didn't really care. I'd been spiraling in L.A., bouncing between my mother's house, Tiffany's in Long Beach, and my car. But after a month, Daniel threw me a lifeline and offered to put me on as a line cook in his Bay Area restaurants. So, in the winter of 2017, I moved back to the Bay.

The first night I got there, I was supposed to stay at an Airbnb in West Oakland. When the Uber pulled up to my destination, I noticed I was deep in the hood. The house I was staying at was on a dead-end street where the only way out was through a sketchy-ass alley. On top of that, in the front yard of the house across the street sat five dudes wearing hoodies and black sweaters, all staring at me from under the shadow of a big-ass tree. It was fucking spooky.

The energy, the vibe—there was some janky shit going on there. It was a scene very familiar to me, and not in a good way. I mean, if you can see a fire is hot, you don't want to put your hand in it, and here I was getting out of the car with a suitcase like a damn tourist.

Hell no.

As soon as I got inside the house, I called Daniel. "Look," I said. "If I'm gonna die in a hood, it's going to be my own. But right now, I need to get the *hell* up out of here."

From there, I spent time in South San Francisco and the Hunters Point and Lower Nob Hill neighborhoods. Eventually Daniel's company rented an apartment for me and a couple of other chefs in the Castro. We would stay up late after work, drinking and talking about cooking and restaurant culture.

For the first few months, I picked up shifts across three of his restaurants, basically filling in wherever I was needed. It wasn't always easy to fit in. The chefs felt like Daniel was forcing them to work with someone who didn't have much experience, so they weren't always cool with me being in the kitchen. (Plus, I still didn't like taking orders.) I didn't get into the flow of a specific kitchen until a couple months in, when I got my own station working the open-flame wood-fired grill at Alfred's Steakhouse, an old-school San Francisco joint that Daniel's restaurant group had taken over a few years before.

There, with the help of the sous-chef Tyler, I got a full education in meat. Tyler taught me how to properly break down animals; how to age meat and deal with temperature, climate, and moisture; how to grill steaks by touch and when to move them toward and away from the flame; how to properly cook aged beef; how to caramelize meat instead of just grill-marking it; and how to rest it. Before Alfred's, I could barbecue, but after Alfred's, I could grill.

I was getting schooled in other ways, too. While working at the various restaurants, I spent a lot of time traveling around with Daniel. Sometimes he'd pick me up and drive me to work.

Sometimes I'd roll with him in a U-Haul to offload furniture or new equipment into a restaurant. And sometimes we'd go to the Farmers Market at San Francisco's Ferry Building.

I'd never been to a farmers' market or even a farm. Before this, the closest I'd ever been to either was the smell of cow shit at Calipatria or the animals in my Granny's backyard. But at the Ferry Building market, I was blown away. We would walk past stand after stand selling everything from pan dulce and pizza to fruits, vegetables, herbs, flowers, meats, and eggs, all from local ranchers and farmers. It seemed like Daniel knew every farmer and rancher working at the market, and as we wandered, he'd tell me their story and get me to handle and taste all their goods, from satsuma mandarins to purple-top turnips to Pink Lady apples. He taught me to keep a notebook and, after I tried something new, write down the flavor profiles.

From time to time, Daniel would get invited to cook at private events, and occasionally asked me to help. One night he agreed to cook a few courses for an experimental vegan dinner, along with Corey Lee from Benu and David Kinch from Manresa. I had no idea who they were, or why anyone would pay $700 a person for dinner, but when we got to the event it made more sense.

It was held in a giant mansion on what looked like a plantation in Saratoga, south of San Francisco. And those chefs were making some pretty incredible dishes. For one of ours, we made cabbage leaves stuffed with a filling of chanterelle mushrooms and leeks, flattened into a half circle shape, and steamed until firm. Then, just like we did with the LocoL foldies, we browned them on a griddle with plenty of oil so that the cabbage blistered on the outside. For a sauce, we used LocoL's green juice, blended it with some herbs, and then thickened it.

Another time, Daniel was cooking a multicourse charity dinner at his house, and asked me if I wanted to help. He had a garden out back where he grew a ton of herbs and flowers for Coi, and we sat out there in the sun that morning, tasting plants and talking about what we wanted to make. We were planning a mushroom and potato dish that needed the right herb to complete. He thought for a minute and said, "Let's take a drive."

We went to a redwood forest not far from where he lived, and walked a little ways into the trees. "Taste this," he said, handing me a light green bud growing off the end of a branch. I'm not big on eating shit off trees, but I trusted him. The bud tasted sweet and a little acidic, like lemon, and kind of reminded me of a Christmas tree. When we got back, I watched him blend it into a bright green oil. With each of these experiences, I was trying to soak everything up to further my own knowledge.

ONE DAY, WHILE WE WERE driving away from the Farmers Market, I asked Daniel, "You think you'd be willing to partner with me in a restaurant by the time I turn forty?" I was thirty-seven at the time and had been having dreams about opening my own restaurant and holding my fortieth birthday party there. Because I went to prison at twenty-two, I never had a chance to properly celebrate my birthday. And after being locked up for ten years, the idea of having an elegant, big-ass party at my own restaurant seemed like a fantasy.

Daniel told me I should write a three-year business plan to map out how I could potentially do such a thing. Although I never put pen to paper, I began mentally sketching out my idea for a concept over the course of our drives together. I thought about it like building a house. Now, in my mind, I can picture my ideal house. But I'm not an architect or a contractor, so all I can do is give someone like that my vision and see how they translate it. And that was how it worked with Daniel and me. I would lay out ideas, and he would try to figure out how to execute them.

I might say, "Damn, man, I want to do collard greens in a special way. Not just a bowl of mush, but presented properly on a plate. Like how we worked with that cabbage at that charity event."

Daniel would nod and think for a minute. "Oh okay," he'd say. "What if we made the greens, then took one of the prettiest leaves, blanched it, and stuffed and folded the greens inside?" He'd discuss presentation and flavor profile, but also the importance of narrative, how it wasn't just about how the dish tasted or looked on the plate, but also the story you could tell about it. We'd want to use local greens from a Compton farmer and make sure the servers knew their story. He helped me see that, in the best restaurants, all of these factors matter.

Over the course of these trips, in bits and pieces, we talked through what I really wanted. We were planting the seeds for my ideal cuisine—and those seeds came primarily from three places:

One was my ancestors in Africa. Before they were enslaved and dragged to America in chains, they cooked with certain techniques that they then brought with them to the New World. As slaves, they worked the fields all day. At the end of the night, they'd get together and count heads. Maybe that day, they hadn't lost anybody. And with that small victory, that small joyous moment, they'd start singing their hymns and telling stories. While that was happening, they'd take the remnants from the master's house—the tail of the ox, the guts and belly of the pig, all the discarded parts the white people didn't want—and make their own meal.

During that meal, they were in good spirits because they were creating this food out of love, with the intention of nourishing, sustaining, and feeding their souls in order to carry themselves over into the next day. They didn't know how long this journey would be. They couldn't have known it would last four hundred years. They just took it day by day. And though they continued using the techniques their ancestors brought with them from home, they didn't have the same ingredients. This showed me that soul food isn't about using the "correct" meats, vegetables, and spices. It's about the technique and the love you put into cooking them.

Thinking like that, I didn't feel bound by the limitations of traditional soul food. I'd started reading West African cookbooks that Daniel had given me, and they made me want to get closer to the way we cooked back in Africa. More grain- and vegetable-centric. Braising beans and vegetables with meat, with the meat acting as a flavoring agent and not the main focus of the dish. But I also wanted to pay respect to the Asian influence in California cuisine, which meant not being afraid to use ginger, miso, soy, and other ingredients I'd gotten comfortable using at LocoL that my Granny would have told me to get out of her kitchen. My food would always be inclusive, not exclusive. And anyway, soul food didn't need to be limited by cultural boundaries. After all, why would we, as Black folks, purposely limit ourselves when so many others were more than happy to do it for us?

Prison was the second seed—not only because making spreads had opened my eyes and my palate to all sorts of flavor combinations, but also because I noticed that the processed shit I had been forced to eat in prison was the same shit most people ended up eating on the outside. Soul food especially had gotten a bad rap as a central culprit in the health problems of poor Black America. I wanted to show that this wasn't true, that it was the *quality* of the food available, not the style, that should be changed. Soul food could be made with better, healthier ingredients and still be "authentic" and flavorful.

After I got out of prison in 2014, I noticed something else. While trying to change myself, I spent time wandering into other neighborhoods, and when I wanted soul food, it was always the same thing: served on Styrofoam plates as takeout or in these little restaurants with no ambience. I would look around and see these cool fine-dining restaurants serving New American, French, Japanese, and Latin foods. But it was hard to find Black-owned restaurants serving Black food in an atmosphere that matched what these other cultures had going on. I wanted to change that.

The final seed was Watts itself. Thanks to the Great Migration, thousands of southern Blacks, usually the kids or grandkids of slaves, came to California and settled in Watts. Coming from the rural South, a lot of these folks were used to growing their own fruits and vegetables, and the Southern California climate encouraged them to keep doing it. Everyone had fruit trees and vegetable gardens in their backyards.

My mom remembers walking down the alleys to school and

being able to sample fruits right off the branches and vines hanging along the way—green grapes, peaches, plums, apples, kumquats. But that wasn't the only thing giving Watts a southern vibe. When I was growing up, there was a market in my neighborhood that sold live chickens. When they stopped keeping their own chickens in the backyard, my Pa Pa used to take us there, buy a couple, bring them home, chop their heads off, pluck their feathers, and have my Granny fry them up.

I wanted my restaurant to reflect the natural connection people had to their land, but with the vibe of that fortieth birthday party I imagined. It needed to be elegant, joyful, and filled with people eating delicious food and having a good-ass time. It needed to showcase the beautiful bounty of local shit we could grow right here in Southern California; keep it healthy and fresh; pay respects to our ancestors by using the techniques and styles they brought with them from Africa; and do it all with the intention of nourishing, sustaining, and feeding the soul.

This, to me, was the essence of my cooking. This *was* California soul food.

IN EARLY 2018, DANIEL WAS working on opening a new Alta down in L.A., in the West Adams neighborhood. At the time, the company that was paying for the restaurant wanted him to do the same sort of cool modern Californian American cuisine he was doing at the other Altas. He tapped a white chef named Shawn, who'd worked for David Chang, to develop the menu, and he let me know he wanted me for the sous-chef role.

That February, I came back down to L.A. and spent a month working on recipes with Shawn out of the old commissary kitchen in the back of Watts LocoL. During that time, I was kicking it with a homie in Long Beach I'd known for years. Though I knew he was a hustler and sold crack in the LBC, I normally didn't inquire about his business, but because of my cocaine addiction, I called him up one night and asked if he had any coke.

He said he did and hooked me up with an eight ball for free. And because he did me that favor, I felt compelled to offer him something in return.

"You know I know how to cook this shit, if you ever need somebody."

He nodded and told me he appreciated that and that he'd be in touch.

There was no premeditation on my part. I wasn't trying to get back in the game. And frankly, I didn't think he'd take me up on it, as I didn't hear from him the rest of my time down in L.A. After the month, I went back up to Oakland to help Andrew, who was trying to open a Middle Eastern restaurant called Dyafa in consultation with the Palestinian-Syrian chef Reem Assil in Jack London Square. But while I was in Oakland staying on Andrew's couch, the homie in Long Beach called me up.

"Yo, Fresh," he said. "You still down to cook?"

Part of me wants to pretend I struggled with the decision, that I was genuinely conflicted. But that wasn't how it went down. In truth, I wanted to see if I still had it. I missed the energy around cooking dope. The music on, the girls around—it was an event. I was good at it, and after grinding in all these kitchens over the last six months, I wanted to feel like I was good at something again.

"Yeah," I said. "Let me know when you need me."

Once a week for the next few months, I would get off my shift at Dyafa, head to the Oakland airport, and catch the last flight to Long Beach. From there, I'd go straight to the dope house; stay up all night doing cocaine, cooking, and partying; and then catch the earliest flight back to Oakland the next day in time for my shift. One way or another, for nearly twenty-four hours straight, I was cooking.

Meanwhile, Daniel started to attend community meetings in West Adams and learn about the neighborhood. Though West Adams originally had white-only "covenants" just like all the other wealthy L.A. neighborhoods—clauses in real estate contracts preventing homeowners from selling to Blacks—during the Great Depression, desperate homeowners in need of cash sold to anyone, and professional Black folks saw their chance and bought homes in the area.

By the 1940s, West Adams Heights, which was also called Sugar Hill, had a fancy hotel and beautiful mansions owned by Black actors, producers, musicians, and other professionals. According to the West Adams Heritage Association, the neighborhood won the first court case in America that ruled against "the enforcement of covenant race restrictions," setting a precedent that could be used across America. Like Watts after 1965, West Adams/Sugar Hill became a point of pride for Black people everywhere. (Of course, white L.A. wasn't going to just sit there and let Black professionals have nice shit. And they figured if they couldn't kick them out, they would build the Santa Monica Freeway right through that beautiful neighborhood, chopping it in half, displacing residents, and ruining home values.)

Today, you can still see some of that beauty and swagger in the homes across West Adams, and as Daniel met the proud residents and fully took it all in, he realized the restaurant should be more reflective of the history of the neighborhood it was in. A restaurant for the future that could honor the past.

Soon after, Daniel pulled me aside in the kitchen at Dyafa. He told me he'd let Shawn go and that he wanted to talk to me about something important.

"What's going on?" I asked.

"Remember the concept you were thinking about?"

"Of course."

"You ready to make it happen?"

One of the voices inside my head was shouting no. That I had a serious drug addiction, which I was funding by cooking work in Long Beach. That while my skills as a cook had improved dramatically from my days turning mustard greens to mush, I still wasn't where I needed to be to develop recipes on my own. That the idea of running a professional fine-dining kitchen was fucking terrifying.

But the voice that answered was the other part of me. The hustler. The survivor. The Watts nigga who knew damn well that these sorts of opportunities basically didn't exist for formerly incarcerated Black men from the projects. After all, We Are Taught To Survive. So, when opportunity knocks, you let that fucker in before he realizes he came to the wrong door.

"Hell, yeah!"

Right there in the Dyafa dining room, we sat down and worked out a deal. I would move back down to L.A. full-time to be executive chef and a partner in Alta West Adams with a percentage of the restaurant, and we would implement my vision.

Just like that, California soul food went from being a theoretical idea of what a menu could be, to something I needed to come up with and execute in a matter of months.

Later on, Daniel would tell me that many people questioned his decision. And I don't blame them. From a skills and experience perspective, I wasn't a pro. I was still playing amateur ball. But as I said before, what was I supposed to do? Just admit I was in over my head and give up what might have been my one chance to do something of my own?

We agreed that, over the course of the first year, I would work side by side with more seasoned chefs, who would show me the ropes. The first was Ed. Ed would help me get the restaurant open, show me how to work with vendors, and get everything set up. We spent lots of time at the farmers' markets. Some days, we'd go to Torrance. Some days, Santa Monica. I was trying to do what Daniel had taught me, trying to understand these different farms and farmers, see what they valued, see how they treated their fruits, vegetables, animals, and employees.

I was learning the difference between working with farms and working with purveyors. Take an avocado. If you buy avocados from a purveyor, they might be getting them from a reputable farm, but that farmer potentially harvested the avocado early, to factor in truck travel, hold, and delivery time. Whereas, if you bought avocados straight from the farmer, there'd be a chance they were picked the day before and would be fresher, creamier, and not already turning brown. It's not rocket science. From age thirteen, I'd known that better raw materials gave you a better final product.

I was thankful we were going to use a charcoal grill, which

I'd gotten comfortable working with at Alfred's, but there were a lot of other things I needed to learn. One of the most crucial elements that needed strengthening was my palate. In prison, I'd always talked about different textures, but I'd never understood or even realized that there were dimensions to flavor. Growing up, we'd take the renderings from the chicken, drain the grease off, add flour, and make our gravy out of that. But working with Daniel and these other chefs taught me that if I wanted to bring more dimensions to that gravy, I needed to play with other, subtler notes. I might add shallots for sweetness and aroma, and cognac to add acidity to enhance the other flavors. I was learning that in a great restaurant dish, the flavors behind the scenes were just as important as the lead actors.

I liked thinking about things like dimensions and balance because, for me, cooking isn't about just recipes. I think of cooking more like a horn player playing jazz, or an action painter slinging paint at a canvas. The musician or the painter isn't thinking of the end; they're thinking of the rhythm, the moment, what they're going to do right now. To lose myself in the moment is rare for me. My entire life is about planning ahead, making sure I'm scanning for danger, evaluating risks, noting the things that seem out of place. That's how I know I love cooking. Because it takes me out of my head and puts me in the moment.

Some chefs can think about a dish and create a recipe in their head. They can see it, almost like a math problem or an algorithm. That's not how I do it. At least not at first. I need to be in the kitchen. I need to open the fridge and see what I have and throw it in the pot. Maybe I know I want to use oxtails. There's the meat, but what's the flavor? Let me see what I have.

I grab a little of this and a little of that and . . . Boom! It's all in the rhythm, the improvisation. Unscripted.

I need the process. What it is, I'm not exactly sure, but I'll put on music and start chopping and balancing and dancing and having fun, just like I did when I cooked work. My synapses don't start firing until I turn that fire on and get the dish going—because then there's pressure. You're racing against overcooking that meat or burning what's at the bottom of the pot. I live for the moments when I bring the dish to the edge and pull it back. That's good pressure, the type of creative pressure that gets my adrenaline and cortisol and all that shit going. And that's when I'm having the most fun.

It's only when I'm done that I'll step back and start to critically evaluate it, in the same manner a painter might. *Do I outline it? Do I patch the color here?* That's where the collaboration came in. Daniel or Andrew might taste what I'd just made and say, "Okay, this is good. How do we take it to the next level? How do we make it great?" And we'd work from there.

That's how we started to build the menu at Alta. The process was entirely collaborative. I was creating dishes, Daniel was creating dishes, and then we would talk through our vision of the dishes with Andrew, or Gwen (who'd come over when LocoL closed), tweaking and elevating and offering feedback on what we were trying to do. Watching Daniel work was an education all its own. At the beginning, I'd just watch him work his way through a problem, watch him moving and tasting and flavoring all the while, teaching himself in real time. Then, after the fact, he'd take me through the steps. He's one of the best chefs in the country, so I could see where the bar was, where I needed to get to.

The fried chicken is a good example of how we worked. These days, I think we have the best fried chicken around. A shattering crisp exterior and a juicy, flavorful interior. Just the right amount of spice. But like a lot of great recipes, it began with a mistake. A couple, actually.

We started with Daniel's ratio of salt and water to brine the chicken overnight, 1.75 percent salt to the weight of the chicken. Then we drained the chicken and put it in buttermilk for a day. After a while, I figured out I could skip the brining and just stir the salt into the buttermilk, pour it over the chicken, and let it sit for twenty-four hours. I made a seasoned flour mix and we were ready to go. Or at least that's what we thought.

I showed Daniel how I made my chicken at home, cooking it from raw in deep cast-iron skillets, and he got this fantasy that we could cook like that in the restaurant. It lasted one night. Our pre-opening dinner was generally a shit show, but the fried chicken was the biggest disaster. Not enough pans, too many orders, and it took way too long. And we undercooked it half the time. So the next day we did it the normal restaurant way, by pre-frying.

Traditionally, restaurants that serve fried chicken prepare it in two stages, so it's cooked through without getting too brown. They first fry it at a low temperature, like 275 degrees, to cook it all the way through. Then they cool it down and hold it, and then fry it to order at 350 to crisp the outside and heat it through.

That led to the second mistake—we only had one fryer. That would have been fine for the upscale California cuisine Daniel designed the kitchen for, but not for the forty orders of fried chicken we would eventually need to be putting out every night. (We would learn this the hard way once Alta actually opened.)

But Daniel had a great idea: Let's just put the chicken in the fryer for a minute to make the spices stick, then bake the chicken at a low temperature in our combi-oven, so we could control both heat and humidity. He cooked it at 250 degrees with 30 percent humidity to keep it moist until it was just cooked, using a medium fan to move the air across the skin and avoid making it soggy. This worked great. But after a few days, I started to wonder why we needed to even fry it first. It got the fryer dirty and it didn't seem like it was doing anything for the flavor. So I asked Daniel, What if we just bake it right after dredging it in the flour, and only fry once someone orders it? He thought for a minute, and said, "Yeah, that sounds right. Let's do it."

The baking let the flavor go all the way through the chicken, so every bite was evenly seasoned. The crust was thin and perfectly crunchy. And it worked with one fryer and was faster to produce, which made it easier for the cooks. We served it with a hot sauce made from Fresno chiles, marinated for days in vinegar, salt, and sugar.

Even our mistakes seemed to turn into something good. Like Miles said, when you hit a wrong note, it's the next one you play that counts. Our adjustments to the chicken also had the effect of making the dish lighter and healthier without sacrificing taste, which was an important element of the menu for me. Again with health in mind, when I started to develop a cornbread recipe, I used almond milk instead of regular. It was good, but it was missing something, so Daniel suggested brown butter to bring out the nuttiness in the almond milk. With that addition, it was perfect. I also wanted to serve it warm in whole loaves, so I used a metal nine pan, which ended up being the perfect size for two people.

We were constantly finding ways to create new things that were rooted in tradition. In one of the West African books, we found a recipe for *akara*, black-eyed pea fritters. It called for raw, soaked black-eyed peas, blended with ginger, onion, and chile. I made the recipe, then Daniel suggested we sprout the peas to make them more digestible. For a dipping sauce we took the zhoug recipe he made for Dyafa, bright with herbs, chiles, and lemon, and mixed it with buttermilk mayo to smooth it out.

For brunch we made cornmeal pancakes, light, fluffy, and as big as hubcaps, with a perfected version of the maple/salted caramel/brown butter syrup I'd made at LocoL.

One dish I really wanted to feature was oxtail. Daniel suggested that I try it with miso and soy to add umami. Then, because so many African recipes used ginger, I decided to add that, along with the holy trinity of onions, celery, and carrots. I thought I nailed the recipe, but since oxtails are such a powerful taste memory in my community, I needed to be sure. When I cooked some up for some of the grannies in Watts and they loved it, I knew I had something special.

We flipped the sweet potatoes in a way that would've caused my Granny to start swearing. In jail, I remembered watching Rachael Ray do a potato pavé, and that thinly sliced style intrigued me. I grew up eating cubed sweet potatoes cooked down in a pot with sugar, brown sugar, a pound of butter, cinnamon, and nutmeg. It was very sweet and very rich. I wanted something lighter, and since almond milk and brown butter were part of my vocabulary now, I used them instead of the cream and melted butter, and cut the sugar by half. We shingled the sweet potato in a baking dish, poured the cooking liquid over the top, and put it in the oven. Once it cooked through, we poured the liquid off, pressed it, put it in the freezer, let it stiffen, and then cut it like a pavé. After that, we seared the top on the griddle to get caramelization and texture, and finished it with candied pecans and some of the excess liquid. This was my way of having candied yams without the mush.

I looked for ways to keep shit classier and defy expectations. Traditionally, if Black folks are going to a barbecue, there are going to be ribs and watermelon. But those are sloppy eats, park food. That shit won't fly on a date at a nice restaurant. So, to combat that, we smoked ribs and made a BBQ sauce from scratch, with watermelon that had been cooked in the BBQ sauce and then pureed back in to give the sauce that watermelon flavor. Then we took the rind, pickled and julienned it, and made it into a cole slaw. We put that watermelon rind cole slaw over the watermelon BBQ ribs, and there you had it: a Southern California Black barbecue all in one dish, and without the mess.

Pickled pig's feet was another important dish for me, because they were a part of my life growing up. After talking it over with Daniel, he pulled out a recipe for a pig's head terrine that he served at Coi. To make it, we took the pig's feet and the head and put them in a pot with charred onion and some other vegetables and boiled them slow for hours until all the meat started falling off the bone. Then we put that meat together, chopped it, put it in a hotel pan, and let it seize up like hogshead cheese. After that, we sliced it thin and put it at the bottom of the plate, with a frisée salad on top with a champagne vinegar and olive oil vinaigrette. The idea was that, when the oil and vinegar hit the pig at the bottom of the plate, it would give you just a taste of that traditional pickling flavor inherent in pickled pig's feet.

As it all started to come together, I was damn proud. While I was locked up, I had talked about how I wanted to be the Crip Suge Knight in the music industry. Well, I realized that collaborating on recipes breeds the same kind of creativity— except, with chefs, everyone is a little bit the artist and a little bit the producer. But as with music, when it works, you can feel that energy. And, in my opinion, the menu we were putting together to open Alta was nothing but bangers.

TWO MONTHS BEFORE WE OPENED, I cooked work for the last time. Almost immediately after I started cooking again, however, the romance and excitement of being back in the kitchen and being that old Fresh wore off. I needed the money, and I wanted the drugs to support my habit, but I started to see the predicament I was putting myself in every time I flew down to Long Beach to cook. When I was in the streets and traveling across the country to cook work, it was a source of pride that I controlled the situation; dictated the spot, the time, the date. But in Long Beach, I wasn't doing any of that. I wasn't picking the location. I didn't know if the feds were already watching the house. I had a restaurant I was opening and a family to support, and yet I was still going into a bad situation blind, all just so I could get some extra money and free cocaine. It was shameful, but more than that, it was stupid.

After the last cook, I told my boy that he didn't need to pay my fee, that it was on me, but that it would be the last time. To his credit, he was cool with it, and the break was clean. But even now, just thinking about the terrible risks I was taking and the possibility that, if I'd gotten caught, I could've been put away for life on some three-strikes shit, shakes me to my core.

As we moved toward opening, I got a crash course in all the things that went into operating a restaurant. Setting up point-of-sale systems, choosing music, a thousand little details. The biggest, as we got closer, was hiring staff.

In 2016, not long after LocoL opened, a woman named Saru approached Daniel and asked if he'd like to be involved in an experimental program designed to create systems to reduce discrimination in fine-dining restaurants. The nonprofit she ran, Restaurant Opportunities Center, had a big grant, and they needed a restaurant to test out the program in. Naturally, Daniel volunteered.

Together, they developed systems of hiring, training, and advancement designed to remove implicit bias, and met with staff to talk about systemic racism in fine dining. The white servers were uncomfortable, and when the restaurant switched to a system of pooled tips, they quit. No one likes it when you fuck with their money.

But Daniel and his team kept with it, and when we opened Alta, it was what we used. Like LocoL, we tried to hire from the neighborhood. We didn't require résumés. We used re-entry programs (at one point, almost the entire kitchen staff had a prison record), and since LocoL had just closed, we brought over a bunch of staff from there. We wanted people to feel safe and seen. I was damn proud of our staff.

———

ONE NIGHT AFTER WORK, DANIEL asked me to dinner with him and Ed at Delicious Pizza, a block from Alta. It was about a month before opening, and I figured they wanted to talk through what the next few weeks would look like, but when we got out on the patio in the back, I could tell by the discomfort on Daniel's face that something was off. At some point, we started to talk about my salary, and I brought up the question of ownership.

Daniel looked at me and then looked away.

"Well, Fresh," he said. "I've been advised by the executive team that it isn't a good idea at this time to involve you as an owner right now."

This news hit me like a blow to my solar plexus. "What?"

"You'll still be executive chef, but you'll be a salaried employee to start."

Now that I know how the business works, I realize Daniel didn't have the right to act on his own, and he never should've offered me so much in the first place. At first, he didn't tell me what was going on behind the scenes, that there were other partners who had control and none of them were in favor of giving up equity to make space for me. Objectively speaking, that was probably the right business decision. I was inexperienced, I didn't know how to run a restaurant, and I had a drug addiction. But, at the time, I wasn't objective. All I could think of was the deal we'd made in the booth at Dyafa. Where I come from, your word was everything, and in that moment, Daniel was reneging on his word.

Hearing this news only reinforced my cynical side, the side that said trusting people was for fools and suckers. I could just see Fresh going in on Keith. *Whatchu think, nigga? You really believed you were gonna have a restaurant? Nigga, you? Get the fuck out of here!*

And that's what it felt like. Like some street shit. Like it was my bad I hadn't seen this coming earlier. I felt deflated. Betrayed. Trapped. Because, the thing was, I needed this job, badly. I needed the money and the stability, so I was in no position to just walk away. But, strangely enough, they needed me, too.

The canned, media-ready story of my life, the one that had been written about so much when LocoL started, was out there. And when Alta was opening, and I was supposed to be a chef/ owner, it had been a nice talking point with the media. *Look at this guy! He gets out of prison, works his way up through the ranks of LocoL, and now he has his own restaurant.* It was the classic "pull yourself up by your bootstraps," American Dream narrative. And thanks to the media attention I'd already gotten, I knew how to play that song. Shit, I'd memorized the lyrics. I didn't understand why Daniel hung back on the publicity, so I thought he had some angle. That he was pushing me out into the spotlight for his own gain. He'd never said I was an owner in the press, but people had assumed it.

But now that I wasn't actually chef/owner, that beautiful story became a false narrative. But, by then, I'd bought in, the community had bought in, and it was almost impossible to retract.

ALTA ADAMS OPENED ON OCTOBER 11, 2018.

The restaurant never had a grand opening. Unlike at LocoL, Jim Brown didn't roll up in a fancy car to cut the ribbon. Lena Dunham wasn't there. We just threw our doors open. But, from the beginning, it felt like a party. I remember being on the line with Daniel that first night, the two of us working side by side, in the zone, cranking out dishes. From my vantage point, looking out upon the restaurant, I could see people hanging out all along the all-black bar, sitting on our heavy wooden stools, admiring the beautiful glass-fronted oak cabinets filled with liquor as they sang along to the nineties R&B playing in the background.

In the next room, where the music was a little more muted, I saw these big Black and white families engaging in conversation, no phones on the table, and couples on intimate dates thrilled by each dish our servers brought out. John Legend and a few other Black actors and producers were there. If I was allowing myself to dream, I might've thought we were creating *the* happening spot for the new version of Sugar Hill.

I loved looking around such a beautiful restaurant and seeing all these people eating my food and having a damn good time. I tried to come by every table and be friendly, funny, and welcoming. You could see how proud the Black people in there were, to be eating at this cool restaurant with a Black chef/owner. Not some fancy-ass culinary school–trained Black chef with a famous father from Beverly Hills, but a Black chef from Watts who grew up in the projects, went to prison, came out, and did this shit. That should've filled me up from top to bottom.

But it wasn't true.

Over the course of the next few months, I became increasingly bitter and resentful. The worst part was that my attitude validated their decision not to make me an owner. I could've taken the initial news and, through hard work, shown them that they had to give me a percentage because I was a star and was showing up and showing out. But I didn't do that. I wasn't performing to the best of my abilities as executive chef. I was unfocused and dealing with my emotions, my resentment, a steep learning curve, and a drug habit. I wasn't taking initiative, and it only made it look like they had made the right choice.

I was performing, though. When dinner service started, I was acting like I was the brand, visiting tables and talking up the food. And I had to bring some high energy, because Alta was blowing up. Night after night, we were packed, with reservations booked for weeks and a three-deep wait at the bar.

The restaurant was already designed when I started, but it was perfect for what I wanted. The slightly worn look we opened with felt right, with its vintage pieces and imperfections, like it had always been there. We kept the lights low and the music loud, the prominent bar at the entrance pumping out good drinks: the feeling of a late-night party vibe. The team was inexperienced but they were having fun, and you could tell.

We started to notice we were becoming *the* late-night spot. A lot of our reservations were for nine or ten P.M., the time you'd normally go to a club. It was a restaurant, but I loved that people were thinking of it during club hours. That was what I wanted: to make it feel like a party.

More important, it gave Black people a cool, hip place to go where they could also feel comfortable. I always told everyone, "When you're here at Alta, you don't have to tell your kids 'shhhh' because you're embarrassed they're loud. The kids next to you are loud, too. Everyone's Black; they get it." Everyone was welcome, but it was a place to showcase how we as

Black people ate, drank, and partied. A lot of fine-dining spots are so quiet that it almost feels like you're eating in a church. But Black people don't eat like that. Actually, Alta *did* sound like a church—but a Black one. Because we don't church like that, either.

The food was like nothing else happening then. We had taken dishes I grew up with out of the Styrofoam boxes, out of the malls and cramped, fluorescent-lit rooms, and put them on handmade plates in a beautiful dining room. We took back the connection to the land around us, the farmers' market vegetables and pastured meats that you never see in Watts. We took back the creativity other cultures were allowed to have in their food. We were making dishes my Granny would have been proud of, and we were doing it in our own style.

One of the cornerstone dishes of soul food is mac and cheese, and you know I wanted my fingerprints all over that. I noticed in the Coi kitchen that they used a whipped cream dispenser to pump air into a potato puree. Why couldn't we do that with a cheese sauce to make it feel lighter? I made a four cheese and jalapeño base for the noodles, then Daniel made a smoked Gouda aerated cheese sauce to put on top, followed by garlic breadcrumbs. It was somehow dense and light, creamy and crunchy. I'd never seen anything like it before. Then one day, a few months after opening, I saw the same dish on a local chef's Instagram. I showed Daniel, expecting him to be as mad as I was, but he just laughed.

"Get used to it," he said. "If it's good, it will get copied. Welcome to fine dining."

We were making good use of the charcoal grill. There was a smothered hangar steak with a mushroom gravy like the one I made for the cauliflower mash at LocoL, but made using the cooking liquid from the oxtails. There was a simple grilled fish fillet from one of the best seafood purveyors in Los Angeles, which we served with a vinaigrette of ginger, habanero, shallots, tarragon, and palm oil, with tons of lemon. A giant brined pork chop with chow chow, jalapeño, and cilantro.

We were *cooking*.

When the reviews came in, they were good—and not in the praising-the-mission-but-not-the-food type of way. Critics definitely appreciated the vibe, but they especially loved the food. In his *Los Angeles Times* review, Bill Addison said he was obsessed with the fried chicken. Jeff Gordinier put Alta on *Esquire*'s "Best New Restaurants 2019" list, saying, "Keith Corbin's cooking makes you keep waving the server back to your table for more." Thrillist named it as one of the "Top 12 Best New Restaurants in America." I was going to *L.A. Times* events as the face of Alta. We hosted Amazon executives, the Underground Museum, and the likes of Diddy, Jay-Z, and Tiffany Haddish.

Occasionally, though, Alta's popularity, my visibility, and my past in the streets would collide. Early on, I remember looking at Alta's reservation system and seeing that someone had made a reservation under "Top Dawg Entertainment." A lot of people know Top Dawg as a record label with a roster that includes Kendrick Lamar, SZA, and a bunch of other famous musicians. But what they don't know is that Top Dawg was started by a dude from the Nickersons.

Once I saw the reservation, my mind immediately jumped to the streets. What was happening here? Had some Nickerson OGs done this on purpose, to come through and flex at my

place of business? Were they coming for me? I stared at the
little reservation box, trying to decide whether I should decline
the booking, but immediately, I tossed that idea out. If I turned
them down, they'd have a right to feel disrespected. I decided I
needed to approach this from a business perspective. Everyone's money would be good at Alta.

The whole rest of the day, I was on edge, trying to figure
out their strategy, thought process, and what they might be up
to. I could think about little else. A few minutes before their
reservation, I positioned myself in the back of the restaurant,
facing the host stand, so I'd have a view of the whole place.
Because I was paranoid, everyone knew where to find me. I
used to carry my Glock .45 at work, and I had it on my hip that
day. I was ready for anything.

A few minutes after the reservation time, I heard the host
say, "Reservation under Top Dawg."

I looked up.

It wasn't killers. Or shooters. Or dealers. Or OGs. Or young
boys.

It was a couple of college kids.

I'd been tripping, setting up for war, ready to die on some
Sun Tzu shit, over a dinner reservation made by some interns
in skinny jeans name-checking their place of work in the hope
that it might get them some free black-eyed pea fritters and
cornbread.

I was relieved—but after all they'd put me through, I wasn't
comping them shit.

———

"HE'S ELEVATED IT IN AN extraordinary and beautiful way."

It was March 2019, and this was the incredible actress Tracee Ellis Ross, standing next to me on Alta's back patio, talking about *my* food. The first time she'd come in, she told me she would definitely be holding an event there, and true to her word, she was responsible for our first private party, renting out the entire place for the women of her hit show *Black-ish*.

We were serving up cornbread with honey butter, pimento cheese dip with pickled vegetables, shrimp and grits, grilled fish, fried chicken, BBQ cauliflower, collard greens, glazed carrots, mashed potatoes, red beans and rice, and coconut cake for dessert. Seeing the family-style plates of food piled high on those glossy wood tables on the patio, surrounded by vine-laden high wooden walls and Edison bulb string lights, I felt like I was in a country home oasis in the middle of the city.

Before the dinner really got going, Tracee pulled me up next to her in front of the crowd and gave a brief welcome. There's a video of it on Instagram. You can see me up there looking nervous. Meanwhile, Tracee, in a bright yellow shirt, was cool as hell.

"I've been very moved by coming here," she said. "Take time to ask questions about Keith's story. He'll be coming around."

During that first hour, as we passed cocktails, I played host, making jokes and taking pictures with the actors, hairdressers, makeup artists, and producers from the show. After we served dinner, Tracee brought me back out, talked about the importance of supporting Black-owned businesses, and congratulated me on the success of Alta. And in that moment, I loved it.

I'd almost tricked myself into believing I was that successful Black business owner she was talking about. But anytime I stopped to think on it, my anxiety spiked.

It wasn't paranoia. I had Black people in my comments on Instagram calling me out, saying, "You're not the owner, we looked up the documents, and it just has CIM and Daniel Patterson Group on it," and calling me the face of gentrification. Meanwhile, other Black folks were commenting back, supporting me, saying Alta *was* Black-owned. And the whole time, I was reading this shit like, *What the fuck have I gotten myself into?*

I kept telling myself that I would respond once I got the matter rectified. I always prided myself on knowing how to navigate situations in the streets and in prison, but out here, I was completely lost. I felt in my heart that the matter would eventually get fixed, but in the meantime, I didn't know what to do.

So, I started getting higher and higher and drunker and drunker.

Truly, I was more fearful over this situation than I ever was in the streets with people actually trying to kill me. This was worse than being locked up in Calipatria or even spooky-ass Folsom. But because I'd created the environment I now had to work in, I'd built my own fucking prison cell. Emotionally. Mentally. Physically. Spiritually.

In the past, I would've been selfish and angry and blown it all up, but I'd already seen from my experience at LocoL just how that affected everyone's else's jobs. Owner or not, as executive chef, I had a real responsibility to watch over the people working for me, especially because a lot of them had come with me from LocoL. I didn't want them to feel I was continually choosing myself over them. Plus, there were certain things I could rationalize. After all, Alta may not have been Black-owned, but it was Black-run. It gave a lot of Black people jobs in the community. That had to mean something, right?

So, instead of sabotaging the restaurant, I sabotaged myself. When the women of *Black-ish* left and the party was over, I did what I always did: went to my car, snorted cocaine, and tried to numb all that pain away.

17

Substance

AS I STRUGGLED TO HOLD IT TOGETHER, THE RESTAURANT KEPT getting busier. When we opened, my skills were still developing. It was a tough situation. I couldn't learn how to truly run a kitchen yet, because I was still stuck on perfecting basic shit like knife skills. Setting up a station. Showing up on time.

The trained chefs Daniel brought in to help weren't always that helpful. I could see that they didn't really care the way that I did, that they thought the food wasn't as challenging or important as the fancy shit they usually made. It pissed me off, and Daniel, too. He came to cover my days off every week, and every week he'd have to fix their mistakes. He wasn't hard on them like he was on me, though. He was trying to train me on cleaning and organizing walk-ins, ordering, prep sheets. How to wrap herbs in damp towels and cover the greens so they didn't dry out. Making sure that the meat vendor wasn't screwing us over on pricing or that the dishwasher remembered to clean the bathrooms before service or that the bar wasn't juicing citrus too far in advance. It was frustrating, because he was always on my ass. "You gotta learn the basics to be a good chef," he would always say. And though I knew he was right, I really hated him telling me how to do shit all the time.

One day, Daniel brought in his waterstone and showed me how to sharpen knives. Soak the stone first, then draw the knife across the stone at the right angle, scraping tiny bits of stone into a paste, which helped with the sharpening. I had a reference point.

"This sounds exactly like someone sharpening a shank on the concrete floor in prison," I told him. "When you heard that sound at night, you knew shit was going down the next day."

No matter how hard my schooling in the kitchen was, I still found joy in cooking for people. When the dining room was packed and the music was bumping, Alta was magic. I loved the dining counter next to the open kitchen, where people would sit and watch us cook. Every night it was like we were onstage. Sometimes when we fired an extra dish by mistake, I'd give it to someone sitting there, just like when I was on the line in the prison kitchen. We got a lot of first dates, and I could always tell when it wasn't going so well, so I'd try to crack jokes and make them smile to break the ice. I think I helped out a lot of relationships that way. But they weren't the only ones. That dining counter changed my life. It's how I met Renee.

I WAS COOKING ON A busy weeknight in the summer of 2019 when I noticed a beautiful Black woman and her friend sitting up at the chef's counter. The friend was loud, talking and flirting with everyone within range, but the other woman kept to herself. I was intrigued. Something about her looked familiar.

As I cooked, I started making small talk. When she told me she was into real estate, I offered to take her outside and show her all the new development around West Adams. While we were standing out on the sidewalk, I helped her step off the curb, and when she took my hand, I felt an electrical charge course through my body. Our magnetism was undeniable—at least on my end.

I asked her if she had a boyfriend.

She looked at me. "No."

"Well," I said. "You do now."

It was corny and juvenile, but that's what this woman did to me.

She gave me a look, her eyes narrowing a little, then reminded me that we'd met before. Two months earlier, she said, she'd come into Alta for the first time and asked me if the mac and cheese I was making was "white people mac and cheese or Black people mac and cheese."

Apparently, I'd responded, "You see a Black motherfucker cooking it, don't you?"

She didn't find that very charming.

The night we met again, she'd tried to convince her friend

to go somewhere else for dinner, saying, "That chef is so rude. There's a bunch of duds who work there."

Despite the rocky start, she ended up giving me her number, and we officially introduced ourselves. Her name was Renee. I wasn't trying to play any games or wait a certain number of days to call. That night, as soon as I got off my shift, I called. She told me she was watching a movie and that I could come over to her place to say hi. She lived in what she called "Historic View Park," which to me had always been Baldwin Hills, aka Black Beverly Hills. But Renee corrected me, explaining that View Park had its own specific history and prestige. Ray Charles, Ike and Tina Turner, and Nancy Wilson had all lived there.

When I got to her house, she introduced me to her big-ass pit bull, Enzo, which made it fucking hard to do any sort of relaxing, and she told me about herself. She grew up in a rural Southern California community called Fontana, on a big property with a bunch of cows, horses, and chickens. She and her younger sister would shoot rifles with their dad, who—I shit you not—was a lifelong correctional officer. She'd grown up conservative and religious—no makeup, no jewelry, no cussing, no smoking, no drinking. Her Seventh-Day Adventist parents were going on forty-three years of marriage and had raised their daughters to believe that the two worst things in the world were criminals and drugs. They had even voted for Reagan.

Renee had gone to college and gotten an MBA in finance. She was divorced with a daughter in college who was studying to go to medical school and a teenage son with special needs at home. Her ex-husband was a lawyer.

The more I learned about her, the more it felt like I didn't fit into her world at all. Plus, there was that pit bull. But, for some reason, Renee the person put me completely at ease. Within a half hour of being at her house, I was lying with my head on her lap, telling her my life story. I didn't leave anything out—except the drugs. I could tell her about hustling, but something in my gut convinced me that if she knew I was using now, she would be out. I couldn't risk it.

Over the next few months, as we started to date, my mood improved dramatically. I was no longer stewing in my anger and feeling sorry for myself. Renee set up and mediated meetings between me and Daniel to discuss Alta's ownership situation and helped me articulate my frustrations and expectations around the business—which helped secure a new deal giving me a percentage of the profit share when the restaurant started making money.

I went from floating around with no set address to living in Renee's beautiful house in View Park. This meant my daughter Cali could come stay with me more often, and she and Renee took to each other from the start. All this newfound stability balanced out some of the damage I kept on doing to myself with the drugs. I was still using and addicted, but my downward spiral seemed to be flattening out.

Until July.

One night, while I was at my mom's house, Tiffany somehow got ahold of Renee's cellphone number and called her. During that conversation, she told her all sorts of shit about me—which, thankfully, I'd mostly already told Renee. But then she started talking about the drugs. "Keith is a dopehead," Tiffany said. "He stays high off that stuff all day. He can't function without it."

Renee, figuring this was a woman-scorned situation, didn't

buy it. But Tiffany kept going in. "Test him if you don't believe me! Go test him right now!"

So, she did.

When she first called and told me what Tiffany had said, I denied everything. I figured she'd have to believe me over an angry ex. But Renee called my bluff. At eleven o'clock that night, she drove to a twenty-four-hour pharmacy, bought a drug test, and then showed up at my mother's house in Watts.

"Okay," she said to me when she got there, holding the bag. "Here's the test. Take it."

I was out of moves. "Wait," I said. "I did get high."

Renee was shattered. My mother tried to talk to her, tell her my addiction was a disease, something I could get through with treatment, but she just sat there in shock. She stayed up the entire night quietly crying, occasionally talking about how she felt she didn't really know me. It was July 15. The next day was Renee's birthday.

FOR THE NEXT SIX MONTHS, Renee tried to work with me to kick the drugs. She was regularly drug-testing me. She put me on her health insurance and enrolled me in an intensive outpatient program, but I got nothing from the classes. I barely went to them, and while there, I could feel myself checking out. Nothing clicked.

I used to tell her, "Look. I can do this shit on my own."

And I would try, but every time I got twenty-five, twenty-six, twenty-seven days clean, I'd crack and sneak off to buy drugs from my connect, not reappearing until many hours later. The honesty and vulnerability I had shown that first night we met, when I laid (almost) all my cards out on the table, had brought me closer to her than I'd ever been to anyone. But now I was defensive, frustrated that I couldn't change, and embarrassed to show her my weakness. I even started cheating on the drug tests in my own damn house. Renee was a successful professional woman used to finding solutions to problems, but I was a problem she couldn't solve.

It wasn't just that the drugs were fucking with our personal life. Renee could see me deteriorating professionally as well. Throughout the fall, she and Daniel conspired to try and get me into inpatient treatment, but I was too far gone. One day, we all sat at a picnic table on the back patio. I was furious, looking around at everyone I thought was trying to fuck me over. Daniel had a distant look, part angry, part sad. Like me, he could be a cold motherfucker when he had to be, and on this day, he got right to the point.

"You need to take a leave of absence," he said quietly. "You need to take care of yourself. Your job will be here when you come back."

I didn't believe him. I was sure this was just a cowardly way to fire me. I slammed my fist on the table and walked off.

I was past trying to get my shit together. And to be honest, I was done. I was done with the outpatient programs and the drug testing and even with pretending I was going to overcome this shit. Without a job to report to each day, any threads of normalcy and stability in my life slipped out of my grip. This was now beyond self-sabotage. I was human napalm, engulfing everything in my life in my anguish, self-pity, and addiction— fucking with Renee's money by overdrawing from her accounts; embarrassing her in front of her friends; coming in and out of the house all night, bug-eyed, talking fast, and sweating; show-ing no regard for anything.

I was back on my "the world has fucked me, so fuck the world" bullshit. It was the same feeling I'd had after Truett was killed, and when I was on the run from the police after the record store robbery—except, this time, I was supposed to be a grown-ass man, a professional, a father.

I thought I was low, but I wouldn't hit bottom until the night of March 6, 2020.

AT FIRST, I DECIDED I would do just a little bit.

I did a bump or two before I got in the house. Renee could tell I was high, and at this point, she wasn't angry and she wasn't yelling. She was done.

She sat me down and calmly told me that she couldn't be in a relationship with me anymore, that I was taking everything from her and giving nothing in return, that I was bringing her down with me.

I got loud, but she never raised her voice. She looked beyond sad. Numb. Emptied out. "Right now," she said, "I have to love me more than I love you."

Hearing us arguing, Cali came into the room. I wanted to leave, to get out of there, to go get high, but Cali didn't want to let me go. She was tugging on me. "Daddy, just lay down with me, or take me with you."

I looked at her. "All right," I said. "Let's take a ride."

I put her in the car and drove her around, thinking she might fall asleep. But she stayed awake. Kids aren't stupid; they can sense when things are off, and she could probably feel my manic energy. There was no way she would relax enough to sleep. We kept driving. At some point, she started pleading with me.

"Daddy, let's just go to sleep before the sun comes up." This was a four-year-old telling me this. "Can we please go in the house before the sun comes up?"

But, no. First, I had to stop by my connect, so I could grab more drugs. When I got back to the house, Cali still wouldn't go to sleep. Now I really couldn't sit still. I was fidgety as a motherfucker. I called Tiffany and told her, "I'm gonna bring Cali to see you. You can spend some time with her while I go hang out."

It was two in the morning.

The whole ride over, Cali still wouldn't sleep. I realize now that she could feel I was troubled, and that made her afraid, afraid to close her eyes because, if she let me out of her sight, who knew what would happen?

Before I got to Tiffany's house, something told me to stop. Whatever flicker of reason was left in my body told me I needed to take Cali back to Renee's. So, I went back and dropped her off with Renee, but I still wasn't ready to stop chasing my high. I kept driving, and on the freeway, I had a panic attack. I couldn't stop shaking, pulling the steering wheel from side to side. Scared I'd get pulled over and be sent back to jail, I turned the car around and, once again, went back to Renee's house.

This was what it had come to. I had exposed my daughter to this shit. She was the one I was supposed to be fighting for, the reason I was working, improving myself, so I could give her a better life. And what had I done? I'd chosen drugs. Over my own daughter.

I couldn't live with it anymore. I screamed and hollered and broke. I didn't break down. I broke open. The tears I cried came from a place inside me that I had spent my whole life sealing off. It wasn't catharsis. It was pain.

Finally, I asked for help.

"I can't do it myself," I told Renee. "It's too much. I can't do it. I need help. Help me. Please. Help me."

She told me she would, but that it wouldn't be for me. It would be for my daughter.

I could live with that.

THE HILLS TREATMENT CENTER LOOKS like a mansion because it is one. Set on three acres up on a bluff in the Laurel Canyon section of the Hollywood Hills, it's like the estate in *The Fresh Prince of Bel Air*, but with more white people. The Hills has hosted a who's who of famous people with addiction issues: Mike Tyson, Lindsay Lohan, and, as of March 2020, Keith Corbin from the Jordan Downs projects in Watts.

When Renee dropped me there a couple of days later, there was no hug, no goodbye. She just looked at the counselor who met us at the car and asked if we were good. When he told her they'd take it from there, she was out.

As the counselor walked me inside, I felt like I was watching myself in a movie. After the last forty-eight hours, I had no more emotions left. But when they took my phone and told me I wasn't going to get it back for seventy-two hours, as I "refocused," I felt my anxiety spike again. I *needed* my phone. I *needed* to reconnect with the outside world. More than anything, I *needed* to talk to Renee. So, using some of my old prison tactics, I ducked into someone's room and convinced them to let me borrow theirs.

Panicked, I called Renee.

When she heard it was me on the line, she wasn't happy. "How are you even calling me right now?"

Renee would tell me later that I sounded desperate. Scared. I have no idea what I said to her on that call, but it was probably me at my most honest.

My time at the Hills was all about routines. One day bled into the next. Physically, I felt weak and tired. I felt old. The place may've looked fancy, but it was another prison—though the food there was better than in the other institutions I'd been in. During my stay, I had a hard time turning off my chef's brain. At each meal, I found myself evaluating the food critically, wondering why the potatoes were oversalted, or the green goddess dressing too saucy. Part of the problem was the inconsistency: the Hills had two chefs. The chef at breakfast was excellent, but the chef at dinner was horrible. And because I can never just sit back and not try to take a leadership role anywhere I'm at, I lobbied for the staff to let me work in the kitchen with him and cook a couple of dinners a week. (Or, to fire his ass and let me take his job.) Other patients even circulated a petition to get me hired.

Two weeks in, I had a pass to go home on a Sunday from noon to six P.M. Renee and Cali came to pick me up. We went shopping to get some zoom zooms and wham whams, and I even drove over to Inglewood by myself to get a haircut. During the drive, I thought of almost nothing but getting high. The temptation was intense.

When I came home and sat down for dinner with my family, I started to get itchy. I could feel myself wanting to go out again. I could feel the excuses in my brain start to take hold.

In the middle of dinner, I stood up. "You know what?" I said. "I'm just gonna go back and check myself in before it gets too late."

"Now?" Renee asked.

"Yeah," I said. "Now."

Forty-five minutes later, I was back at the Hills.

The only other time in my life I'd been voluntarily locked up was when Branden was killed while I was in prison—but that was my family telling the guards to do that for my own good. This time, it was me. And considering how much I hate feeling penned in, it spoke to just how badly I wanted to beat my addiction that I returned to rehab early.

AFTER THAT, I REALLY STARTED to put in the work. I took the classes and learned about all the ways drugs flip your brain and how long it takes to heal. I went to all the group therapy sessions and, just like at LocoL, had no problem telling my story. I appreciated how the counselors and the other patients seemed to connect to my experience in ways they found helpful.

Truth be told, though, my actual saving grace was the COVID-19 pandemic. For one thing, it shut everything down and made it so I didn't have to think about any of the restaurant stuff. At the time, there was no restaurant to think of. Along with everything else in the country, Alta had been temporarily closed. With the world truly paused, I had nothing else to do but think of myself.

During that time, Daniel called to check in. I was surprised to hear from him, and even more surprised when he asked when I was coming back. I really thought I was gone for good. We

talked about the lockdown and when we might see a government relief check. He thought by the end of April we could be
back in action. I told him I'd be there.

"Are you sure it's not going to be too much stress?" he
asked.

"Yeah," I said, like I always did. But this time I meant it.

Another way the pandemic helped me find the tools to fight
my addiction was through an unexpected angle: butting heads
with the Hills administrators.

Normally, these frustrations would've pushed me to go get
high, but in rehab, I had to face them head-on and deal with
them sober. And I truly am thankful for that. If the entire time
I was at the Hills had been smooth sailing, as I took classes and
therapy in a beautiful facility overlooking a canyon, it wouldn't
have prepared me in any way for my real life. But being forced
into conflict battle-tested my sobriety.

And then, forty-two days in, I got kicked out.

At this point, it was only a matter of time. So, when the
coordinator brought me into his office to let me know I was
being discharged, I stood up and informed him that there was
no point in going through all the formalities.

Then, as politely as possible, I swore at his ass and told him
I'd see him on the streets.

I was out.

A FEW DAYS LATER, I went back to Alta and started working
alongside Daniel and Gwen, doing takeout and fulfilling contracts to feed frontline workers through a community-based
initiative Daniel started with Saru called High Road Kitchens.

I also used the opportunity to restart my relationship with Daniel as we worked side by side each day, fine-tuning and tweaking the restaurant. Our smaller size meant that everything needed to be more organized and streamlined, and it felt good to throw myself into something. We revamped our fried chicken, upgrading the chicken itself to the same shit the most expensive fine-dining restaurants use. We moved the grill to make room for another fryer. We put a smoker out back, and developed a smoked brisket cured in a salt and spice rub and served with our own apple barbecue sauce, which has become one of our most popular dishes. We simplified our sides. I even changed the mac and cheese.

But it wasn't just the menu. In the kitchen, our dynamic changed, too. Now when we developed recipes, I noticed that Daniel was looking to get my input as he worked his way through it, instead of showing me his steps after the fact. Eventually I started to run the creative process on my own, getting feedback only when I needed it.

Once I had a certain level of control in the kitchen, I could finally truly invest in learning the other aspects of running a restaurant.

WHILE I WAS BATTLING MY drug addiction and so absorbed in my own struggles, I hadn't noticed that Daniel was going through his own shit. He'd made bad decisions with business partners, and as his businesses failed, so did other aspects of his life. His wife divorced him, and the dudes who lent him money took over his company. When he came back to reopen Alta during the pandemic, he did it as an employee. It was ironic that he ended up in the same place I'd started, doing owner shit, but not being an owner.

We both worked our asses off and started building the business back up a little at a time. Daniel was working in the front as a line cook, and I was running the back kitchen. For the first time in my career, I felt like I was in control of my own destiny. Every day we did an emotional check-in before service with the team, where everyone could share how they were feeling. Most of the time I answered with one word: motivated.

A MONTH OR SO LATER, I was driving on Crenshaw when I saw a big, fit Black dude in his late forties carrying himself like he was not to be fucked with. He was on the phone. I pulled up alongside him and rolled down my window.

"*As-salaam-alaikum.*"

He put his phone down and turned toward the car. Before he could even see inside, he responded, "*Wa-alaikum-salaam, my brother.*" Then he recognized me, and the expression on his face changed. And in that moment, I knew it was really him.

"What up, Shaq?"

Standing in front of me was my old mentor from Calipatria State Prison, Tobias Tubbs, aka Shaq. Last I'd seen him, he'd been serving two life sentences for murder without the possibility of parole. But, as he explained to me, in 2017 Governor Jerry Brown commuted his sentence to twenty-five to life, and the following year, he was granted parole. I wasn't surprised. Shaq was and still is a force of nature. This was a dude who ran an entire prison kitchen, commanding so much respect that inmates of all races followed his lead even when he wasn't physically there. If anyone could rehabilitate themselves and earn a release from prison through willpower and discipline, it was Tobias Tubbs.

I got out of the car, and we kicked it for a bit. Shaq told me he was now a motivational speaker, visiting prisons and schools all over California. After that first random run-in, we started hanging on a regular basis.

Shaq's not the only one from my time in prison I get to see again. QT and Tiny Wood Rat are out now, too, and both have good jobs driving big rigs all over the country. Every once in a while, we'll all get together. There's something genuinely comforting about the four of us chopping it up over a meal like we used to.

Except, this time, the food is a lot fucking better.

BECAUSE OF COVID, MY FORTIETH birthday didn't take place in my restaurant. I wasn't wearing a tuxedo. We didn't pop bottles of champagne. I just invited some friends and family over, and we ate takeout, then went outside to kick it. Montana, the twins, and my brothers Marlon, Kevin, and Gerald were all there. Out on the porch, the conversations got deep. We talked about love. We talked about trauma. And we talked about the life transitions everyone went through as they tried to figure out what to do now. We'd grown up on some different shit, and were the lucky few who made it out.

Because I'd had to make a change in my life to survive, I often felt separated from the people I grew up with, so seeing all of my brothers and homies on similar paths was dope. I remember looking at Montana and Marlon, both thriving and happy, and it made me think about that morning outside the Nickersons, when I'd decided not to get out of the car. That decision saved at least five lives, including my own.

Then, as if on cue, the universe tested me again. Our cell-phones all started buzzing at the same time. My little cousin (Branden's nephew), a promising high school athlete, had just been shot in Watts. It was random, not directed at him specifi-cally, but at the time we didn't know that. I saw my homies' reflexes take over. Violence called for retaliation. The energy in the place changed as they got up and paced around, making calls, getting ready to leave. I wasn't going anywhere, though. I told them I was staying out of it, and reminded them of every-thing they had to lose by getting involved. They thought on it and decided to stay out of it, too.

I don't know if that was the fortieth birthday present I thought I'd get, but I was glad to take it.

WHEN WE REOPENED IN 2020, we lost money for a year while we focused much of our energy on feeding people in need, but it paid off. Our work in the community during the pandemic helped us stay connected, and when we were finally able to open at full capacity, we became busier than ever. One of the most rewarding aspects of reopening has been seeing the ways the clientele has and has not changed. During our initial opening as a hot new "best restaurant" in the city, people from all over L.A. came to check us out—and we were happy about that. But, as we knew from LocoL, those one-off patrons weren't going to keep our doors open. Now the majority of the custom-ers were either regulars from the neighborhood or Black professionals and creatives from across the city, who all thought of Alta as "their" restaurant.

What we didn't expect was how many people wanted to throw parties here. At the height of the pandemic, we were desperate for more outside seating, so Daniel applied for a permit to build a parklet. When the city came to mark off the area, I convinced them to let us take a ninety-foot space on the quiet side street, next to the restaurant. We built a beautiful, shaded structure that felt like an extension of the patio, connected to it by an open door. And as soon as we opened it up, we started booking events. We hosted private parties for Issa Rae, Lena Waithe, the cast of *Grand Crew* on NBC. We cooked at wrap parties for *Black-ish* on ABC, and *Insecure* on HBO. There was even a *Hollywood Reporter* story detailing how Alta "became Black Hollywood's top restaurant for power dining." We had three Black couples get engaged while eating at the restaurant, *and* we hosted a wedding. I'd always wanted my restaurant to be a place to party, but the fact that it seemed like *the* place to party made me feel so damn proud.

When we finally opened again for good in the spring of 2021, I was fully engaged. I knew how to run the kitchen, cook every station, wait tables, even seat the floor. After a few false starts, I began to put together the team we have now. Each of them is talented and smart, and excited about the restaurant. That middle management, team-building shit? Well, it was actually starting to work. Alvaro, Rae, and Pete putting dishes on the menu. Rashad running the drinks program, Jaela selling wine, Asia charming everyone in the place. We changed the tip share so that all our hourly employees make at least $25 an hour. We continued promoting from within, and we not only kept the great vibe we always had, but we gained better teamwork and a higher level of performance and commitment.

I never thought I'd use the shit I learned in the gang intervention training, but it had a lot in common with how Daniel had set up our HR systems: finding solutions, not blaming; de-escalating emotional situations and letting people cool off before approaching them. It didn't work for me when I was younger, but now I was starting to see how effective it was with the team. Now I'm the guy making sure that they take breaks, that the schedule is fair, that everyone stays on their game. I show the cooks how to fix their mistakes when they burn something, and how to properly put away greens in the walk-in. It's given me empathy for what Daniel went through with me. When people don't show up or fall short, it puts extra pressure on the team. But I have empathy for the team, too, because I've failed in more ways than they can imagine.

Of course, there were still some really tough moments. After Coi closed, Daniel convinced his friend Ruben Morancy, the master sommelier who ran the wine program there, to move to Los Angeles. Originally from Haiti, Ruben moved to the States in his youth, and would go on to spend decades in the wine business. He loved what we had created at Alta, and he brought his passion for great wine and service, teaching the staff and elevating our standards over the next year and a half.

As a Black man in a very white industry, Ruben saw how Black customers were always left out of wine marketing and education. For the last few years, he'd been working on plans to help change that, and in a way the pandemic gave him just the right opportunity. We couldn't use the coffee shop next to the restaurant, so he suggested that we turn it into a wine shop. It was a brilliant idea. We called it Adams Wine Shop, and Ruben created a selection focused on BIPOC and women winemakers. Our customers loved it. By the summer of 2021, we were taking meetings with developers about opening more of them around the city. Ruben would run the shops as an owner. It was his dream come true.

One day at the beginning of October 2021, Ruben didn't show up for work and wasn't answering his phone. Worried, I went over to his house in Culver City to check on him and was devastated to find him in his bed, passed away from natural causes. Ruben was such a beautiful human, always with a kind, thoughtful word for anyone who came into his shop. I still feel his loss as I'm writing this now.

In the weeks that followed, Daniel and I partnered to put together a celebration of Ruben's life. More and more, after I came out of rehab, he and I were finding ways to collaborate successfully. I always told him we'd take over L.A. together, but it wasn't until I was sober and he was living here that things really started to come together. We'd worked with Snoop Dogg's business partners on a Red Ranch hot sauce and had developed an apple barbecue sauce and seasoning mix to sell in grocery stores.

Daniel jokes that, because of the way I've progressed, I no longer need him around, but that's not what it's about for me. If you ride with me, and show loyalty, I will ride with you. Say what you want about me and all my faults, I am loyal. I was loyal to my generation, and I'm loyal to the people with me. So, you can fuck up—hell, you *will* fuck up, because we all do—and I will still ride with you. Because I know there's going to be a time when I'm fucking up, too, when I'm not getting accolades and am not in the news, when I'm going through a rough patch fighting my addictions. It's during that time when you figure out who your people are. And Daniel is one of my people. That's just how it is.

After I was back from rehab, I asked him why he stayed with me through everything, when he should've cut me loose so many times.

"A lot of experience being on the wrong end of abusive relationships," he laughed. Then he thought for a minute. "I don't know, partly it was the strength of our relationship. I just couldn't walk away and see you back on the streets. I guess I thought with all the shit you went through that maybe you deserved extra chances to figure it out. I know it was a stupid idea. I know I artificially advanced you and it stressed you out. But I saw something special in you."

"Yeah," I said. "But that's a bad bet. Most people don't make it."

He shrugged. "You did."

In April 2021, my ownership in Alta was finally made official. With Daniel's encouragement, CIM, which owns 50 percent of Alta, came through with an operating agreement giving me an actual ownership stake as a fully vested partner, not contingent on my employment, with the flexibility to sell my share of the company back if I ever want to leave.

So, now, when someone asks me if Alta is Black-owned, I can look them right in the eye and say, "Hell, yes. Welcome to my restaurant."

18

I Do This

ON JUNE 17, 2020, MY FATHER, SAMUEL CORBIN, WAS MURDERED. He'd been living in an RV in the driveway of my aunt's house in Compton, and that night, he borrowed her car to drive to the bodega a couple blocks from her house for a soda. After getting his drink, he was almost back home when someone pulled up next to him in a truck and emptied their pistol through the driver's-side window, killing my father. He was seventy-six years old.

As soon as I heard, I drove to the scene of the crime and spent the next few hours talking to detectives, trying to piece together what had happened so I could update my family. After many hours and no definitive answers, I watched them load the white bag containing my father's body into the coroner's van and then drove to Alta to start my morning prep. I tried to bury myself in my work, but I couldn't shake the feeling that, even as other things change, death would never let me go.

My father's murder still hasn't been solved, but the working theory is that it was a case of mistaken identity. After all, nothing was stolen from him. His days in the streets had long since passed. He was a threat to no one. Where I'm from, if you make it to his age, you've earned the peaceful dignity of an old man's death. Yet, even by street standards, his killing seemed unusually cold. My father had already been dying. He was sick with multiple forms of cancer related to his exposure to Agent Orange in Vietnam. Hell, he was pissing into a colostomy bag. But it wasn't just his body that was in pain.

The year before, his youngest son, Joshua Glover, was killed. Josh was thirteen years younger than me. He'd been raised primarily in the Springdale projects in Long Beach, by his mother, who was white. He'd been living in Las Vegas at the time of his death, but had come back to visit my father in Compton and gone out to a dice game. While there, he got into an argument, was stabbed multiple times, placed in a wheelchair, and left by a bus stop to bleed out. By the time an ambulance came, there was nothing more that could be done. Josh was dead. He was twenty-five.

When my sister called to tell me Josh had been killed, the first person I thought of was my father. That was his baby boy, and it had always bothered him that he couldn't reach Josh in the way he had his other sons. He knew Josh was getting in trouble, which was why he'd sent him to Vegas in the first place. My father was a realist. He'd been in the streets, he'd seen his other sons in the streets. It wasn't that he thought he could save him, but he knew Josh didn't have the same support system around him as his other kids, so he tried to intervene as much as he could. Even the last time he saw Josh alive, he'd told him, "Don't go back up there around that gambling house." But sure enough, on the last visit, that was the first thing he did. And when he got killed because of that decision, I think something in my father broke.

In the days leading up to Josh's funeral, my father had been quiet. This wasn't like him. He was Big Sam, big in stature and personality, a man who was always talking and teaching. That day was the first time in my life I ever saw my father cry.

After Josh's murder, I'd been seeing my father more frequently than in the past. I could tell he was suffering and in pain, but he never wanted to talk about that. You'd ask him how he was doing, and he'd always turn the conversation around to you, your plans, the future. He stayed positive. He'd always been the father you wanted, according to your needs. If you needed him to listen, he was there to give his ear. If you needed counsel, he was there to speak. And if you didn't need him around, he wasn't.

As one of his kids who didn't spend a lot of my childhood with him, who didn't get him before Vietnam changed him, I harbored resentment and envy toward my older siblings. It took dealing with my situation with my oldest son to recognize that it wasn't always so simple, that I couldn't just blame Big Sam for being an absentee dad. Maybe he'd wanted to play a bigger role in my life. Of course, we never talked directly about these things, but being on the other side of it made me appreciate him more.

For his funeral, I tried to take the lead on making sure all his kids were included and involved in every aspect. We had a beautiful service at my brother Bo's church in Los Angeles. It invigorated me to hear all the kind words and good stories being told about my dad. The mayor of Compton gave the family a certificate on behalf of the city for Big Sam's service to the community. As a decorated war hero, my father received military honors at his burial. His casket was draped in an American flag, which was then folded and presented to the family. The military detail shot rifles into the air and concluded the ceremony with taps.

Big Sam's name rang out through both the Hub and the Dub. To this day, the old heads refer to me as "Big Sam's son." I'm still hearing stories about my father that I've never heard before. After talking to my mother, I now see parallels between how I was feeling and how she felt after my Granny's death. Granny was finally able to let go only after my mother was sober, when she knew she could safely entrust her with the keys to the family. Obviously, my father didn't choose to go out the way he did, but he and I had been close to the end of his life, and in our final conversations, I could sense that my newfound sobriety and stability gave him comfort. In his own way, I think he was letting me know he had confidence in me. It was time for me to hold the keys.

ON JANUARY 22, 2022, MY son Samuel Benjamin Corbin was born.

Less than two years earlier, the idea that I'd be having

another child seemed really fucking unlikely. When Renee dropped me at rehab, she had every intention of also dropping me for good. That wasn't me reading the tea leaves; she'd said as much. But I was desperate to change her mind, and not just because I needed her strength and support to get through rehab. Ever since I took her hand as she stepped down from the curb that day at Alta, I felt we had this instant connection, something so spiritual that it almost felt like divine intervention. Not having her in my life wasn't an option for me, which was why I resorted to prison tricks to secure a phone and call her that first day at the Hills. She was my lifeline.

Throughout my time in rehab, Renee and I did couples counseling over Zoom, using my counselor at the Hills to facilitate. Renee was able to express her hurt and frustration, and with the counselor as referee, I finally learned to really hear her without getting defensive, feeling attacked, or attacking back.

This gave us the head start we needed so that, when I returned from rehab, we wouldn't be starting from the place where we left off. Due to COVID-19 restrictions and the lockdown imposed, Renee had taken care of Cali the entire time I was away. Seeing her show so much love and care for a child who was not hers, while also taking care of her own special-needs son, made me see her not just as a woman I wanted to be with, but as someone to have a family with.

Upon my return from rehab, I moved back in with Renee, and we began slowly rebuilding our relationship. Throughout our struggles, she'd always said there were glimpses of me that were so loving and caring, that no one had ever been as real or as vulnerable with her as I was that first night we met, when I put my head in her lap and the story of my life poured out.

Renee had always wanted to have another child, and as I started to see my own future taking shape clear of drugs, I wanted that with her. Taking care of Cali and Renee's son, Kaleb, together, we could see I had become more capable. Because Kaleb has a hard time communicating, especially when he's upset, he has taught me to be vigilant for other types of cues and more aware of what other people might be carrying. When I drop him off at school each morning, I can't help but feel ashamed about how I used to tease kids at school who I thought were not as smart or capable as me. There was no room for compassion in the person I had to be at such a young age. But being around Kaleb has changed all that.

When Renee got pregnant and we found out it was a boy, I was overjoyed. And considering the loss of my father and the major role Renee's grandfather Samuel had played in her life, we both knew instantly what the perfect name would be.

But the journey to pregnancy was difficult for us. We tried naturally but had two miscarriages, so we started IVF. It was incredibly expensive and intensive. Renee had to take shots at all hours and monitor everything. And even after all that, the first implementation failed. Then we had a third miscarriage. We did another round and had another miscarriage, but we both wanted a child together so badly that we kept going. When it finally worked, we felt our faith had been rewarded.

Of course, another part of me was terrified. We'd had so many miscarriages that there was this sitting fear that at any moment we might lose this baby. I've never done so much baby-sitting before I had a baby to sit. There were special pillows. Certain ways to lay. And you best believe there was no sex.

But when that doctor pulled Samuel out, and I heard my

son cry, it was a moment of relief like I'd never felt before. I didn't cry in the moment, but I think there are tears back there just waiting to come out. Before he was delivered, we filled out a list for the hospital of what we wanted, and I wanted to cut the umbilical cord. I'd never done that before. In my three previous experiences having kids, there was a lot I'd never done. A lot I wasn't proud of.

But I know that with Samuel, I want to raise him different. Just like the way I felt when my oldest brothers would describe my father before Vietnam, I want Samuel to not recognize the stories his older siblings tell about his father. With my other children, I dreamt about doing things in another way, but I didn't know how to, what that meant. But this time I do. Having a partner like Renee has been crucial to that. She just thinks differently.

We stayed in the hospital with Samuel for two extra days just to ensure we got all the information possible, all the proper nurturing and lactation training, and we talked to all the doctors. We want to set ourselves up for success. If there is a thing to be done, we're going to do it. I'm taking paternity leave right now, so I make sure I'm bonding with him. I usually have the night shift, which I've discovered is a lot more difficult when you don't have a drug keeping you awake. But I'll just put on Anita Baker and rock him, stare at him, rub noses and cheeks, massage his feet, and pray the love I have inside is pouring into him.

I want him to be happy. To enjoy his childhood. To experience all his life progression and changes as they should be. I want him to walk in his time. I don't want him to move faster than life says he should. I don't need him to think he's grown at thirteen.

A few months before Samuel was born, we'd sold Renee's place in View Park and bought in Westwood. Surrounded by Brentwood, Bel-Air, Beverly Hills, and a bunch of bougie country clubs, Westwood was only twenty miles from Watts, but as far as I was concerned, it might as well have been on another planet.

It's a trip to think that that's going to be the only home Samuel will know.

Before I had Samuel, I never realized there was prep to do before a child was born. It's no different from planting something—even before you lay the seed, you need to pull the weeds and till the ground to set it up for success. On top of that, you have to pay attention to the seasons. Yes, you can grow something out of season, but it won't be at its best. Try to grow a summer fruit in the winter, and it'll struggle under the harder light. It's the same way with kids.

With Keith Jr., Keivionna, and even Cali, I wasn't tilling the ground, pulling the weeds, or planting in the right season. Now, because I'm in the season of my life where I'm clean, focused, driven, and financially prepared to have a kid, that imbalance eats at me. I can't change who I was at the time, but I can recognize that it wasn't fair to my first three kids.

The Bible says the children will not pay for the sins of their father, but looking at my own kids, I believe they're suffering for them. As a young man living in Texas, Keith Jr. was incarcerated for a few years. He's out now and living close to San Antonio, but we don't have much of a relationship, at least not in the way I wish we did.

Keivionna is nineteen, living in Long Beach, and every bit as hardheaded as I was at the same age. When I try to kick game to her about staying out of the streets, she just comes back asking me how I can even say that, considering the life I've lived. And she's not wrong. Even after she was shot in the leg during a drive-by at a party in Compton last year, her opinion has not changed.

Even my youngest daughter, Cali, has suffered. Though we're trying to give her every opportunity to succeed now—sending her to a great charter school, filling her after-school schedule with voice lessons, acting classes, gymnastics, all those activities I would never even have known about a couple years ago—I still see her struggling. I watch her falling behind her classmates academically, needing tutors just to keep her head above water, and I wish I'd given her a better foundation.

The other night, Cali had a dream in which she was flying. Not just flying, but jumping from roof to roof, then falling into a deep pool of water. It was strange. I used to have almost the exact same dream as a kid, over and over—though I loved waking up before the falling part. I would just be soaring.

That's what I want for my kids moving forward. I want to establish a legacy. In a movie I remember watching as a kid, an old man builds a gate along his property line. At one point, his grandson asks why he's doing it, considering they have no live-stock or anything to keep in. The grandfather looks at his grandson and says, "I'm building this gate for you."

I think about that grandfather all the time. I want to build that gate. I want my portrait on the wall above a fireplace in a house our family has owned for generations and has passed down, because I want my grandkids and their grandkids to know that their grandfather started something that has been sustained, that he built something that lasted. I don't want their dreams to end with them falling. I want them to fucking soar.

WE KNEW THE WHITE PEOPLE were coming when they changed the name.

It first started happening way back in 2003, when the L.A. City Council voted to change "South Central" to "South Los Angeles." But no one except real estate agents and the media paid it any mind. Since then, I haven't heard a single person from South Central refer to it that way. You can't rebrand history.

They said they wanted to change the name because there was a stigma attached to "South Central," because that name scared away investment. What they were actually saying was that it scared away *white* investment. It wasn't the first time they tried this shit, either. The casino in Compton *still* tries to claim it's in "Crystal City."

But now, with the L.A. Metro's Crenshaw Line opening up and the NFL stadium in Inglewood, the floodgates are finally open. As of 2020, Inglewood had more than half a dozen separate townhome and condo projects in development, with starting prices at around $900K. Baldwin Hills Crenshaw Plaza sold in August 2021, to the local developer Harridge Development Group, for around $140 million. White people are even jogging on Crenshaw.

Of course, being from Watts, I didn't think anything of the name change or any of this. I figured Watts was gentrification-proof. The last frontier. But they're finally coming for Watts, too, starting with a name change for Jordan Downs.

"Cedar Grove at Jordan Downs" is the first phase of the Housing Authority's billion-dollar redevelopment plan. The Jordan Downs I knew is being demolished. The new version will be "mixed-use, mixed-income," with double the housing. Cedar Grove is now open and has all the development buzzwords you can handle: *LEED Silver certification . . . maximizes solar opportunities . . . environmental sustainability . . . a vibrant urban village.* There will be new green spaces, a bank branch on-site, and that field I used to sleep out in with the bats is being redesigned as a community park with barbecues.

The old factory where I knocked holes in the wall is now Jordan Downs Freedom Plaza. This past year, they opened a Nike store, a Starbucks, a fitness center, and a 31,000-square-foot grocery store. In the press release on the L.A. Housing Authority website, they celebrated the opening of the grocery store as evidence of Watts's "no longer being a food desert after 30 years." Guess they forgot about LocoL.

Part of me is sad. That's to be expected. Anyone would be sad if they saw the place that held their history and shaped their identity being wiped away. But I'm not trying to pretend that nostalgia for my youth is more important than improving Watts—Watts, and Jordan Downs, *should* be improved. I'm just trying to figure out whom they're improving it *for*.

When my grandparents came to Southern California during World War II, business was booming. There were plenty of jobs paying real money, and my grandparents and their friends were happy to use that hard-earned money to live in nice communities wherever they pleased. All the Black people didn't *have* to stay together. Maybe some of us wanted to be by the beach, or others preferred the hills. But those weren't options.

None of those communities would let us in. We *had* to live in South Central.

So, we tried to make it work. We tried to make Compton into a nice, professional-class Black suburb, but when the white people left, the banks stopped loaning, and none of our development plans was approved. We succeeded in making Sugar Hill our own beautiful neighborhood, filled with rich Black people, but they put a freeway through it and blew it all up.

So, can you *really* blame me for being a little less trusting when white people, well meaning though they may seem, start coming into our communities making promises?

No one is going to argue *against* better housing or increased access to hourly wage jobs. But that shit is Revitalization 101. That's the most basic package, and yet it always seems to be the only one we're offered. And we take it. But when you take something that's offered, it's not really yours. We're trying to own our futures. But we can't if our only option is to rent them from you.

We're tired of being just employees. We want to be partners. We want something tangible, something to be able to pass down, something generational. Working in a Starbucks is a nice start, but how about *owning* a Starbucks? Or the plaza housing the Starbucks?

They say, "Give a man a fish, you feed him for a day, but teach a man to fish, and you feed him for a lifetime." Fuck that. Keep your fish. I want the contracts to sell all the fishing licenses at that lake.

ABOUT SIX MONTHS AFTER ALTA first opened, a server came back to the kitchen and said that two white men had requested to speak to the chef. I came out, and they introduced themselves as Rick Moses and Jeff Appel. They told me they loved their meal and were building something in Culver City involving restaurants. Rick, I found out, had restored downtown's Grand Central Market in 2013.

"Give us a call," Jeff said, handing me a card. "We'd love to talk to you about a potential opportunity."

Two weeks later, I called. They told me more about their plans to build the first food hall in Culver City, in the Citizens Publishing Company Building—and that they wanted a Keith Corbin restaurant in it. I called it Louella's Cali Soul, a fast, casual spot serving up bowls and sandwiches, named after my Granny, of course.

While I was still in the drug game, the planning for Louella's happened in fits and starts. Sometimes Daniel was in and sometimes he was too fed up. But by the summer of 2020, we were back to the original plan—do everything together. While we were in the kitchen cooking at Alta, we went into full creative mode. With the failures of LocoL in mind, we decided to keep the menu simple and fast to execute. Sandwiches, sides, and salads. A lot of the new items came out of our cooking at Alta. A perfected version of the fried chicken. The smoked brisket with apple barbecue sauce. A marinated, smoked, and fried tofu sandwich with spicy tartar sauce and slaw that I think is the best vegetarian sandwich around. And a purple sweet potato soup, aromatic from ginger, lime, and cilantro; sweet with coconut milk; and energized with a fiery kick of habaneros. As it came together, we realized that in a way we'd discovered, five years later, a menu that would have killed it at LocoL.

Citizen Public Market officially opened for business at the

end of 2020. It was beautiful, with wood floors flown in from a French farmhouse and eateries from big names like Nancy Silverton. On paper, it was a great opportunity for me, but Louella's lasted only five months before the landlords and I mutually agreed to part ways. I'm thankful for the opportunity I was given, but I wasn't in the right season (or neighborhood, really) to open my second place. Since then, I've realized that, if I'm going to open another place cooking California soul food like my Granny's, I need to be back home. I need to be in Watts. I can't think of anything better than paying homage *to* the place I grew up *in* the place I grew up.

To that end, Daniel and I are in the process of leasing space in Jordan Downs Freedom Plaza in the hope of opening a new Louella's. The idea is to make a hybrid of the community-driven ethos of LocoL with the cool vibe and delicious food of Alta. Now that I've gotten the experience and the actual cooking chops, I can already picture it. I've been spending a lot of time in my garden, working with vegetable and spice seeds from Africa, seeing if I can cultivate them here. What I'd really love is to have some version of a live garden *at* this new Louella's, so guests can pick herbs and spices and add them to their dishes the same way you might add salt or pepper or chile flakes. I want them to understand the difference between farm-to-table and having a farm right next to your table. I want a place my Granny would've been proud to come to for her birthday. And you best believe we're gonna have cake, motherfuckers.

A FEW WEEKS AGO, I was at Alta when I got a FaceTime call from the big homie Nardo. When I saw all the fellas he was with, I realized that it was BE-K's birthday, and I told them, "I'm on my way."

Once I'd finished up work, I got in my truck and drove the fourteen miles on the 10 and the 110 to a house across from Jordan Downs, on Grape Street. I double-parked and put my hazards on. I was planning to stay just long enough to show respect and pay tribute to BE-K.

All the fellas were there: Nardo, Bolo, Bow Wow, Moe-C, and Miney. They had a propane griddle to cook up carne asada and ground beef and to griddle tortillas for gringo tacos. Everyone was outside kicking it, drinking, smoking, and, in some cases, snorting.

When I told them I was sober now, they respected that—though, of course, they also had to give me shit. "Nigga, you couldn't go one day without snorting, and you're clean? *You?*"

I was supposed to stay for only a couple of minutes, but before I knew it, it had been nearly two hours, and I was still in the mix, telling old war stories and chopping it up. It was so easy to be around homies I'd known for decades, doing what we'd been doing since we were kids. Those men are my brothers. We've been through too much shit together. You can't replace that.

But, at the same time, I felt out of place, a little uncomfortable. For one thing, I was exposed, putting myself at risk, hanging around dudes with drugs and guns, not knowing when or if some shit might pop off. And if the police came through, it wouldn't matter that I was Chef Keith Corbin or that my restaurant had received a great review from Bill Addison in the *L.A. Times*. I would just be that nigga Fresh from Grape.

When I finally got back in my truck to leave Watts, it was

past nine P.M. Driving away from the barbecue, I turned the corner and passed my aunt's house, the place where I was almost killed three years before. The memories of that white Camaro flooded back into my brain like a rising tide. I could feel the steering wheel getting sticky with sweat from my palms. Even with everything I've experienced in my life, I'd never felt a panic attack like that before. My heart seized up. I couldn't feel the streets. I couldn't see the threats around me in the dark. Checking my mirror and blind spots, I gunned the engine and got the fuck out of there.

As I drove down Wilmington Avenue and got onto the 105 heading west, back to Westwood, my grip loosened, and my mind finally stopped racing. Traffic on the highway was light, and as my nerves settled, I zoned out and thought back to the month before, when I'd been at a different barbecue. This one, in our Westwood neighborhood, had featured hummus, burrata, pink wine, and indie rock. Though I was the only Black man there, the crowd was decently diverse, a mix of mostly white, Indian, and Asian folks. Renee, who has much less discomfort about this shit, was immediately in her element, and from the beginning, she seemed to know everyone.

It took me longer to warm up, but people there were welcoming, and by about an hour in, I was holding court at a table, captivating everyone with my story. They seemed genuinely impressed to hear it. As we were leaving, I felt I'd made a good impression, that we would be invited to future barbecues, that other residents at the barbecue might go home and talk about my story and maybe even feel good about themselves. But though I live in Westwood, I'll always be *from* Watts.

And because I'm from Watts, I know about the door. I know

that owning a hot restaurant and a beautiful house in a nice neighborhood with a loving partner and family are one side of that door. And I know people think that once I've walked through it, my life will turn into a fairy tale with a happy ending. But they don't realize that, for us, the door never closes.

And it shouldn't. Because on the other side are parts of my past I can't let go. I still have friends and family struggling. I still get calls as consigliere. Only a few of my homies can still reach me, but when they do, I try not to give advice. I try to just listen. But it's hard.

There are still days when I'll be prepping dinner or playing with my kids and get a text that another friend or family member was shot. Every time, my blood pressure spikes and the PTSD kicks in. I find myself needing to get outside, to get air, to remember to breathe and come back to the present, without the drugs to block out the pain. I'm not mad about it. It's just how it is—part of what I mean when I say I'll always be from Watts.

After all, if I'm going to move forward in this life, I need my present to coexist with my past. I need to find a way to be comfortable living with that door open.

Wouldn't it be easier to believe I can?

ACKNOWLEDGMENTS

One day in the summer of 2019, a writer named Kevin Alexander called to interview me. He said he and a panel of judges across the country were picking the best new restaurants in America for a website called Thrillist, and Alta was on his list. At the time, he knew nothing about me; all he knew was he liked my food, so he started asking questions for his article. I was high on cocaine, so I just started running my mouth, giving him a little taste of where I'd come from.

When I finally stopped talking thirty minutes later, Kevin was silent for a minute. I thought I'd lost him. Finally, he asked me a question: "Have you ever thought about writing a book?"

Ever since then, we've been on this journey together. Over the last three years, I've spent over five hundred hours talking to him about my life (and those are just the taped calls) through rehab, my father's murder, my son's birth, and everything in between. We've fought and cried and laughed and pushed each other to be better. We've become brothers, and this is just the beginning of our creative partnership. There's a lot more to come. (I also want to thank his wife, Wendy, for her patience as

Kevin spent many nights on the phone when he was probably supposed to be doing other things for their three children. I also want to thank her for the beautiful baby gifts for our son Samuel, as I know Kevin's ass isn't that thoughtful.)

Our partnership wouldn't be nearly as strong without our excellent literary agent David Granger. Granger is a journalism legend, one of the greatest magazine editors in American history, and having his expertise and experience on the team has been crucial for my path to publication. He's grouchy in all the best ways, and we love him for that.

Speaking of the team, I've got to thank Alessandra Lusardi, who has been with us from the beginning of the proposal, and whose keen eye and insights helped shape, tighten, and build this book from the ground up. She's one of the real ones. I also want to thank Julia Richardson, who transcribed nearly every interview and organized them so we could actually find things, and also happens to be a crazy gifted singer. And I want to thank our fact-checker, Chris Massie, who checked the hell out of all the facts, and found out things about me I didn't even know.

At Random House, thanks goes out first to our editor, Mark Warren, for believing in the book enough to buy it, significantly improving the book throughout the process, and just being a solid, thoughtful dude. The same with Chayenne Skeete, whose insight, organization, and perspective helped make the book much better. We're all overdue for a meal together.

I want to thank everyone from Watts who helped me on my path (sorry but I'm using y'all's real names): Greg, Rodney, Terry (GIP), Charlie, Bruce, Jerry, Bobby, Leonardo, Carlton, Frank, Tyrell, Cleve (Buddy), Bernard, Donte, and my entire PRS family. I also want to thank some of the older women in the neighborhood and at my schools who helped me out, including Miss Margaret, Mrs. Banks, Sheryl Day, Lainey Foster, Carolyn Jenkins, and Mrs. Clark.

From my time in prison, I need to shout out a few people in particular: Shaq, QT, Tiny Wood Rat, Peabody, Big Cisco, Ant Dog, and Peter Wallace. When you're locked up, you keep everything and everyone at arm's length for your own self-preservation, but all these people went against those practices. They took it upon themselves to invest in me, and see me come home and do something, and I'll be forever grateful for that.

From my years at LocoL, I need to thank Andrew, Bambu, Roy, Carnisha, Nartrella, Wayne, Imani, Rob, and everyone else who held it down even when we didn't know what the hell we were doing.

I want to thank the entire Alta family, both past and present, for all we've been able to accomplish. All of you have played a crucial part in Alta's success, and I couldn't be more grateful for that. And to my ride or die Gwen, who has literally stood back to back and side by side with me in these trenches fighting for every inch of success, both at LocoL and Alta: thank you for your love and loyalty.

And of course I'd like to make a special shoutout to my chef, partner, and friend Daniel Patterson. He always asks me why I still call him Chef, but to me, he'll always be my chef, the person in the industry I look up to the most, the man who not only taught me how to cook, but also how to understand even thinking about cooking. If it wasn't for his bravery, stepping outside his comfort zone to do something different with Roy and start LocoL, there would've been no opportunity for me. And since we both know opportunity without support isn't real, I want to thank him for his tireless support and for believing in me, especially when I wasn't ready to believe in myself. I also want to thank him for opening up and sharing his own experiences and traumas, which helped me see that those type of struggles weren't unique to my situation. He is one of the few people in this world who has truly helped change my legacy and narrative, and I'm bonded to him for that.

As we get to wrapping this up, I obviously want to thank my family. My mother exemplified for me how someone can transform their life in our community. She also showed me that I didn't need to be just one thing, that I could be several things and still be myself, and for that I have so much respect and love. I want to thank my stepdad, Mitchell, who stepped in as a father figure in the absence of my dad and worked tirelessly putting up with my mother and taking care of and loving on her kids. I want to thank my Aunt JoJo for being my biggest cheerleader and always seeing the good in me, even when I didn't deserve it. To this day, she continues to root for me the most.

I'd like to thank all my siblings: Samuel; Nedra; Manuel; Mitchell; Kadeisha; Kevin; Gerald; Marlon; my twin cousins who were raised like my siblings, Victor and Victoria; and my brother from another mother, Pope. Some of you helped raise me. Some of you helped me survive in and out of these streets. Some of you helped show me other paths through this life. But through all my trials and tribulations, you all continuously loved me. And I love you all.

I want to thank my children. I want to thank Keith Jr. for his ability to keep me honest about my own failures as a parent. I'm grateful that he can only express that, because without that dialogue, there is no healing, no rectifying, and I'm looking forward to the opportunity to keep building more with him, and to make up for our lost time. I want to thank my older daughter, Keivionna, for being so independent, strong-minded, and opinionated. The most frustrating thing about her is, through her, I recognize so much of myself. She's a hustler and a go-getter, and I know she wants something out of this life. If she puts her mind to it, I know damn well she can get it. I'm rooting for her.

I want to thank my younger daughter, Cali, for being so incredibly loving, sweet, and creative. Between the Fresh and Keith sides of my personality, she definitely got all Keith. She never wants to see anyone get hurt; she's just full of love, intuitive, and thoughtful. One of the things I love about her is that you can have an adult conversation with her, and if she doesn't understand something, she'll go away, chew on it a minute, and come back and ask you to clarify. I love that thirst for knowledge.

As for my son Samuel, he's only a couple of months old, so his personality is still forming. He's just starting to crack smiles, but the thing I've noticed about him is just how alert he is. He wants to see what's happening, see what's going on in the world, and if he feels like he's missing out, no matter how tired he is, he's gonna stay awake to be in the mix. And though it's a pain now when that boy won't take a damn nap, I hope he always keeps that energy up.

And last and certainly not least, I want to thank Renee. Judging by where I was at in my life when I met her, I can only say it must've been divine intervention. She was heaven-sent. Everything I was dealing with in my life, all of my struggles, Renee had no life experiences with those things. And yet she was so supportive of me that she would research my issues, and talk to people about them, and try to learn to deal and help. She attacked my problems tirelessly and ferociously in ways I couldn't. Even when she felt she had to give up on me for her own self-preservation, she couldn't. She cared for me. She loved on me. And she taught me that it's okay to lean on someone when you're in trouble. It's okay to ask for help. She literally changed my mindset.

With Renee, I felt like I was back in school. I've learned so much from her. Seeing Renee with her kids Kaleb and Kaelyn made me admire her as a mother. I knew immediately that if I was lucky enough to have another child, I wanted it to be with her. She was already the best mother. But it went beyond that. She helped me navigate this new life. She helped me stick up for myself. She's been my mediator and communicator. She's taught me boundaries. She's encouraged me to rebuild relationships with my children. Hell, she even taught me how to take someone on a proper date. Renee has helped rebuild me from the ground up as a grown-up who could not just function outside these streets, but thrive. I love her. She helped save my life.

ABOUT THE AUTHORS

KEITH CORBIN is the James Beard Award–nominated executive chef at and co-owner of Alta Adams in Los Angeles. His modern California soul food restaurant was named one of the best new restaurants in the country by both *Esquire* and Thrillist and, since opening, has consistently been on the *Los Angeles Times* best restaurant list. A native of Watts, Corbin was formerly director of operations for Roy Choi and Daniel Patterson's LocoL restaurant group and also worked for Patterson at his Michelin-starred fine-dining establishment Coi in San Francisco.

Instagram: chefkeithcorbin

KEVIN ALEXANDER is the author of *Burn the Ice: The American Culinary Revolution and Its End,* a James Beard Award–winning food journalist, and recipient of the Society of Professional Journalists' Mark of Excellence Award. His work has appeared in *Esquire, Elle, Men's Journal, The New Republic,* and *The Boston Globe,* and he is a 2018 and 2020 Association of Food Journalists Award winner. Born in Texas and raised in New England, he now lives in Northern California with his family.

Twitter: KAlexander03

ABOUT THE TYPE

This book was set in Ehrhardt, a typeface based on the original design of Nicholas Kis, a seventeenth-century Hungarian type designer. Ehrhardt was first released in 1937 by the Monotype Corporation of London.